This pioneering ethnoarchaeological study is of contemporary ceramic production and consumption in several villages in the Los Tuxtlas region of Mexico. While many archaeologists have identified ceramic production zones in the archaeological record, their identifying criteria have often been vague and impressionistic. The present book's contribution is to use ethnographic research to suggest how archaeologists might consistently recognize ceramic manufacturing. It also places ceramic production in larger cultural contexts. The author provides details of the ecology, production, distribution, use, discard, and site formation processes. His critical observations on some of the serious weaknesses in archaeological interpretations of ceramic production will interest Mesoamericanists and all other archaeologists grappling with these, and related, issues.

NEW STUDIES IN ARCHAEOLOGY

Domestic ceramic production and spatial organization

NEW STUDIES IN ARCHAEOLOGY

Series editors
Colin Renfrew, *University of Cambridge*
Jeremy Sabloff, *University of Pittsburgh*

PHILIP J. ARNOLD III
Visiting Assistant Professor, Department of Sociology,
Anthropology, and Social Work, Skidmore College, Saratoga
Springs, New York

Domestic ceramic production and spatial organization

A Mexican case study in ethnoarchaeology

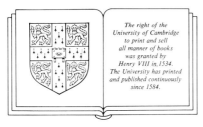

The right of the
University of Cambridge
to print and sell
all manner of books
was granted by
Henry VIII in 1534.
The University has printed
and published continuously
since 1584.

Cambridge University Press

Cambridge

New York   Port Chester   Melbourne   Sydney

Published by the Press Syndicate of the University of Cambridge
The Pitt Building, Trumpington Street, Cambridge CB2 1RP
40 West 20th Street, New York, NY 10011–4211, USA
10 Stamford Road, Oakleigh, Melbourne 3166, Australia

© Cambridge University Press 1991

First published 1991

Printed in Great Britain at the University Press, Cambridge

British Library cataloguing in publication data

Arnold, Philip J.
    Domestic ceramic production and spatial organization: a Mexican
    case study in ethnoarchaeology.
    1. Pottery. Making. Primitive techniques
    I. Title
    738.14

Library of Congress cataloguing in publication data

Arnold, Philip J.
    Domestic ceramic production and spatial organization: a Mexican case study in
    ethnoarchaeology/Philip J. Arnold III.
        p.   cm,   (New studies in archaeology)
    Includes bibliographical references and index.
    ISBN 0–521–39199–7 (hardback)
    1. Indians of Mexico – Mexico – Tuxtlas Region – Pottery.
    2. Pottery craft – Mexico – Tuxtlas Region.
    3. Indians of Mexico – Mexico – Tuxtlas Region – Antiquities.
    4. Ethnoarchaeology – Mexico – Tuxtlas Region.
    5. Spatial behavior – Mexico – Tuxtlas Region.
    6. Tuxtlas Region (Mexico) – Antiquities.
    7. Mexico – Antiquities.
    I. Title.   II. Series.
    F1219.1.T84A75   1991
    972'.62–dc20   90–15075 CIP

ISBN 0 521 391997 hardback

CE

TO MY MOTHER,
FOR HER COURAGE, STRENGTH,
AND LOVE

CONTENTS

FIGURES

TABLES

ACKNOWLEDGMENTS

This book was completed while I held a one-year teaching position at Skidmore College. At Skidmore I encountered exceptional colleagues and a wonderful working environment. I would like to thank Jackie Azzarto, Sue Bender, Bill Fox, Debbie Sutherland, and Jill Sweet for their encouragement and all-around support. I would also like to express my gratitude to the Skidmore Media Services, John Danison at the Computer Center, and Sue Martin for their assistance with various aspects of manuscript preparation.

Funding for this and related research was obtained from several agencies. These include the National Science Foundation (no. BNS 8505041, no. BNS 8120430, no. BNS 8302984, no. BNS 8403810), the Tinker and Mellon foundations (both through the Latin American Institute, University of New Mexico), Sigma Xi, and the Student Research Allocations Committee at the University of New Mexico. I am extremely grateful to these institutions for their financial support.

My largest debt of gratitude is owed to those individuals who have challenged me to learn while teaching by example. A few merit special recognition. Jeremy Sabloff has been the driving force behind this research. His unfailing support and guidance have made a demanding task much easier. It would be a grievous oversight not to acknowledge the contributions of Lewis Binford, Robert Santley, Mari Lynn Salvador, and Flora Clancy. This manuscript benefited from a merciless, yet extremely fair review by Dean Arnold. Arnold's comments dramatically improved the quality of the final product.

Friends and colleagues who have contributed along the way include Christopher Dore, Pamela Hong, Veronica Kann, Janet Kerley, Ronald Kneebone, Thomas Killion, Patricia McAnany, Barbara Mills, Christopher Pool, Matthew Schmader, and Michael Smyth. Rani Alexander, James Boone, and Raymond Thompson were kind enough to furnish copies of unpublished and/or hard-to-get manuscripts. I would also like to thank Mellisa Hagstrum and Ben Nelson for permission to cite their unpublished data. Shannon Fie contributed her extraordinary energy, skills, and patience to this volume. That contribution has made the single greatest difference in the manuscript and in my life.

Fieldwork was greatly facilitated through the kindness and hospitality of Mexican colleagues. Ponciano Ortiz C., at the Instituto de Antropologia e Historia in Xalapa, helped me gather unpublished data on ceramic production in Los Tuxtlas. Bernd Fahmel-Bayer instructed me on the complexities of the library system at the Instituto de Investigaciones Antropológicas, UNAM, in Mexico City. Letters of introduction to the study communities were supplied by Gabriel Arnau O., Presidente Municipal de Santiago Tuxtla, and Luis M. Dias del Castillo R., Presidente Municipal de San Andres Tuxtla. Special thanks are reserved for Marcos Rodriguez R., who served as field assistant and friend.

A final note of appreciation goes to the potters of Los Tuxtlas. These individuals opened their hearts and homes, and with dignity and kindness showed me much more than simply how to manufacture pottery.

1

Introduction

Most archaeologists would agree that craft specialization is an integral component of increasing socioeconomic complexity. The occurrence of specialized craft production has served as a perennial favorite for discussions involving social stratification, economic exchange, and ultimately state-level organization (e.g. Brumfiel and Earle 1987; Childe 1950; Wright 1986:323–324). In fact, craft specialization could be characterized as the workhorse of archaeological investigations into complex society. Specialized production, as exemplified in an almost bewildering variety of material manifestations, has been used to monitor administrative influence over production (Feinman, Kowalewski, and Blanton 1984; Spence 1986), the development of inter- and intra-regional trading networks (Rathje 1975; Wright and Johnson 1975), and various characteristics of the producer/consumer relationship, including the degree of producer competition (Feinman et al. 1981) and the existence of elite consumers (Rice 1981:223).

Given its central role in interpreting social complexity, it is not unreasonable to also consider how craft specialization is viewed archaeologically. What methods have been advocated to identify craft production? What interpretive models have been advanced to meld these archaeological data into an understanding of the past?

The present work employs ceramic production data to address these questions. Ceramics were chosen for several reasons: (a) their positive correlation with sedentism and complex society (e.g. Rice 1987:190; Skibo et al. 1989:126); (b) their almost exasperating quantity as archaeological data (e.g. Willey 1961:230; Sullivan 1988: 23); and (c) their potential as vehicles for interpreting past production organization (e.g. Arnold 1985; Kramer 1985; Rice 1987). These characteristics make pottery and pottery production extremely relevant to research into socioeconomic complexity.

This study presents ethnoarchaeological information on the ceramic production and consumption behaviors of nonspecialized traditional potters in Veracruz, Mexico. It responds to the recently identified need for middle-range theory devoted to ceramic production (Rice 1987:171–172). Such a theory would aid in the identification of production loci as well as contributing to more general socioeconomic interpretations of production organization. Middle-range research (Binford 1977:7, 1981:26) is the necessary first step in developing theory of this type. Middle-range research is actualistic and attempts to link the dynamic properties of extant behavioral systems with the material patterns encountered by archaeologists. As an example of middle-range research, the present work seeks to establish "signature patterns" (Binford 1981:26) of pottery manufacture.

Like many ethnoarchaeological studies devoted to pottery making (e.g. Kramer 1985) this research discusses production materials and techniques and supplies data on household ceramic assemblages and vessel use-lives. These comparative data are instrumental in facilitating the generalizations that form the basis for generating laws and building theory (e.g. Hempel 1977:244, cited in Binford 1982a:130; Kaplan 1964:84; Nagel 1961:179–181). Unlike most other studies, however, this research also investigates the spatial organization of production, as reflected in the arrangement of activities and facilities within production areas. Concurring with recent statements by Stark (1985:172) and Rice (1987:171), the present study argues that all too often research emphasis is placed on tools and production output rather than focusing on production organization. A concern with the organizational properties of production moves research beyond documenting *what* occurred and toward more theoretically satisfying issues of *how* and *why* a specified pattern was generated.

Evaluating ceramic production
Although characterizations of production scale and organization abound in the archaeological literature, there is a growing climate of critical self awareness directed at these inferences (e.g. Brumfiel and Earle 1987; Muller 1984; Rice 1987:170–172). Some archaeologists have become concerned that our methodological reach is beginning to exceed our interpretive grasp. Traditionally, archaeologists have cited ethnographic studies to substantiate their interpretations, but as Rice (1981:219) observed a decade ago: "Archaeological definitions of craft specialization are poorly developed and virtually impossible to correlate with these [ethnographic] criteria . . . It is clear that some operational definition of craft specialization needs to be developed for and by archaeologists."

Nowhere is this difficulty more apparent than in the area of ceramic production studies. Despite a wealth of data describing all phases of pottery making (e.g. Arnold 1985; Kramer 1985; Rice and Saffer 1982), there are few consistently reliable methods that link these contemporary observations to the material record. The limitations of our knowledge are clearly seen in reference to pesky "cautionary tales," statements demonstrating that material patterns documented in one example contradict the patterning observed in a purportedly similar context. Archaeologists studying the manufacture and use of pottery are particularly fond of demonstrating just how variable production systems can be (e.g. Adams 1979; Hodder 1982; Stanislawski 1978).

Unfortunately, cautionary tales do little to rectify the problem. The fact that a contrary argument can effectively negate an interpretation merely underscores our ignorance of how the variables are causally related. Cautionary tales simply beg the question of why the observed variability exists. Still lacking is an understanding of the variables selecting for a particular production decision; that is, a theory of ceramic production.

Basic to this theory is our knowledge of the articulation between the activity of pottery making and its material consequences. The importance of this articulation is manifest at several different levels. First we must have confidence that our identification of production evidence is justified. Like other archaeological phenomena, production "evidence" does not speak for itself. To identify an object as a polishing stone or mold, for example, is to generate an inference about how that item functioned in the past. How we justify that inference is dependent upon our methlogical and theoretical approach to ceramic production and artifact analysis.

But let us assume, for now, that a valid identification has been established. The next step would be to place that evidence into some interpretive framework. How do we move from a site containing certain categories of inferred production phenomena to a statement about how production was conducted in the past? How do we use production evidence to interpret production activities?

Certainly the most common procedure is to reference a hierarchical classification of production scale. In these models production comprises a number of distinct "states" or "modes" representing the ethnographically established range of production activities (e.g. Peacock 1981:8–11, 1982; van der Leeuw 1976:392–404). Differences in pottery making follow a general progression from part-time household production to full-time industrialized manufacture (Rice 1987:183–191). Each discrete type is associated with certain production characteristics, often with an emphasis on technological differences. These models should not be construed as representing a unilineal evolution of ceramic production, however. They are simply typological schemes attempting to categorize a continuum of behavior.

As typologies, however, these models are subject to the same regulating conditions noted for other classifications (e.g. Brew 1946; Dunnell 1971; Rouse 1960). One condition is the need to stipulate those characteristics necessary for class membership (Dunnell 1971:15–17). Attention, therefore, focuses on shared, definitional characteristics while variations in nondiagnostic attributes may be ignored. Consequently, these models can obscure considerable intraclass variability that may be extremely relevant to the dynamic properties of the production system. While such typologies have considerable utility as heuristic devices, they should not bear the full weight of synchronic interpretations of ceramic production.

Nor does this approach lend itself to analyses of diachronic variability. The ability to perceive change through time is one of the great strengths of archaeology. Yet a perspective that presents variation as a static concept is of little use in this regard: "Clearly, such juxtapositions cannot in any way be construed as representative of actual changes in the organisation of pottery-making. They remain an *a posteriori* construct of the researcher, and they say little about the real nature of changes which are or were taking place" (van der Leeuw 1984:720). As a consequence, it can be extremely difficult to determine at what point variability has reached critical mass, requiring a restructuring from one production state to another. Under such typologies, attention is diverted away from the boundaries between types in favor of the types themselves. This problem has been likened to the "drunkard's search" (Kaplan 1964:11), in which research efforts are concentrated in a certain area, not because it is potentially informative, but rather because it is easier to manage (Rice 1984a:233).

Ceramic ecology, middle-range research, and spatial organization
The limitations discussed above justify attempts to establish a theory of ceramic production. Since *theory* has worn a haberdashery of definitional hats, its use deserves some explication. In the present context theory refers to a "device for interpreting, criticizing, and unifying established laws" (Kaplan 1964:295). The construction of theory goes beyond collecting generalizations, although as noted above these empirical data can be extremely informative. But theory is not built from empirical observations. Rather, theory is invented to account for those observations. A theory, therefore, is more than the sum of its generalizations; theory enables the researcher to anticipate potentially undocumented variability. Theory building is learning *from* experience as much as learning *by* experience (Kaplan 1964:295).

This study uses ethnoarchaeological experience to learn from ceramic producers. Ethnoarchaeology "systematically defines[s] relationships between behavior and material culture not often explored by ethnologists" (Kramer 1979:1) in the hopes of applying these relationships archaeologically. The ethnoarchaeological experience discussed here derives from a study of traditional potters inhabiting the low sierra along the southern Gulf Coast of Veracruz, Mexico. A total of fifty potters, residing in four communities, provides the data base. Production data were generated through interviews, observation, household inventories, mapping, and houselot excavation. Potters in and around this area have been the subject of previous attention (Foster 1955:22; Krotser 1974, 1980; Stark 1984); this present work builds upon that research while supplying new information on the character of production in this area.

CERAMIC ECOLOGY
The present work employs a two-pronged approach in furthering the cause for a ceramic production theory. First, this study uses the tenets of ceramic ecology to focus on the interaction between potters and their natural and social environment (e.g., Kolb 1989:335). A call for research that placed ceramic studies squarely in an environmental context was initially made by Frederick Matson (1965). Dubbing this approach "ceramic ecology," Matson suggested that it be viewed as a "facet of cultural ecology, that which attempts to relate the raw materials and technologies that the local potter has available to the functions in his [her] culture of the products he [she] fashions" (1965:203). Matson's goal was to advance archaeological perceptions of pottery; releasing ceramics from the tyranny of culture history and relating ceramic studies to the broader anthropological issues of the day.

Since then ceramic ecology has provided a strong paradigm for contextualizing pottery production systems (e.g. Kolb 1976, 1989). Through an explicit concern with the environment, ceramic ecology supplies a method for cross-cultural comparisons that may also be used to investigate past production activities (e.g. Arnold 1985:14).

At the core of ceramic ecology is an emphasis on the natural environment, including the natural resources available to the potter and the climatic forces acting on production (e.g. Arnold 1975; Rice 1987:314). The most relevant natural resources for the potter include clays, temper, and fuel. A ceramic ecological perspective thus requires information on the geology of the region, as well as data on hydrology and land-use practices (Rice 1987:314).

In addition to raw materials, a region's climate may also provide mechanisms for regulating ceramic production. Some of these variables have been recently discussed by Arnold (1985:61–98). Precipitation and temperature are obvious concerns; other factors include humidity, prevailing winds, and cloud coverage. Climate may affect the schedule of production, the intensity of manufacture, and the production technology (Arnold 1985:98).

The social and economic environments of the potter are also of interest; the so-called "human aspects" of ceramic production (Matson 1965:216; also Arnold 1985). Ceramic ecology calls for data on production tools and techniques, the social organization of potters and rates of pottery production and consumption (e.g. Rice 1987:316). Ceramic ecology seeks information on all factors relevant to the study of pottery making. By adopting a perspective in keeping with the goals of ceramic ecology, this study establishes archaeologically relevant relationships between ceramic production, ceramic consumption, and both the natural and social environments of the potter.

MIDDLE-RANGE RESEARCH AND SPATIAL ORGANIZATION

This present study is also an exercise in middle-range research (Binford 1977:7, 1981:25). As noted above, research of this type is designed to link the dynamic properties of contemporary systems with archaeological patterns. Since the cultural activities that contributed to a given archaeological deposit are unobservable, we must look to the present for insights into the behavior generating the material patterns:

> What we are seeking through middle-range research are accurate means of identification and good instruments of measuring specified properties of past cultural systems . . . We are looking for "Rosetta Stones" that permit the accurate conversion from observations on statics to statements about dynamics.
> (Binford 1982a:129)

Such a research program, in turn, is designed to contribute to middle-range theory. This theory serves to link the observations made in the present with the potential archaeological record; it is concerned with the formation processes responsible for patterning in material remains (e.g. Schiffer 1987, 1988; cf. Raab and Goodyear 1984).

Middle-range theory enables the researcher to anticipate archaeological variability, based on an understanding of causality established through middle-range research. Anticipation as used here is not interchangeable with prediction. Prediction can occur without understanding why two variables are causally related; "statistical" or "probabilistic" explanations (e.g. Nagel 1961:24; Salmon 1982) for example, are essentially a series of generalizations that require no underpinnings of theory. Since probability implies more than one possible outcome, these explanations also provide a breeding ground for "spoiler" arguments (e.g. Yellen 1977:133). Middle-range research generates empirical data but also seeks to establish causality.

An additional step is required when making justified statements about the past. Archaeologists, explicitly or implicitly, employ certain uniformitarian assumptions.

These assumptions hold properties of the natural and/or cultural systems constant; they serve as moorings for inferential arguments. Any study that proposes to use contemporary data to evaluate the archaeological record must also justify the uniformitarian assumptions that are in use.

For this reason the present study also focuses on the spatial organization of production activities. To what degree can spatial organization serve as a viable uniformitarian assumption? A concern with spatial organization is characterized by an emphasis on those variables affecting the management and scheduling of activities across space (Kent 1987a, 1987b). Most research dealing with activity organization has been conducted by archaeologists interested in mobile cultural systems. Ironically, complex systems, with their penchant for sedentism and wealth of architectural data, have traditionally received far less attention in this regard. One wonders if there is not a degree of empathetic interpretation involved; our personal experience is certainly more attuned to the use of space in a sedentary system. Are we less inclined to challenge our conceptions of complex societies than our models of mobile cultural systems?

An evaluation of this possibility is outside the scope of the present study. Regardless of the answer, the utilization of space is a crucial variable for production studies. Ethnographic research suggests that full-time producers display a very different spatial organization than potters adhering to a more irregular production schedule (e.g. contra Peacock 1982:25–31; Reina and Hill 1978:50–64). The number of producers, the quantity of output and the need for task simultaneity will similarly affect the spatial organization of production (e.g. Wilk and Netting 1984:7). The important point to remember is that space presents certain limitations on production organization – the greater the scale of production, the greater the demands on space. A desire for greater production efficiency will usually be reflected in a reallocation of space and/or a reorganization of the activities utilizing that space. Tasks performed simultaneously cannot be conducted within the exact same location. As part of a middle-range research program, this study investigates spatial organization as a potential uniformitarian assumption for studies of ceramic production.

Organizational requirements of pottery making also affect decisions concerning production tools and techniques. Rather than viewing technological change as a simple concomitant of increased consumer demands or the need for more efficient production, this research argues that technology is also regulated by the spatial resources of the producer. And since evidence for this same technology frequently anchors archaeological interpretation of specialization (see discussion in Stark 1985), this study calls for a re-evaluation of the models used to characterize craft production in the past.

These research interests serve as the basis for the organization of the present work. Part 1 presents three main sets of data relevant to ceramic ecological studies. The production environment, including both natural and social characteristics, is discussed in Chapter 2. This presentation makes the case for relative homogeneity throughout the producer environment. Climatic variability is minimal and potters generally have access to the same suite of raw materials. Moreover, the socioeconomic circumstances of the potters is comparable.

This ecological similarity makes the discussion of production activities in Chapter 3 all the more interesting. In contrast to their environment, the potters of Los Tuxtlas display some important distinctions in production techniques. One such distinction is the use of kilns by a small number of producers while the remaining potters prefer open firing. Another difference is exhibited in vessel forming. Chapter 4 considers variability in household assemblage attributes and identifies important relationships between the size of assemblages and the life span of pottery.

Part 2 focuses on how production differences might be evaluated archaeologically. Chapter 5 presents a critique of conventional procedures for identifying and interpreting ceramic manufacture. This discussion makes the point that current methods for giving meaning to the archaeological record are ambiguous and difficult to reconcile with questions of culture process. This problem is addressed in Chapter 6, which argues for an emphasis on activity organization when addressing pottery production. This approach focuses on the organizational structure of production; how tasks are spatially and temporally scheduled and what factors condition those decisions. Chapter 6 also uses this perspective to re-examine the firing variability noted above. This analysis suggests that spatial constraints can have crucial implications for the kinds of tools and techniques adopted by the potter.

If spatial constraints are genuinely influencing activity organization, other domestic activities should be similarly affected. This possibility is investigated in Chapter 7 with an analysis of refuse disposal within producers' houselots. Through a comparison of surface and subsurface material patterning, this chapter reaffirms that spatial constraints can significantly alter activity patterns and in an archaeologically visible manner. Spatial organization is thus a legitimate variable in investigating ceramic production archaeologically.

In Part 3, Chapter 8 places these findings in the broader context of production studies by applying them to the archaeological site of Matacapan. An understanding of spatial organization permits a view of both diachronic and synchronic variability across the site. Chapter 9 discusses the role of middle-range research in production studies and offers a justification for emphasizing spatial organization as a relevant link between the present and the past.

PART 1

Ceramic production and consumption in Los Tuxtlas

2

The ceramic production environment

Although central to the study of ceramic ecology (e.g. Matson 1965), the role of the environment in ceramic production has only recently been addressed in a systematic fashion (Arnold 1985). Arnold's ethnographic synthesis demonstrates how both the natural and social environment are intimately related to the character and tempo of pottery manufacture. For example, the availability and quality of clay, temper, and fuel can help determine the location and scale of production efforts (Arnold 1985:20–60; Nicklin 1979). Climate can regulate drying time, firing opportunities, and the length of the production season (Arnold 1985:61–98). Population pressure and market demand may also contribute to the development and trajectory of a production industry (Arnold 1985:171–201; Rice 1984a:249–250, 255–257).

This chapter describes the Tuxtlas production environment from the perspective of ceramic ecology. It places the potters and production communities in a natural and social environmental context and explores some of the factors regulating pottery manufacture. These factors include weather patterns, the quality and accessibility of raw material, and the demographic and labor organization of the Tuxtlas potters.

This ecological discussion underscores the relative homogeneity in the Tuxtlas production environment. Potters have access to similar suites of raw material and there are minimal climatic differences between the production communities. The potters' social environment is characterized by comparable household demographics and subsistence activities. Given this overall similarity, one might also expect consistency in the potters' tools and production techniques. The fact that significant distinctions do occur, both in the production and consumption of ceramics, is addressed in the following chapters.

Study region
The Sierra de Los Tuxtlas is a low range of volcanic mountains rising abruptly out of the Gulf Coast Plain of southern Veracruz, Mexico (Figure 1). The Tuxtlas region is located along the Gulf of Mexico, about 80 km southeast of the city of Veracruz and almost 60 km west-northwest of Coatzlcoalcos. In its entirety, the sierra occupies an area between 4500 and 5000 sq km (Andrle 1964:6; Tamayo 1949). To the north and east the Tuxtlas abut the Gulf of Mexico; to the south and west the sierra slopes gradually downward to meet the salt marshes and sand dunes of the Gulf Coast Plain. At the center of the region are numerous cinder cones, craters, and volcanoes providing mute testimony to a violent geological history (e.g. Pool 1990; Rios Macbeth 1952).

The cinder cones that punctuate the sierra's skyline lie along an axis running from the northwest to the southeast. The more prominent volcanoes include San Martin Tuxtla (1660 m) and Cerro Vigia (*c.* 700 m) in the western Tuxtlas, and Santa Marta (1600 m) and San Martin Pajapan (1270 m) in the eastern part of the region (Andrle 1964:11). Near the center of this axis is Lake Catemaco, the third largest natural lake in Mexico. Heavy precipitation and natural springs maintain the level of this fresh water lake (Rios Macbeth 1952:330).

Lake Catemaco provides a convenient means to divide the Tuxtlas into separate sections: (a) the northwestern San Martin massif, and (b) the southeastern Santa Marta massif (Andrle 1964; Killion 1987). Although this division may not reflect distinct geological differences between the respective areas (e.g. Williams and Hiezer 1965), it might indicate slightly different rates of geological development (Arnold 1987:65; Pool 1990:159). This possibility is consistent with the continued activity of the San Martin

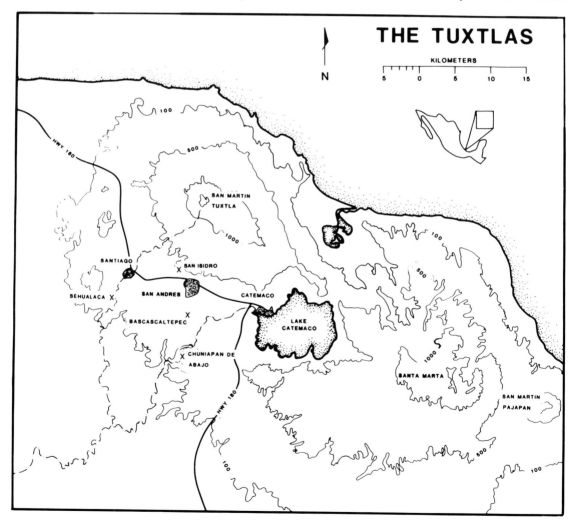

Figure 1   Sierra de los Tuxtlas study region.

volcano into modern times (Andrle 1964:16; Tamayo 1949), while Santa Marta and San Martin Pajapan are considered to be extinct (West 1964).

San Andres Tuxtla, Santiago Tuxtla, and Catemaco are the population and administrative centers of the region (Killion 1987). All three are situated within the San Martin massif. San Andres contains the most inhabitants, with over 64,000, Catemaco has a total of 35,000 persons, and Santiago Tuxtla has a population of about 20,000 (Arnold 1987:67). Potters may come to the local markets within these centers to sell their goods.

The remaining population of the San Martin massif is scattered throughout the sierra in a number of small, sometimes isolated, communities. Communication with these communities varies greatly, and during the rainy season some villages may be effectively cut off from the regional centers. Along the major highways the primary means of transportation is by bus and taxi. As one moves away from these major routes, however, travel on foot and occasionally horseback are more prevalent.

Killion (1987) has divided the San Martin massif into three main zones, based on the distribution of settlements and the agricultural economy of the inhabitants (Figure 2). Along the southern slopelands are the wetlands, rolling hills, and coastal plain of southern Veracruz. The easily cultivable, productive soils of this alluvial bottomland are generally restricted to areas adjacent to major river courses, creating a pattern of dense but dispersed rural settlements engaged primarily in subsistence agriculture.

The central zone, comprising the area between the basal escarpment of San Martin Tuxtla and the alluvial bottomlands of the Rio Grande de Catemaco, is the major zone of occupation. Highway 180, the main thoroughfare in the region, passes through this central zone. Many small, but dense, communities occur along this route or along dirt roads connected to it. The area to the west of Lake Catemaco is relatively level and is also highly fertile. Agricultural producers take full advantage of this combination; agriculture in the central zone tends to be intensive, with both subsistence agriculture and plantation and cash-crop farming (Killion 1987).

The northern portion of the San Martin massif includes the upland area around the San Martin volcano and the steep northern slopes that ultimately meet the Gulf of Mexico. Farming in this region is difficult, due to a number of factors including heavy annual rainfall and rugged topography. The soil matrix includes coarse volcanic sands, tuffaceous sediments, and basalt flows. While these volcanically derived soils are fertile, thirty years of deforestation have exposed this zone to increased erosion. Along the coast to the north, estuaries and grasslands provide little additional farmland. As a result, settlements in this zone are small and widely dispersed; shifting agriculture is common, as is some cattle grazing near the coast.

Production communities

The research presented in this study was undertaken in four communities, all bordering the central zone. Potters in these settlements belong to the same *mestizo* cultural tradition that characterizes most of the rural population in the Tuxtlas (Arnold 1987; Killion 1987). While the Popoluca and Zoque Indians living on the southern slopes of the Santa Marta massif remained relatively isolated until the middle of the twentieth century (e.g. Baez-Jorge 1973; Foster 1966; Holmes 1952), the indigenous population of the San Martin massif was impacted more directly. In addition to the depopulation brought about by smallpox and other Old World diseases, this area was rapidly settled by Spanish, German, and Cuban immigrants drawn by tobacco production and cattle ranching (Andrle 1964:130–135; Medel y Alvarado 1963). Consequently, the modern inhabitants of the region exhibit a thorough mixture of European and native Mexican cultural traits.

The community of San Isidro is situated to the northwest of San Andres on the upland south-facing slopes of the San Martin massif. San Isidro is located at an elevation of about 400 m above seal level and contains approximately 750 inhabitants (SPP 1982). A dirt road, passable during the dry season, connects San Isidro with San Andres. Bus service is unpredictable, however, and the potters generally carry their goods to the market. This round-trip takes about two hours.

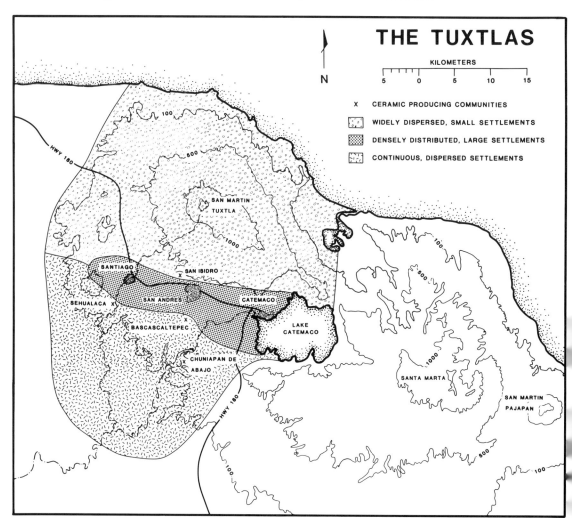

Figure 2   Major habitation zones of the study region (after Killion 1987).

The terrain around San Isidro is steep and uneven. Houselots are generally cut into the sides of hills, giving the community a terraced appearance. Much of the natural vegetation around the community has been cleared as the result of *milpa* agriculture. Two main factors affect soil fertility in this community. The steep grade produces rapid run-off, causing erosion of the soils which, in turn, often exposes a soil matrix that is distinctively argillaceous. High erosion and low-productivity soils have been attributed to encouraging ceramic production in other parts of the New World as well (e.g. Arnold 1985:171–190).

In contrast to the uneven terrain of San Isidro, the three remaining communities are situated within relatively flat areas between the central zone and the southern portion of the Tuxtlas. Sehualaca lies to the southwest of Santiago Tuxtla along the levee of the Rio Tepango, one of the major streams draining the southern slope of San Martin. Sehualaca, with a population of about 640 persons and situated at an elevation of 160 m above sea level, is the only study community adjacent to a main thoroughfare (SPP 1982). Potters in Sehualaca are more likely to use bus or taxi service to transport their ceramics to the Santiago market. In addition, persons wanting ceramics may also visit the home of the potter, thereby receiving a better price for the items.

Bascascaltepec is located about 4 km south of San Andres at an elevation of 240 m above sea level. A dirt road is the main transportation artery linking this community and San Andres. Bascascaltepec was the largest community visited, with a population near 1000. Unfortunately, the potters of this village practice their craft infrequently, so the opportunity to gather comparative information on production techniques was limited.

Chuniapan de Abajo is situated about 10 km south of San Andres, adjacent to the Rio Grande Catemaco downstream from the Salto Eyipantla. Chuniapan de Abajo is situated within the relatively flat bottomlands of this river. The community's population of 600 makes it the smallest settlement studied. The potters of Chuniapan de Abajo seldom take their products to the market of San Andres. No scheduled transportation reaches this community, although some adventurous taxi drivers will brave the trip for the right price. Potters feel that the distance to San Andres is too great; instead they take pottery to the surrounding localities of Cuesta Amarilla, Chuniapan de Arriba, and El Salto de Eyipantla.

Natural environment
The potter's natural environment has important implications for the ceramic product and production activities (Arnold 1985; Rice 1987). The location and quality of clay and temper are ultimately the result of the specific geological and climatological circumstances of the region. The raw material, in turn, can determine the kinds of vessels that are manufactured and may even restrict manufacturing techniques (e.g. Arnold 1985:29). Moreover, temperature and precipitation can affect how production is organized and scheduled. A comparative analysis of pottery production in Los Tuxtlas must be firmly grounded in a working knowledge of the natural production environment (also see Arnold 1987; Pool 1990).

WEATHER PATTERNS

Weather patterns provide a critical mechanism in regulating ceramic production. Arnold (1985:61–77) has demonstrated how the climate provides obstacles to most production phases, from raw-material acquisition to vessel firing. Clay and temper sources may be submerged during certain seasons or mines might be susceptible to collapse (e.g. DeBoer and Lathrap 1979:116; Reina 1966:63; Reina and Hill 1978:32). Weather may also affect vessel production, especially as reflected in formation and drying schedules (Arnold 1985:63–65, Table 3.1). As Arnold (1985:71) observes, the "most favorable weather and climatic conditions for pottery production thus occur during a time of sustained sunshine, warm temperatures, little or no rainfall and low relative humidity."

The Tuxtlas climate cannot be considered "favorable" for production. In fact, only warm temperatures are generally assured. Rainfall is another matter completely. Potters rarely work during the summer, due to the often intensive and lengthy periods of precipitation. Production during the winter can also be difficult. Although winter rainfall is less intensive, the winter is also the time of the greatest variation in rainfall (Sierra M. 1969, 1971). Such variation often presents problems for organizing and planning production activities because winter storms are less predictable. The ability to schedule manufacturing episodes is especially important, since the potters are rarely able to complete production activities in a single day. In addition, winter storms (*nortes*) associated with the dry season can produce high winds and significant drops in temperature, all of which may jeopardize successful production.

Temperature

There is comparatively little variability in the temperature regimes throughout the Tuxtlas mountains. Higher elevations do exhibit lower average temperatures throughout the year, but these differences are usually on the order of 2°C or less per month. In terms of ceramic production, this difference is not expected to be behaviorally significant.

Average yearly temperature for the region is about 25°C, with the minimum remaining above 20°C during the winter months (Table 1). The coldest period in the Tuxtlas generally runs from November to March. This period is characterized by *nortes*: polar air masses that move southward and westward across the Gulf of Mexico into the region (Andrle 1964:37). These air masses produce distinct drops in temperature; up to 10°C in a twenty-four hour period (Andrle 1964:38). These periods of colder weather appear to last about three to six days and average about four per month during the winter season (Andrle 1964:37).

Highest temperatures in the region generally occur during either May or June. There is a noticeable (but often slight) drop in temperature during July, when the rainy season is usually at its height. Temperatures tend to level out after this month and then begin a gradual decline toward the winter lows.

Temperature variation is most pronounced when weather extremes are considered. Under these circumstances elevation plays an important role. Andrle (1964:30–31) noted that the record low for San Andres was 6.8°C. Based on a projected decrease of

Table 1 *Mean monthly temperature data from fourteen Tuxtlas weather stations*[1]

Station	Jan.	Feb.	Mar.	Apr.	May	June	July	Aug.	Sep.	Oct.	Nov.	Dec.	Mean Annual
Catemaco A	20.4	21.2	23.7	26.1	26.9	26.3	25.1	25.2	25.0	23.6	22.1	20.7	23.9
Catemaco B	20.2	21.9	24.3	26.2	27.2	26.7	25.6	25.5	25.4	23.8	22.4	20.6	24.2
Coyame	20.7	21.2	23.6	25.6	26.6	26.7	25.8	26.1	25.9	24.3	22.7	21.2	24.2
Lauchapan	21.6	22.4	25.2	27.7	28.9	28.5	27.0	27.2	26.8	25.3	23.4	22.1	25.5
Los Mangos	21.8	22.4	24.2	26.7	27.5	27.0	25.9	25.8	25.5	24.6	23.3	22.5	24.8
Morillo	21.7	22.8	25.5	28.5	29.6	29.1	26.9	27.4	27.0	25.5	23.7	22.4	25.8
San Andres	20.8	22.2	24.9	27.4	28.1	27.5	26.3	26.0	25.3	23.9	22.2	21.1	24.6
San Juanillo	22.0	23.0	25.7	28.8	29.8	29.1	27.6	27.5	27.3	25.7	24.0	22.8	26.1
Santa Rosalia	21.8	22.5	24.8	27.5	28.6	28.4	27.2	27.1	27.1	26.0	24.3	22.8	25.7
Santiago	21.1	22.1	24.4	26.7	27.8	27.5	26.2	26.2	25.8	24.1	22.7	21.7	24.7
Sinapa Bajo	21.4	22.2	24.6	27.0	28.1	28.2	26.9	26.8	26.6	25.6	23.5	22.2	25.3
Tapalapan	20.8	21.3	23.6	25.9	26.8	26.2	25.5	25.5	25.1	24.7	23.7	21.3	24.1
Tres Zapotes	21.7	22.8	25.3	27.8	29.1	28.7	27.3	27.4	27.1	25.8	24.0	22.7	25.8
Zapotitlan	21.9	22.9	23.4	24.5	25.8	26.3	26.2	26.4	25.8	25.8	23.8	22.9	24.6

[1] In degrees Celsius.

0.5°C for each 100 meters of elevation, he suggests a minimum of 0°C for the highest point in the Tuxtlas. On the other hand, the warmest reading recorded at San Andres was 42.6°C. Under situations of temperature extremes, therefore, the varied topography of the Tuxtlas can produce wide differences. On the average, however, this variability is minimal.

Precipitation

Precipitation in Los Tuxtlas is primarily orographic; that is, rainfall quantities increase with elevation (Figure 3). A rainshadow on the sierra's southern side, however, results in comparatively less precipitation of this area. Rainfall levels vary from an annual range of about 5000 mm at the highest elevations to 1000 mm per year on the inland side of the range.

In addition to the regional variability in annual precipitation, there are distinct

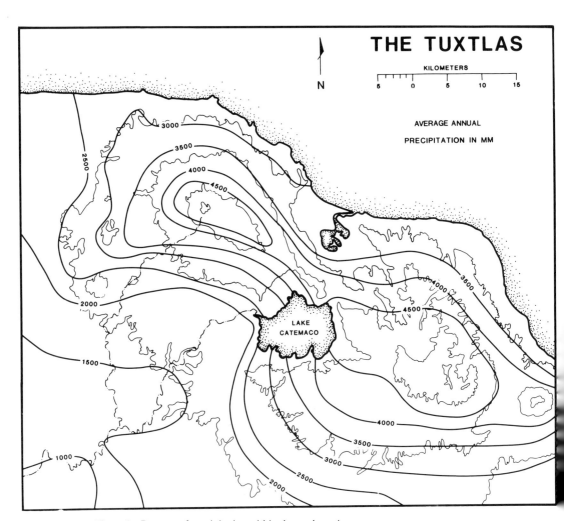

Figure 3   Patterns of precipitation within the study region.

Table 2 *Mean monthly precipitation data from fourteen Tuxtlas weather stations*[1]

Station	Jan.	Feb.	Mar.	Apr.	May	June	July	Aug.	Sep.	Oct.	Nov.	Dec.	Total Annual
Catemaco A	42.6	31.0	26.9	36.7	62.0	280.4	410.9	313.0	432.9	291.2	151.0	71.5	2150.2
Catemaco B	55.3	37.4	25.6	25.7	63.5	234.2	368.5	291.3	407.6	287.0	146.8	88.4	2041.3
Coyame	263.7	190.3	138.9	119.7	102.2	448.8	686.5	547.6	760.2	718.0	488.0	341.3	4795.2
Lauchapan	24.6	18.8	24.6	23.5	61.6	175.5	282.4	241.6	354.9	234.1	86.5	58.1	1586.2
Los Mangos	53.7	26.5	15.3	15.0	44.4	169.2	316.4	254.8	317.5	253.7	132.2	67.3	1666.1
Morillo	26.4	20.5	18.2	16.6	47.0	171.7	236.7	188.0	257.4	255.5	112.0	63.6	1413.6
San Andres	44.6	23.2	26.4	39.6	67.7	218.2	299.8	288.8	453.9	322.2	142.2	70.8	1993.3
San Juanillo	24.2	21.1	21.9	24.8	53.8	182.0	304.2	237.8	226.8	169.6	69.0	43.6	1378.9
Santa Rosalia	38.1	36.5	23.1	20.0	19.9	168.9	234.2	228.1	294.8	250.7	134.1	81.7	1530.1
Santiago	86.5	37.2	31.9	44.4	72.2	282.0	321.2	263.9	455.8	394.7	190.9	134.4	2314.6
Sinapa Bajo	98.2	54.3	38.6	29.8	67.6	217.3	433.0	337.3	468.0	403.0	210.6	144.1	2511.8
Tapalapan	237.2	129.6	97.0	83.8	130.1	258.0	323.0	278.4	524.0	680.0	457.4	325.9	3560.6
Tres Zapotes	94.3	40.1	34.6	26.6	51.0	170.5	278.5	220.0	329.9	429.9	178.9	132.1	1986.4
Zapotitlan	159.3	103.6	89.2	50.1	70.0	357.4	360.8	349.3	521.0	606.4	321.5	348.4	3228.0

[1] In millimeters.

Table 3 *Mean monthly precipitation data by season from fourteen Tuxtlas weather stations*[1]

	Season	
Station	Dry	Wet
Catemaco A	39.8	278.2
Catemaco B	41.5	260.5
Coyame	162.9	570.0
Lauchapan	30.6	204.7
Los Mangos	30.9	215.8
Morillo	25.7	183.5
San Andres	40.3	256.5
San Juanillo	27.2	176.1
Santa Rosalia	27.5	198.9
Santiago	54.4	291.8
Sinapa Bajo	57.7	316.1
Tapalapan	142.7	406.6
Tres Zapotes	49.3	248.5
Zapotitlan	94.4	409.2

[1] In millimeters (SPP 1981).

seasonal patterns of rainfall (Table 2). The dry season occurs between January and May, coinciding with the coldest time of the year. April and May are frequently the driest months in Los Tuxtlas. In addition to lowering temperatures, *nortes* also affect precipitation; these periodic storms produce highly localized rains and make the largest single contribution to winter rainfall (Andrle 1964:36).

The wet season encompasses the period from June through December, with the heaviest rain generally falling between September and October. Increased precipitation often reflects the contribution of tropical depressions and hurricanes, which are more common toward the end of the wet seasons. A short dry period during the summer (usually in August) is called *el veranillo* (Andrle 1964:35) or *la canicula* (Gomez-Pompa 1973).

A comparison of these seasons based on average monthly rainfall is even more striking (Table 3). The mean monthly precipitation during the dry season varies from under 30 mm to over 150 mm, with an average of almost 60 mm. During the wet season these amounts range from a low of 176 mm to a mensal high of 570 mm. Thus, wet season precipitation for any given community is from three to six times greater than the dry season rainfall.

PRODUCTION RESOURCES
Clays
The clay-containing deposits in Los Tuxtlas are the result of continuous volcanism coupled with a series of marine transgressions and regressions (Arnold 1987:72–80;

Table 4 *Distance to clay sources used by Tuxtlas potters*

| | | Distance[1] | | |
Community	Clay type	Kilometers	Hours	N
San Isidro	*Colorado*	1.2	0.30	11
	Amarillo	1.0	0.25	5
	Both			2
Bascascaltepec	*Amarillo*	1.6	0.40	2
Chuniapan de				
Abajo	*Amarillo*	4.0	1.00	15
	Negro	8.0	2.00	2
Sehualaca	*Blanco*	5.0	1.20	10
	Amarillo	3.0	0.80	1
	Both			2

[1] Measured as round trip distance to source.

Pool 1990:148–161; Rios Macbeth 1952). These episodic inundations resulted in the formation of a thick bed of sedimentary clays, known as the Concepcion Formation (Rios Macbeth 1952). Based on in-field examinations, kaolinite appears to be the dominant clay mineral within this deposit (Pool 1990:150). These sedimentary clays are fine grained, probably the result of size sorting during transport (e.g. Rice 1987:45).

Clays containing kaolinite possess several functional properties that are important to the traditional potter. Plasticity, or the clay's ability to retain a shape after it has been molded (Grim 1962:54), is perhaps the most significant. Kaolinitic clays are generally considered to exhibit good plasticity levels (Rice 1987:Table 2.7). Excessive shrinkage, on the other hand, is a property to be avoided (e.g. Arnold 1971:30–31; Shepard 1956:18). Shrinkage occurs when absorbed water molecules are driven off as the raw material dries. For traditional potters, high shrinkage rates can result in vessels cracking (Arnold 1985:21). Because of their mineralogical structure, koalin clays do not absorb large amounts of water. These clays are less susceptible than other fine-grain, plastic clays to the negative impacts of shrinkage (Grim 1962:81; Rice 1987:49).

Clay-bearing deposits of the Concepcion Formation are primarily exposed in the south and southwestern portion of the San Martin massif. Both contemporary and prehispanic potters have exploited these sources (Pool 1990:161). The average one-way distance from production communities to clay sources is 1.81 km (Table 4). This distance is reasonably close to the 1 km "preferred territory of exploitation" noted by Arnold (1985:38–50). In terms of pheric distances, potters in the Tuxtlas fall toward the lower end of the spectrum, traveling on foot an average of under one hour to obtain their clay. Producers in each community tend to favor a single source of clay, although different deposits are utilized for a number of reasons (see below). Potters rarely pay to mine the clay, but when a fee is charged it is usually rendered in the equivalent of ceramic vessels.

The potters of San Isidro use two clays to manufacture their ceramics. The first clay is called *colorado*; it fires to a dark red, the result of relatively high amounts of iron oxides and organic material. The deposit is located about 0.6 km from the center of town, on the property of a local farmer who occasionally charges a user fee. Seven of the potters using this source are related to the *ejido* owner and do not pay.

Despite the levy, *colorado* clay is preferred by the San Isidro producers. Like all the potters studied, San Isidro producers manufacture primarily utilitarian ceramics, with an emphasis on cooking vessels. Clays rich in organic material are often favored for such products, as the organic matter burns away and the resulting pores in the clay body aid in arresting cracks brought about by thermal stress (Arnold 1985:23–24; Rye 1981). Clays that fire to a dark color are also preferred for cooking vessels due to improved thermal retention (Arnold 1985:23).

About one-third of the producers use the *amarillo* clay: a light tan/brown, fine-grain clay that fires to a medium orange. Despite different clay characteristics, potters using the *amarillo* clay manufacture the same suite of utilitarian vessels noted above. There is no charge for mining this deposit because it is not on agriculturally productive land. Mining consists of digging shallow pits about 1 m wide and 0.5–1 m deep. This clay occurs in a relatively thin deposit, so a number of these small excavations are scattered along the base of the hill.

Only two of the potters studied in San Isidro use both types of clay. In the case of the first potter, the *amarillo* clay was most frequently used. This potter generally manufactures ashtrays, and given the previous discussion there would be little reason to use the *colorado* clay for this purpose. In the second case clays were used interchangeably and there was no apparent selection in terms of the forms made from the different clays. Despite this lack of functional differentiation the potter never mixed the two clays. The purposeful separation of these clays suggests an appreciation for the different firing properties of the raw material (e.g. Arnold 1971).

The clay used by Bascascaltepec potters is also called *amarillo*, although it is not the same material used in San Isidro. The Bascascaltepec *amarillo* is located about 0.8 km to the north of the community. This clay is fine grain and low in organic inclusions. The Bascascaltepec potters do not pay to use the deposit.

In Chuniapan de Abajo two varieties of clay are used. The first is a yellow clay with a sandy matrix (yet another *amarillo*), while the second is a darker clay containing more organic matter (*negro*). In neither case do the potters pay for the raw material. The *amarillo* clay is the most common material used, and the deposit is located about 30 minutes or 2 km to the east of the village on the border of an agricultural field. Of the 17 potters in Chuniapan de Abajo, fifteen use this clay.

The *negro* clay is located at a greater distance and requires a one-way trip of about 4 km. Potters who use this material prefer it to the yellow clay because they feel that the vessels are more durable and they find the fired color more aesthetically pleasing. As one potter put it, "Mas rojos salen los comales," or the comales become a darker red after the firing. Interestingly, the ceramics manufactured by this potter also exhibit some of the highest use life values for this vessel type (Chapter 4). One method of judging material quality thus appears to be based on the chromatics of the finished product (e.g. Shepard 1956:86).

Despite the *negro* clay's superior quality, it is not exploited intensively. Without pack animals or other means to gather the raw material, potters using the *negro* source cannot collect sufficient material on one trip to compensate for the added travel time.

Two kinds of raw material are also used by the potters in Sehualaca. As in the above cases, however, the vast majority of producers favor one clay, and even if both materials are used they are almost never mixed. The first clay is a white, fine-grain material that fires to a pale orange. This clay is obtained from about 2.5 km away in the hills to the southeast. The deposit is situated close to the surface and the potters dig no more than 75 cm to gather the material. The Sehualaca producers consider this clay to be superior, both in terms of workability and the quality of the fired vessel. Of the thirteen potters, twelve use this material.

The second clay is collected to the west of Sehualaca at a distance of about 1.5 km. This material is used by three different potters, but only one of them relies on it exclusively. There are apparently two reasons for using both materials. The first reason is a combination of the distance and labor availability. The potters who use both sources tend to be older women who rely on the inferior clay if they find themselves without assistance when it is time to gather the raw material. The second factor is the accessibility. Several potters mentioned that the closer clay deposit is often inaccessible because of flooding. During these periods, potters are forced to collect their material from the more distant source.

Temper

As used throughout this study, *temper* refers to nonplastics added to the ceramic paste by the potter (Shepard 1956:25). Volcanic material, commonly found throughout the Tuxtlas, provides an excellent source of temper for ceramic production. Layers of ash are often size graded, with the larger, heavier particles located near the bottom of the deposit and the finer sediments situated at the top. Presorted tempering materials are thus available to the potter. The availability of such deposits can significantly reduce processing time (e.g. Shepard 1956:26).

Another advantage of volcanic ash is its low level of thermal expansion. Chemically, volcanic ash is considered a basic material (e.g. Rice 1987:33–34). Basic materials have a lower rate of expansion than many marine sediments containing calcium oxides and quartz (Arnold 1985:24; Rye 1976:116–118). Tempers with the lowest levels of thermal expansion reduce stress during repeated heating and cooling of the ceramic body (Arnold 1985:24). Riley (1984) has recently suggested that the exchange of cooking vessels tempered with volcanic ash throughout the Mediterranean area during Late Bronze and early Iron ages resulted from their superior resistance to thermal stress. This same characteristic could also account for the presence of volcanic ash in some Lowland Maya wares (e.g. Simmons and Brem 1979; Smith 1971:269). The vast majority of items made by the Tuxtlas potters are cooking vessels, which are precisely those items subject to repeated heating and cooling episodes. Volcanic ash constitutes some of the best temper for these utilitarian vessels.

The form of the nonplastic is another consideration; clays attain a weaker bond with smooth, rounded materials than rougher, more irregular materials of the same size (Shepard 1956:27). Because of its irregular shape, volcanic ash bonds readily with clay and improves overall vessel strength. In this regard ash-tempered pottery is superior to ceramics tempered with sand (Rye 1976; Shepard 1956:27). Ceramic producers in Highland Guatemala, faced with a choice between marine and volcanic deposits, overwhelmingly favor volcanic ash as a temper (Rice 1976).

Data on the access and use of temper confirm the Tuxtlas potters' preference for this material (Table 5). It is also apparent, however, that not all the potting communities use volcanic ash. Tertiary and Quaternary sedimentary outcrops segment the geological landscape (Pool 1990:148–161), in some cases significantly increasing the distance to the nearest available ash deposit. When this distance becomes too great potters choose an alternative tempering material.

The potters in San Isidro find themselves in precisely this situation. Although this community is located on the edge of the Tertiary sediment/Quaternary volcanic series, there are no exposed ash deposits in close proximity. Instead of volcanic ash, these potters exploit a deposit of Tertiary sediments that contains quartz-feldspar sands (Pool 1990:151). This deposit is located about 1.50 km to the northwest, on a high ridge overlooking the community. Potters tend to gather larger amounts of temper than clay during a single collection episode, in part because the temper is located farther away. As a result, potters will sometimes 'rent' a friend's burro in order to gather as much temper as possible during a single trip. A potter collecting temper in this fashion may gather up to 70 kg. If either funds or burros are unavailable, however, the potter will simply carry smaller quantities of the material back to her house.

Ceramic producers in the three remaining communities rely on deposits of volcanic ash, which tend to be exposed along stream courses near the villages. Potters are never charged for this material. Pottery producers in Bascascaltepec travel an average distance of 2.75 km to obtain their temper while the average distances for the Chuniapan and Sehualaca potters are 0.48 km and 0.45 km, respectively. The average one-way distance to temper for the entire region is 0.93 km.

Table 5 *Distance to temper sources used by Tuxtlas potters*

| Community | Temper | Distance[1] | | |
		Kilometers	Hours	N
San Isidro	Sand with quartz/shell	3.00	1.00	18
Bascascaltepec	Volcanic Ash	5.50	1.50	2
Chuniapan de Abajo	Volcanic Ash	0.96	0.20	17
Sehualaca	Volcanic Ash	0.90	0.18	13

[1] Measured as round trip distance to source.

Fuel

The fuel used in firing vessels is a third natural resource that must be considered from an ecological perspective (e.g. Arnold 1985:53–54; Matson 1965:210). Like the other production materials, the character of the fuel resources is determined by the geology and the climate of the region. In addition, fuel availability is also a function of agricultural activities and deforestation.

Tuxtlas potters usually rely on easily obtainable wood products to fire their ceramics, although a few potters also employ animal dung when it is available (Table 6). Potters in San Isidro are faced with the most difficult task of obtaining fuel, be it for household cooking or for firing ceramics. The area around San Isidro has been heavily deforested due to agricultural practices (Gomez-Pompa 1973; Killion 1987). Firewood must be obtained from relatively long distances or must be purchased. In fact, San Isidro is the only community of potters that regularly purchases wood to fire ceramics. Wood is sold by individuals who travel to the forest, cut the material, and then use horses or burros to transport it back. Wood is purchased by the *carga*, which is a pile of 100 pieces, each piece approximately 50 cm long and about 10 cm thick. Potters usually use one *carga* of wood per firing. Those potters choosing not to purchase fuel must travel an average distance of 10.6 km to collect wood. In San Isidro, only three potters who fired their own ceramics did not purchase wood from a vendor. The remaining fourteen potters (excluding one who fired her ceramics with a neighbor) all paid for their wood.

The potters of the other Tuxtlas communities have greater access to fuel. These three communities are located in the south where the high evergreen selvas of the sierras give way to the savannas, grasslands, and palm stands of the coastal plain (Gomez-Pompa 1973). In Sehualaca, which lies between these two zones, the potters use a mixture of fuels including hardwood, palm fronds, and cow dung. Potters in this community travel an average distance of 2.42 km for their materials.

Table 6   *Distance to fuel resources used by Tuxtlas potters*

Community	Fuel[2]	Distance[1]		
		Kilometers	Hours	N
San Isidro	Hardwood	21.20	5.00	3
Bascascaltepec	Hardwood and Palm Fronds	15.00	3.00	2
Chuniapan de Abajo	Palm Fronds	5.28	1.20	11
	Palm Fronds and Hardwood	5.60	1.40	6
Sehualaca	Palm Fronds, Hardwood and Cow Dung	4.82	1.00	13

[1] Measured as round trip distance to source.
[2] Listed in order of importance.

In Bascascaltepec, to the southeast of San Andres, the potters rely on palm fronds and hardwood. These potters find their materials at an average distance of 7.5 km, the second longest trip for the study communities. Bascascaltepec is located along the border of the central agricultural zone, and has thus been faced with an increasing amount of deforestation for agricultural land. Potters have yet to begin paying for their fuel, but increased pressure in the future might make buying wood a necessity.

Palm stands become the dominant vegetation in Chuniapan de Abajo and provide the potters of this community with their main source of fuel. Almost 65 percent of these potters use palm fronds exclusively, while the remaining 35 percent use a combination of palm fronds and hardwood. The average distance to fuel for these potters is 2.64 km.

Social environment

Subsistence agriculture constitutes the primary economic pursuit in the ceramic-producing communities. Pottery-making households participate in the *ejido*-based system of land use in which the male head of each *campesino* household is granted a parcel of land to cultivate (Killion 1987). Since the program's inception, however, much of the higher quality land has come under private ownership and the amount of arable *ejido* holdings has decreased. Many *ejido* plots are held by the same extended family for generations, with production rights passing to the male family members (Killion 1987). Married males and their wives often take up residence with or near the husband's family in order to secure their access to the *ejido* holdings.

The women who make pottery must schedule their efforts around the labor demands of the annual agricultural cycle. This requirement decreases the amount of time available for production and reduces the potential for ceramic specialization. As noted previously, the study communities are situated on the border of the central agricultural zones. According to Killion, dry-season farming in this zone is an important activity: "Peak labor loads, due to the overlap in the number of crops planted for household consumption, occur between May and August, but moderate labor loads also occur in the late winter and early spring when *tonamil* [dry season] agricultural activities can be quite demanding" (1987:186). Although the dry season provides the best conditions for making pottery, in many instances ceramic production must be delayed until the agricultural activities have been completed. Potters are thus forced to balance the manufacture of ceramics against the labor requirements of subsistence agriculture.

This balance is reflected in the frequency of production activities. As used throughout this study, production frequency is an index of labor input based on the number of days per week devoted to production tasks. The difficulties in acquiring a *representative* sample of time allotments among the fifty individual potters should be obvious, especially given the seasonal nature of their work. The alternatives were to concentrate on the activities of a few potters and assume they were representative, or establish a scale that potters felt sufficiently comfortable using. Because it included information obtained from all potters, the latter alternative was chosen.

A histogram of production frequency values suggests a slightly skewed, bimodal distribution (Figure 4). The majority of potters work between 1.5 and 3.5 days per week, with only 12 percent of the 50 producers making pottery more than 4 days per week. Despite the bimodal tendency of the distribution, both the mean and median are about the same, with values of 3.06 and 3.00 days per week respectively. This similarity suggests that high outlier values are not adversely affecting these figures.

Even when viewed at the community level, this bimodality is still present (Table 7). The communities fall into two distinct groups: (a) San Isidro and Sehualaca; and (b) Bascascaltepec and Chuniapan de Abajo. In order to determine if this division was significant, production frequency figures were subject to a Mann Witney U test. This statistic is perfectly suited to the task since it does not assume a normal population distribution and works on relatively small sample sizes (Blalock 1972). The results confirm that San Isidro and Sehualaca exhibit significantly higher rates of production frequency than Bascascaltepec and Chuniapan de Abajo ($U=136.5, Z=3.36, p<0.05$). Similar tests failed to produce a significant difference between San Isidro and Sehualaca ($U=89.5, Z=1.10, p>0.05$), while such a difference does exist between San Isidro and Chuniapan de Abajo ($U=51, Z=3.35, p<0.05$) and between Sehualaca

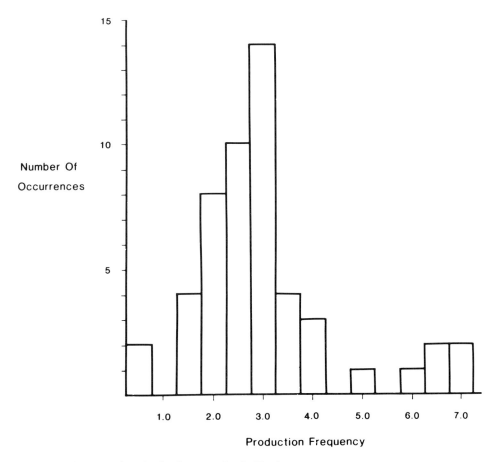

Figure 4   Histogram of production frequency for the Tuxtlas potters.

Table 7 *Production frequency data from Tuxtlas ceramic production communities*

Community	Production frequency		Firing		
	Mean	Median	Mean	Median	N
San Isidro	3.88	3.00	1.13	1.00	18
Bascascaltepec	1.62	1.62	0.75	0.75	2
Chuniapan de Abajo	2.29	2.00	1.26	1.00	17
Sehualaca	3.15	3.00	0.96	1.00	13
TOTAL	3.06	3.00	1.12	1.00	50

and Chuniapan de Abajo ($U=49$, $Z=2.55$, $p<0.05$). In no cases did Bascascaltepec differ from the three communities, an unsurprising fact given its small sample size ($N=2$). Despite the lack of a significant difference, the small value for Bascascaltepec suggests a low production frequency. Based on the difference between the two groups, it appears that San Isidro and Sehualaca make ceramics more frequently than Chuniapan de Abajo and Bascascaltepec.

LEARNING THE CRAFT
The women of the household make ceramics in Los Tuxtlas. Of the fifty potters interviewed in this study, there was only one male. This individual was physically disabled and could not perform the agricultural activities commonly conducted by the male members of the *campesino* population. Ceramic production was apparently chosen as an alternative because he was related to several women in the community, all of whom made pottery. He was able to obtain raw material from his sisters, so he did not have to travel to the sources to collect it.

The majority of potters in the Tuxtlas were taught to make ceramics by a member of their immediate family (Table 8) – twenty-seven producers learned from their mother, three were taught by their mother's sister, and another two learned from their mother's mother. In other words, thirty-two potters were taught by some member of their matriline. In contrast, only four potters learned their craft from members of their husband's family. Seven potters learned by watching a neighbor, while the remaining seven claimed to have been instructed by no one in particular.

Although the majority of producers learned pottery making through kinship ties, those who did not represent an interesting study group. This pattern is especially prominent among the ceramic producers of Chuniapan de Abajo, which contains over half of the potters belonging to the latter category. One possible conditioner of this difference appears to be the mean age at which production is learned.

The average age for learning pottery production throughout the Tuxtlas region is 18 years, with a median value of 16 (Table 9). Producers in San Isidro and Sehualaca begin at an average age of sixteen, while the potters in the other communities do not start making ceramics until they are at least twenty.

Table 8 *Relationship to teacher among Tuxtlas ceramic producers*

| Community | Wife's side | | | Husband's side | | | |
	Mother	Aunt	Grand-mother	Mother	Grand-mother	Neighbor	On own
San Isidro	12	1	1	-	-	2	2
Bascascaltepec	2	-	-	-	-	-	-
Chuniapan de Abajo	6	-	1	1	2	2	5
Sehualaca	7	2	-	1	-	3	-
TOTAL	27	3	2	2	2	7	7

The relatively late age at which pottery manufacture is learned in Chuniapan de Abajo helps clarify why so many producers in that community have learned on their own or from a neighbor. For most of the Tuxtlas potters, marriage and children are quite common by the age of twenty. As noted previously, married couples usually reside with or near the husband's family. When a woman has married and begun a family of her own, she seldom has the opportunity to return to her mother's home for ceramic lessons. Ceramic production may also be adopted as a secondary income, a necessity that would become more likely as the potter's own household continues to grow. In either case these married women are more likely to learn from their neighbor or from a member of their husband's family, rather than someone in their own family. The relatively low production intensity exhibited by the potters of Chuniapan de Abajo indicates that production is a comparatively low-priority economic strategy. Thus, there is less likelihood that a girl's mother will make ceramics. The network through which a potter is taught, therefore, is an indirect function of the potter's age.

There is also a relationship between production frequency and learning to make pottery. The potters of San Isidro and Sehualaca make ceramics more often than the remaining communities and also display the youngest age at which ceramic production is learned. While conclusive data are not available, it does appear that families

Table 9 *Age at which Tuxtlas potters learn to make ceramics*

Community	Mean	Median	Minimum	Maximum	N
San Isidro	16.58	15.00	8.00	27.00	17
Bascascaltepec	25.50	25.50	25.00	26.00	2
Chuniapan de Abajo	20.62	20.00	10.00	37.00	16
Sehualaca	16.33	16.50	9.00	25.00	12
TOTAL	18.27	16.00	8.00	37.00	47

operating at a higher level of production teach their daughters at a younger age. This relationship has also been noted for potters in Guatemala (Deal 1983:51; Hayden and Cannon 1984). Among these Guatemalan potters the majority were taught by some member of the potter's matriline. In addition, daughters of potters working at a higher production output were more likely to learn ceramic production at a younger age than the daughters of less intensive producers. Although comparable data are not available from the Tuxtlas, a similar pattern of learning seems to be in evidence.

LABOR ALLOCATION

The number of individuals within the potter's household can have both detrimental and beneficial effects on ceramic production activities. Ceramic production is just one of the tasks that falls to the peasant women of the Tuxtlas. These potters are also responsible for cooking, cleaning, washing clothes, attending the market, and assisting with cultivation. Consequently, the larger the family, the more time must be devoted to the numerous domestic chores. The demands of these activities can reduce the amount of time available for manufacturing pottery (e.g. Arrot 1967:42). Increases in family size may prove detrimental to domestic pottery production.

On the other hand, the larger the family, the greater the potential pool of domestic labor. Within large households domestic responsibilities can be delegated to other family members. Usually these tasks fall to the adolescent females of the household, who may help with cleaning, cooking, and caring for smaller children. Under these conditions, the potter may have more available time for ceramic manufacture. Large household populations, therefore, might also provide a "deviation amplifying" mechanism for ceramic production activities or specialization in general (e.g. Arnold 1985:234).

The household demographic profiles for Tuxtlas potters suggest that neither possibility is particularly strong in this region (Table 10). Despite the differences in production frequency, there is little intercommunity variability in either the size of the household population or the sexual composition of its members. The average size of a potter's family is slightly over six persons, with a tendency to have more males than females. Median values are similarly distributed. The only community that deviates from this pattern is Bascascaltepec, with an average of eight persons and a higher number of females than males. Spearman's correlations failed to establish a significant relationship between production frequency and either males ($r_s=0.12, p>0.3$), females ($r_s=-0.11, p>0.4$), or total population ($r_s=-0.02, p>0.5$).

While production frequency is not directly related to household size, it does have an impact on labor allocation. Households are more likely to have someone helping the potter on a consistent basis if production was more than three days per week (Table 11). Of the thirteen potters working at a high (i.e. above median) frequency, twelve receive some form of help, while seventeen of the eighteen potters with no assistance operate at a low frequency of production. A chi-square analysis supports this observation ($X^2=6.11, p<0.05, d.f.=1, Q=0.82$).

Also important when considering labor allocation is the number of assistants. Not

Table 10 *Family size/composition data from Tuxtlas ceramic production communities*

Community	Persons		Males		Females		
	Mean	Median	Mean	Median	Mean	Median	N
San Isidro	6.77	5.50	3.44	3.00	3.33	2.00	18
Bascascaltepec	8.00	8.00	3.50	3.50	4.50	4.50	2
Chuniapan de Abajo	5.94	6.00	3.23	3.00	2.71	2.00	17
Sehualaca	5.76	5.00	3.31	2.00	2.46	2.00	13
TOTAL	6.28	5.50	3.34	3.00	2.94	2.00	50

surprisingly, this variable associates significantly with household population (Table 12). Only one of the fifteen households with low populations have more than one helper, while eight of the nine cases with high numbers of assistants coincide with high household population ($X^2=6.43$, $p<0.05$, d.f.$=1$, $Q=0.85$).

Finally, we should consider what tasks are being performed and who is conducting them. Within the Tuxtlas sample, the activities requiring the least amount of technical expertise are most frequently performed by production assistants (Table 13). Material acquisition requires the least amount of know-how, especially when the primary role of the assistant is to transport rather than select the raw material. Of the thirty-two potters who are aided during production, 81 percent receive help during this initial production stage.

Raw material preparation is also a comparatively mechanical process, conducted by 28 percent of the assistance. Vessel forming and vessel firing, the two activities that probably require the greatest expertise, are associated with considerably lower frequencies of assistance. Only about 16 percent of the potters are helped during the formation of a vessel while less than 10 percent of the producers obtain regular help during vessel thinning. No potters are consistently aided during vessel firing.

Table 11 *Contingency table of production frequency by presence/absence of production assistants*

Production frequency	Assistants	
	Absent	Present
Low ≤3	17	20
High >3	1	12

$X^2=6.11$, $p<0.05$, d.f.$=1$, Yule's $Q=0.82$

Table 12 *Contingency table of household population by number of production assistants*

| | Number of assistants | |
Household population	Low	High
Low ≤5	14	1
High >5	9	8

$X^2=6.43$, $p<0.05$, d.f.$=1$, Yule's $Q=0.85$

The overwhelming majority of potters thus received help in obtaining raw material. And although production is a female activity, males make a surprisingly large contribution to this stage of production (Table 14). In fact, in only two instances were females other than the potter involved in gathering raw materials. The majority of males providing this aid are either husbands or elder children. These males are physically strong enough to carry substantial quantities of the material or are sufficiently experienced to watch over the draft animal in the rare instance when one is used.

The second pattern suggested by the data is that males aid more frequently with fuel acquisition than the collection of any other resource. This tendency is interesting when viewed from the perspective noted above, namely that assistants usually conduct those tasks that require the least amount of technical skill. The potter, of course, has the best understanding of the desired raw-material properties. Clay and temper are especially important in this regard, because if inferior material is collected there is very little that can be done with it. Fuel, on the other hand, may not be appropriate for vessel firing (i.e. it may burn too slowly or may not produce sufficient heat), but it can still be used for the family hearth. Thus, if an assistant collects inferior fuel it may be still usable while inferior clay and temper are not. Fuel acquisition, therefore, is an

Table 13 *Production tasks conducted by potters' assistants*[1]

Community	Material acquisition	Material preparation	Vessel formation	Vessel thinning	Vessel firing
San Isidro	7	7	4	2	-
Bascascaltepec	1	1	-	-	-
Chuniapan de Abajo	11	1	1	1	-
Sehualaca	7	-	-	-	-
TOTAL	26	9	5	3	0

[1] Numbers may reflect assistance in more than one stage by the same individual.

Table 14 *Assistance with raw material acquisition*[1]

	Clay		Temper		Fuel	
Community	Males	Females	Males	Females	Males	Females
San Isidro	1	-	2	-	5	–
Bascascaltepec	–	1	-	-	-	-
Chuniapan de Abajo	7	-	1	-	7	1
Sehualaca	4	-	-	-	5	-
TOTAL	12	1	3	0	17	1

[1] Numbers for each community may reflect several tasks performed by one individual

activity embedded in the general suite of domestic tasks. Males who aid in collecting clay or temper are almost always accompanied by the potter, while males gathering firewood often go on their own or with other male friends. Assistants thus tend to conduct the least technical activities and males are responsible for gathering the "safest" raw material from the standpoint of pottery production.

Summary

Tuxtlas potters are confronted with a contradictory production environment. While deposits of fine grain clay and volcanic ash are readily obtainable on one hand, precipitation patterns are less conducive to successful ceramic production. Even the driest months are characterized by periodic *nortes* that bring heavy rains and dramatic drops in temperature. Potters working during this season must be extremely vigilant as these conditions not only impact firing but may also interfere with drying schedules.

This same environment, however, does not vary markedly between the production communities. All potters are faced with comparable difficulties and potential solutions. For example, even though rainfall varies greatly on a seasonal basis, differences among the pottery-making villages are not significant. Similarly, most potters employ the same suite of raw materials and face similar demands on their time brought about by household economics. In this sense the production environment is comparatively homogeneous.

Even when considering the social environment, there is still a wide amount of comparability among the producers. Many of the relationships are relatively pre-dictable. Most producers were instructed in pottery making at an early age and learned from a member of their matriline. The more often a potter worked, the more likely the chance of having some help during production. The number of assistants was related to the household population. Finally, the tasks performed by those helpers were usually the least demanding in terms of production experience. The patterns are relatively straight forward and not surprising.

The most notable difference was in production frequency, in which potters at San Isidro and Sehualaca worked more often than the potters in Chuniapan de Abajo and

Bascascaltepec. It would be reasonable to expect this distinction to be manifest in the kinds of production tools and techniques employed by the various potters. As the following chapter indicates, however, production frequency does not appear to be associated with differences in pottery making. In fact, many of the most interesting differences displayed by the Tuxtlas potters occur between producers who are operating at similar levels of output. Thus, despite overall similarities in both the natural and cultural production environments, important producer distinctions continue to exist. The remaining two chapters in this section explore these differences in detail. The next section provides a method for addressing some of this variability in both contemporary and archaeological contexts.

3

Ceramic production in Los Tuxtlas

The previous chapter characterized the Tuxtlas potters as traditional producers operating on a seasonal basis. Minor variability in the production environment was noted (i.e. clays and temper), but other factors such as climate and subsistence activities did not vary markedly between production communities. Despite the separation of potters into two groups, based on time invested in production, pottery manufacture in Los Tuxtlas is essentially an unspecialized, part-time domestic chore.

This overall consistency in production scale and mode, however, is not mirrored by uniformity in manufacturing activities. In fact, the Tuxtlas potters display certain crucial differences in production tools and techniques. These technological distinctions are extremely relevant, for they constitute one of the primary vehicles for interpreting pottery manufacture in the past (also see Stark 1985). Differences in the number and kinds of tools are often associated with very different production systems (Peacock 1982:8–11; van der Leeuw 1984:Figure 1). Firing technology is a case in point; open-air firing is often associated with small-scale production while oven or kiln firing may be symptomatic of more intensive production industries (e.g. Foster 1955:10; Rice 1987:181–182; van der Leeuw 1976:392–398, 1977). Firing differences may also develop to mitigate climatic conditions (Arnold 1985:213). Kilns are of considerable archaeological importance, in that they are more likely to leave discernible archaeological traces than open or even pit firing (Stark 1985:165; also Deal 1988:124).

As the following discussion demonstrates both open and kiln firing are carried out by the Tuxtlas potters. Interestingly, this distinction does not correlate with significant differences in other variables commonly used to characterize production scale or mode (Kramer 1985:80–81; Rice 1987:170–172). Furthermore, it is not associated with climatological patterns in the study region. The fact that potters, operating at similar production states, may employ such a range of techniques is one effective argument against the conventional scheme for classifying production activities (see Chapter 5). Ironically, the variability masked by these classifications may be crucial to clarifying the relationships between pottery manufacture and the archaeological record.

The following discussion is divided into four general steps of ceramic production. Since accessing raw materials was described in the previous chapter, this treatment begins with the preparation and processing of those materials. Among the Tuxtlas potters this step involves minimal time and labor investment. Vessel formation is then considered. Two techniques of making pottery are documented in the Tuxtlas: (a) a "molding" technique only used for *comales*; and (b) a more common hand-modeling procedure used to make all vessel forms. How pots are dried is the subject of the third section. This section emphasizes the spatial requirements of drying as much as the process of drying itself. Pottery firing is the topic of the final section. The differences in vessel firing are discussed, as is their lack of association with either the frequency of production (i.e. labor input) or the intensity of production (i.e. labor output).

Raw material processing
Once raw materials have been collected, some degree of processing or refinement is often required before they can be used. The potter may pulverize the clay, making it easier to mix and extract large inclusions (e.g. Papousek 1981). Tempers must be sifted, insuring appropriate size and facilitating adequate distribution throughout the clay body. Fuel must be dried and the green portions removed. These green parts often produce steam that can damage vessels during firing.

REFINING
In the case of the Tuxtlas potters, most of the materials occur in a naturally refined manner. The quality of the clay is high and is generally low in aplastic inclusions. Tempers, especially ash, frequently occur in size-sorted deposits, making extraction of desired granule size an easier task. If wood is purchased from vendors, it has already been cut and requires little additional attention. Potters collecting their own fuel select the oldest, driest material possible, thereby reducing processing time. At least for the ceramic producers in the Tuxtlas, raw-material preparation requires little effort when compared to the other production activities.

Drying the material is a necessary first step in processing clay. Given the heavy rains that can occur in the Tuxtlas, the deposits are often saturated, even during the dry season (see discussion of *nortes* in Chapter 2). After the clay has been collected it is spread out in a cleared area of the houselot to dry. In some instances the material is laid out on a piece of plastic, but more often it is simply distributed across a small portion of the patio surface. The presence of the clay does not seem to affect the use of the patio in any discernible way and no attempt is made to keep activities away from the drying raw material.

Depending on the weather, the clay may be left out for several days before it has dried. Once this stage has been accomplished the potter places the clay back into a basket or burlap bag (*costal*). While performing this task, the potter will manually crush any large clumps of clay, but no conscious attempt is made at refining the entire batch by pounding or grinding, as is common in other parts of Mexico (e.g. Diaz 1966; Lackey 1982; Popousek 1981; van de Velde and van de Velde 1939). The clay is simply put aside until it is time to mix it with the temper and begin vessel formation.

Temper undergoes a similar, but even less intensive processing stage. Regardless of type, temper is brought back to the household and spread out to dry, again with little concern that it might be mixed with dirt in the patio. The temper dries more quickly than the clay, so it is rarely left out for more than one day. After it has dried, the temper is also stored in a burlap sack or a plastic tub. No attempt to crush the material is made, although the potter will remove any roots or other organic matter found in the temper.

Fuel undergoes no processing to speak of, apart from the removal of the green portions. Fuel may also be cut into appropriate-sized pieces when it is time to fire, but this activity is more situational than regularized. No attempt is made to dry the wood or otherwise make it more readily usable. In fact, unlike the clay and temper, the wood is rarely covered and protected from rain. Wood, however, is consumed more quickly than the other materials. As noted previously, wood is used for a variety of purposes while clay and temper are not.

MIXING THE PASTE

After the clay and temper have been adequately dried, they are mixed together to obtain a clay body of appropriate consistency. Mixing the paste is performed in two ways, depending on the number of vessels to be manufactured. The potter will wedge small quantities of clay on a piece of flat wood; larger amounts are processed by placing the clay on the ground, adding temper, and mixing the mass with the feet. This activity is usually performed by the potter, although the husband and even the children may assist in this task. Next to gathering raw material, processing and preparation are the most common forms of assistance rendered, occurring in about 22 percent of the cases.

Whether the potter mixes small quantities by hand or uses her feet to produce larger amounts, combining clay and temper is usually performed indoors (Table 15). Of the fifty potters, forty-three mix the ceramic paste inside their houses, five conduct the activity outdoors on the patio, and two perform the task within a separate covered area especially constructed for pottery manufacturing. The time required to complete this activity varies as a function of the amount being prepared; amounts combined by hand (usually under 10 kg) can be finished in about 30 to 40 minutes, while larger quantities may require several hours.

After the body has been mixed, it may be stored at one of several locations. There is a preference for storing clay and temper within the house because dry season rainfall is often unpredictable. It is easier to keep the material indoors than risk the chance of losing production time because the raw material must be dried a second time.

Two potters in Sehualaca conduct production activities within special structures.

Table 15 *Location of material preparation activities within the houselot*

| Community | Inside house | | | Outside house | | | Outside house in special facility | | |
	Mixing	*Storage* Clay	Temper	Mixing	*Storage* Clay	Temper	Mixing	*Storage* Clay	Temper
San Isidro	17	11	11	1	7	7	–	–	–
Bascascaltepec	2	2	1	–	–	1	–	–	–
Chuniapan de Abajo	15	15	16	2	2	1	–	–	–
Sehualaca	9	10	11	2	1	–	2	2	2
Total	43	38	39	5	10	9	2	2	2

These structures are roofed-over areas of the patio that are used entirely for ceramic manufacture. Both of these potters devote more than four days per week to production activities and note that production is more efficient if all materials and tools are located in the same place. It appears that these potters are responding to increased production intensity by establishing distinct activity areas within the compound. The allocation of space in this fashion thus serves to minimize task interruption and helps insure comparatively higher levels of production output. The use of special production areas under conditions of increased production intensity has been documented among other traditional potters (Krotser 1974:136; Reina and Hill 1978:98).

CLAY AND TEMPER RATIOS

The important relationship between amounts of clay and temper, and the subsequent effect on production success, has been noted by ceramic technologists (e.g. Rye 1976, 1981; Shepard 1956). Potters are faced with the task of obtaining the proper temper-to-clay ratio so that an acceptable workability and rate of shrinkage can be achieved without compromising the strength of the clay body. Body strength may be especially important to the Tuxtlas potters, given the manner in which ceramic vessels are formed (see below).

The ratio of temper to clay is surprisingly consistent throughout the Tuxtlas, although the amount of material used by different producers varies as a function of the potter's production frequency (Table 16). Two groups become apparent when production frequency is held constant. The first group includes San Isidro and Sehualaca, both of which use about 4 kg of clay a day. The second group consists of Bascascaltepec and Chuniapan de Abajo, who average close to 1.5 kg of clay per day. This grouping parallels the distinction noted for production frequency.

The amount of temper used in pottery manufacture conforms to the same pattern, with one exception. San Isidro potters using the *colorado* clay employ far less temper

Table 16 *Weekly clay and temper consumption rates for representative Tuxtlas households*

Community	Type of clay	Weekly consumption of material[1]		Ratio of temper to clay	Rate of breakage	Production frequency[2]
		Clay	Temper			
San Isidro	*Amarillo*	25.00	13.33	1:1.87	20%	6.00
	Colorado	12.00	3.00	1:4.00	25%	2.50
Bascascal-tepec	*Amarillo*	4.00	1.50	1:2.66	40%	1.50
Chuniapan de Abajo	*Amarillo*	5.00	2.50	1:2.00	35%	2.00
Sehualaca	*Blanco*	12.50	7.50	1:1.66	20%	3.50

[1] Kilograms used during dry season, with number of potters in households held constant.
[2] Days per week during dry season devoted to production.

than the Tuxtlas potters using the other major clays. Here, it is important to remember that the amount of temper added to a clay is primarily a function of the quantity of aplastics that occur naturally in the raw material (Shepard 1956:25–26). As noted earlier, the *colorado* clay contains more organic material than the other San Isidro clay. Organic inclusions provide natural tempering material thereby reducing the necessary amount of additional temper.

As a general rule, potters use about twice as much clay to temper, by weight. This ratio is somewhat higher than that documented for other traditional potters. For example, in their study of Pakistani potters, Rye and Evans (1976:90) note that the potters of Multan add 20 percent of temper by weight to the clay. The volcanic ash used by potters in Highland Guatemala is mixed with clay in a ratio between approximately 1:5 and 1:9, depending on the raw material (Rice 1976). Other Guatemalan potters, using sand temper, achieve a 2:1 ratio of clay to temper (Reina and Hill 1978:98–99). Potters in Acatlan, in the state of Puebla, Mexico, make their wares from a mixture of 75 percent clay and 25 percent temper (Lackey 1982). The fact that comparatively more temper is used in the Tuxtlas ceramics reflects the fine-grain character of the clays and the utilitarian function of the finished product.

Vessel formation
The ceramic producers in the Tuxtlas practice two methods of vessel formation, although one is by far the more common. In both cases formation is relatively simple; the potter either models the vessel from a solid lump of clay or uses a simple mold to form the object. No separate rotating device is used, such as the potter's wheel or the Mayan *kabal* (e.g. Foster 1955; Thompson 1958). Nor are any vessels constructed in separate episodes, with the upper and lower portion manufactured at different times. The practice of forming over a period of two days, however, was observed by Krotser (1974:136–137) for potters in Ranchoapan, a lowland community to the southeast of the Tuxtlas.

PARADO
The most common method of vessel formation in the Tuxtlas is called *parado* ("standing upright" or "standing on end") and consists of shaping the entire vessel from a single mass of solid clay. This same process and terminology is also used by the potters in the lowland to the southeast of the Tuxtlas (Krotser 1980). This method of vessel formation appears to be unique to the Gulf Coast region (e.g. Foster 1955).

Tools
The potter begins by organizing all of the necessary tools and placing them within easy reach. There are five main production tools used in *parado* construction. The most important is a piece of *jicara* (*Cresentia cujete*), the large husk from the seed of trees available throughout the region. The piece of *jicara* is used during the entire formation sequence, first to shape the vessel body and later to smooth the interior surface. Potters often own several pieces of *jicara* of various sizes, each used for shaping a different portion of the vessel. These tools last about nine months on the average. Potters cite the loss of the item as the most common reason for obtaining a new one.

The second tool is a sieve (*cernidor*) used to add small amounts of temper to the clay and also spread a thin layer of temper on the work surface to prevent sticking. This implement usually consists of a used sardine can whose bottom has been perforated with small nail holes about 1 mm in diameter. Large pieces of *jicara*, coconut shell, and even a piece of burlap bag may also be used to sift the temper. Potters rarely own more than one *cernidor*, which generally lasts about fifteen months.

A small can or plastic cup is the third tool commonly used during vessel formation. This container holds the water that is continually used throughout the formation sequence, as well as to store the pieces of *jicara* when production is finished. Potters seldom have more than one water container at any given time, but these items are easily replaced and do not need to be stockpiled.

The fourth implement is a piece of old cloth (*trapo*) that is used to smooth the rim of the vessel at the end of the construction sequence. Potters will often have several pieces of cloth; they are replaced about every two months.

The final production tool is actually not used until the vessel has dried. Once dry, the vessel is thinned and its solid clay base removed by shaving the exterior with a sharp-edged piece of metal. This item is called a *raspador* and is made from any available metal, including an old *machete*, a worn out knife, a piece of aluminum roof, or even pieces of a discarded car body. The *raspador* is about 15 cm long and 5 cm wide, and can last several years.

Formation

After gathering and arranging the necessary production implements, the potter prepares the work surface by placing a handful of temper in the *cernidor* and covering the work area with a thin lens of sand or volcanic ash. Depending on the size of the desired vessel, a mass of clay weighing between 0.5 and 1 kg is then placed on the board and is wedged with the temper. The potter kneads the mass for about five minutes, occasionally adding temper, until she is confident that the correct proportion of temper has been achieved and is properly distributed throughout the clay body. The potter then forms the clay into a cone and sets it aside while the process is repeated. When anywhere between five and ten of these cones have been made, the potter is ready to begin formation.

A small amount of water is sprinkled on the work surface to keep the clay from sticking to the wood. The potter then inverts the cone, so that the small end rests on the board and the larger end extends upward. It is from this larger end that the vessel will be formed. The small end serves as a support so that the clay mass can be rotated. After the vessel has dried, this lower support is cut away and the clay is reused for another vessel.

Production begins with the potter using her fingers to extract small amounts of clay from the center of the large end; the entire mass is rotated, and the clay is pushed against the palm of the other hand to begin forming the vessel walls (Figure 5a). After several rotations, sufficient clay has been built up along the edges of the cone. At this point, the potter takes a piece of *jicara* and repeats the process, slowly turning the cone while the gourd fragment is used to push the clay wall upwards and outwards. One of two strategies can be followed, depending on the type of vessel. If a *comal* (a relatively flat, circular griddle) is to be made, the potter continues shaping and thinning the vessel walls until they extend at about a 70° angle and the vessel is approximately 28 cm

Figure 5a

Figure 5b

Figure 5c

Figure 5   Vessel formation using *parado* technique

in diameter (Figure 5b). If a jar or bowl is the end product, the vessel walls are pushed upwards and inwards while the lower portion is extended outwards until the desired shape is achieved. At the same time the potter continues to pour small amounts of water on the work surface. The potter will also use various sized pieces of *jicara* to smooth the vessel interior.

Finally, the potter takes a damp piece of cloth and, holding it over the rim of the vessel with one hand, uses the other hand to spin the vessel. In this way a smooth and regular rim is created (Figure 5c). The rim is the only portion of the vessel that is prepared in this fashion, although scraping the vessel interior with the gourd also produces a relatively smooth finish. Once the vessel is finished, it is put aside, another cone is selected, and the sequence is repeated.

The spinning motion attained during this procedure is never pronounced, so it does not provide the centrifugal force achieved with the potter's wheel or even the slower, continuous lathe-like motion noted for some potters using the *kabal* (e.g. Thompson 1958). The *parado* technique does make production somewhat easier and more rapid, however. A potter forming an average size *comal* can finish in approximately ten minutes, while a small bowl (*tecualon*) requires about eight minutes and a larger jar (*olla*) or basin (*cazuela*) can be completed in fifteen or twenty minutes.

PALMEADO

The second, and less common, form of vessel production is called *palmeado*. It is used only to manufacture *comales* and *tostadores* (extra–large griddles). This procedure employs a technique reminiscent of concave mold-making (e.g. Foster 1955:6–7), although the "mold" in this case is a cloth-covered tub or basin. The potter begins by sprinkling a small amount of temper on the work surface, but considerably less time is devoted to wedging the clay. Once the clay body is prepared, the potter uses her palm to flatten out the clay, much like she would a *tortilla* (Figure 6a). The clay is usually set on a circular piece of plastic so it does not stick to the wood surface and can be more easily turned. When finished, the clay has been pressed into a flat disk, about 2 cm thick and approximately 28 cm in diameter.

The potter then places this flat disk into a makeshift mold, consisting of a plastic or metal tub (*palangana*) that has been covered with a piece of cloth (Figure 6b). The cloth is secured by tying its corners together underneath the tub. A piece of string may also be wound around the lip of the tub to further secure the cloth. Even so, the cloth is not rigid and there is slight depression where it is stretched over the mouth of the tub.

Potters practicing this technique own an average of six *palanganas*, although the number varies widely. Some potters may own several tubs but primarily use one or two. Vessel size is determined by the diameter of the clay disk prepared by the potter, not the diameter of the *palangana*.

After the clay has been set atop the cloth, the potter will wet a piece of *jicara* and use it to smooth the clay disk (Figure 6c). The pressure applied during smoothing, in addition to the weight of the clay, causes the cloth to sag and provides the clay disk with a degree of concavity. The potter uses her finger, rather than a wet cloth, to smooth the edges of the clay. When the vessel is sufficiently uniform the tub is set aside until the clay has dried and is ready to be fired. This process results in a *comal* that is similar to those produced by the *parado* technique, although these vessels are usually flatter and more shallow. The *palmeado* procedure requires less skill on the part of the potter. *Comales* can be completed in about six minutes using this technique.

Figure 6a

Figure 6b

Figure 6c

Figure 6   Vessel formation using *palmeado* technique

Table 17 *Formation techniques and associated mean production frequencies*

Community	Parado	Mean production frequency	Palmeado	Mean production frequency	Combination	Mean production frequency
San Isidro	18	3.88	–	–	–	–
Bascascaltepec	–	–	2	1.62	–	–
Chuniapan de Abajo	3	2.16	6	2.66	8	2.00
Sehualaca	13	3.15	–	–	–	–
Total	34	3.45	8	2.40	8	2.00

The vast majority of Tuxtlas potters favor one method of production (Table 17). Of the potters, 68 percent (N=34) exclusively practice *parado* formation, while 84 percent (N=42) practice it alone or in combination with *palmeado* production. The *palmeado* technique alone is used by 16 percent (N=8). While potters using only the *parado* technique exhibit the highest average production frequency, there is no significant relationship between production frequency and vessel formation.

VESSEL DIVERSITY
The vessel forms manufactured by the Tuxtlas potters reflect the utilitarian orientation of their products and the household focus of their economy. Ceramics are made for traditional domestic consumption with an emphasis on food preparation. The Tuxtlecos believe that certain foods taste better when prepared in clay containers. Despite the fact that metal pots and pans are available and are used for other purposes, many households continue to rely on ceramics for cooking *tortillas*, beans, and corn.

The most common form produced by Tuxtlas potters is the *comal*, the flat griddle used to prepare *tortillas*. *Comales* come in three basic sizes, depending on the item to be prepared and the facility used in its preparation. The smallest griddle, the *comal de estufa*, is approximately 21 cm in diameter and about 3 cm deep at the center (Figure 7a). This form represents an adaptation to the introduction of gas stoves used by some households in the central zone of the Tuxtlas. *Comales* produced for these stoves are smaller, due to the smaller heating area of the stove.

The middle-size *comal* averages about 28 cm in width and is 3.5 cm deep (Figure 7b). This vessel is used on the *fogon*, the traditional raised cooking hearth that is common throughout the region. Potters claim that this size vessel can be used to cook about four *tortillas* at one time. Small fish, called *popostes* are occasionally cooked on the *comal*.

The largest griddle, the *tostador*, is used to roast coffee and sometimes corn. *Tostadores* average about 37 cm in diameter and 7.5 cm deep (Figure 7c). Now that coffee is more widely available in the market, the production of *tostadores* is declining rapidly.

Another product that is commonly manufactured is the bowl, or *tecualon*. This vessel serves a multi-purpose function, ranging from mixing ingredients to serving food to storage of small items (Figure 8a). *Tecualones* are usually about 18 cm in diameter with a depth of 6 cm. In certain cases the interior of the vessel is incised, often with a floral design. This decoration only occurs on vessels that are to be used for grinding chile and the vessels are then called *chimoleras*. In rare instances the potter may attach three small nubbin supports to the vessel.

Cazuelas are also frequently produced in the Tuxtlas. These vessels are basin-like with walls 12 cm high and a diameter of 25 cm (Figure 8b). Some potters attach handles to the vessel, while others prefer not to. The presence or absence of handles does not affect the potters' term for the vessel type. Some producers noted, however, that the vessels are sometimes called *frideras*. *Cazuelas* are used for preparing soup and rice as well as for frying eggs, fish, and meat.

Ceramic producers also make two kinds of pots or *ollas*: (a) the *olla de frijol*, used for soaking and cooking beans; and (b) the *olla de maiz*, used for preparing corn (Figure 9).

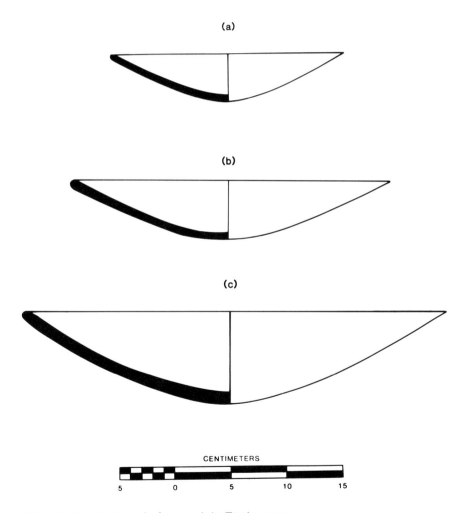

(a)

(b)

(c)

CENTIMETERS

5   0   5   10   15

Figure 7   *Comal* and *tostador* forms made by Tuxtlas potters.

Both types of *ollas* come in two main sizes, one for about 0.5 kg of beans and a second which holds one kilogram. *Ollas* tend to show the greatest variety in terms of shape – in some cases the vessel neck is pronounced and the mouth relatively restricted (<12 cm diameter), while in other cases there is no prominent neck and the mouth is about 20 cm in diameter. *Ollas* are always produced with an out-flaring lip. As with the other ceramics in the Tuxtlas, no glazes are applied to these vessels.

Tuxtlas potters may also produce several other items. One potter has become somewhat of a specialist in producing ashtrays (*cineceros*). These are small items, about 8 cm in diameter and approximately 2 cm deep. This woman sells her ashtrays to the hotels and restaurants of the area, and thus has entered into a market system that exceeds the distributional network of the more common cooking wares. Ashtrays made by this potter have been noted as far west as Alvarado (70 km) and as far east as Acayucan (90 km). This potter claims that working with larger vessels is too physically demanding and therefore specializes in smaller items. Other potters are now beginning

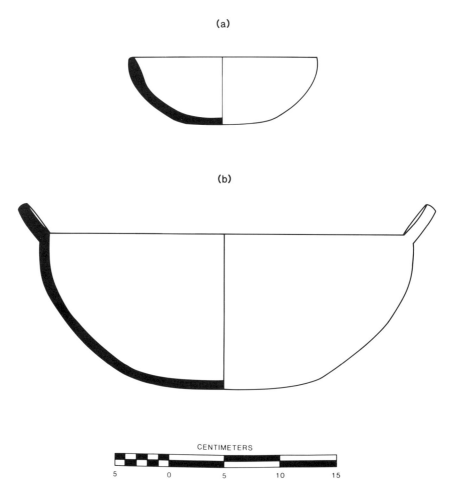

Figure 8   *Tecualon* and *cazuela* forms made by Tuxtlas potters.

to experiment with ashtray production.

Miniature vessels and small animal figures (*jugetes*) are manufactured on occasion. Potters also produce a cone-shaped vessel, set on an out-flaring base. This form is called an *incensario* and is used to burn incense during votive offerings. Potters have also begun making bodies for *pinatas*, based on the form of *ollas*. Finally, some producers are making flowerpots (*maceteras*), which are similar to the *cazuela* form but may be decorated with an undulating rim.

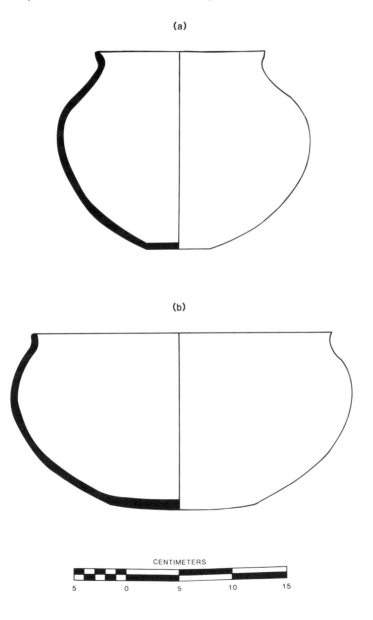

Figure 9   *Olla* forms made by Tuxtlas potters.

Ceramic producers in the Tuxtlas do not make jars for carrying and storing water. Despite the fact that such vessels are produced in Tlacoltalpan, a lowland community to the west of the region (Stark 1984), potters in the Tuxtlas prefer to use galvanized buckets or plastic pails.

The lack of water jars is interesting, especially given that clay vessels are usually preferred for storing water in hot climates (Arnold 1985:139). Two factors appear to curtail their occurrence in Los Tuxtlas. First, water in ceramic jars is cooled as some of the liquid within seeps to the vessel exterior and evaporates (Shepard 1956:126–127). Obviously, the lower the humidity, the more rapid the evaporation and the greater the cooling properties of the vessel. The study region, however, is characterized by high levels of humidity year-round. Evaporation is thus inhibited, minimizing that component of water storage.

The second factor involves the availability of drinking water. Nelson (1985), working in Highland Guatemala, has recently noted an inverse relationship between distance to water sources and a household's reliance on ceramic water storage jars. The Fulani of West Africa display a similar pattern (David and Hennig 1972:8). In these cases, fresh water is readily available, and there is little need to store water for long periods of time. Thus, potentially advantageous storage properties of ceramics are reduced. Fresh water sources are also located throughout the Tuxtlas, and all of the production communities are located adjacent to these springs. For the sampled households, then, plastic and metal containers present a lighter and more efficient means of collecting and storing water.

PRODUCTION DIVERSITY

Production diversity, or the number of forms produced by a household, follows a pattern similar to the frequency of production for the Tuxtlas communities (Table 18). The potters in San Isidro and Sehualaca produce the highest number of forms while producers in Chuniapan de Abajo and Bascascaltepec make fewer forms. San Isidro is not statistically different from Sehualaca in this regard ($U=112.5$, $Z=0.18$, $p>0.05$), while both communities differ from Chuniapan de Abajo ($U=58$, $Z=3.11$, $p<0.05$; $U=32$, $Z=3.26$, $p<0.05$; respectively). Both San Isidro and Sehualaca potters also manufacture more vessel types than producers in Bascascaltepec, while Chuniapan de

Table 18 *Production diversity and frequency among Tuxtlas production communities*

Community	Production diversity		Production frequency		N
	Mean	Median	Mean	Median	
San Isidro	6.22	6.50	3.88	3.00	18
Bascascaltepec	1.50	1.50	1.62	1.62	2
Chuniapan de Abajo	3.76	4.00	2.29	2.00	17
Sehualaca	6.53	7.00	3.15	3.00	13
Total	5.28	6.00	3.10	3.00	50

Abajo potters do not.

These regional data suggest that a positive relationship exists between production diversity and production frequency (Figure 10). A correlation of the two variables also indicates a significant, albeit comparatively weak relationship ($r_s=0.40$, $p<0.05$). This association is noteworthy, given that production diversity has been used to infer production scale and organization as well as degrees of economic competition among producers (e.g. Feinman 1980; Foster 1965; Rice 1984b; van der Leeuw 1984).

A two-way contingency table provides another means for investigating this relationship (Table 19). As this table indicates, there is a definite tendency for low-production diversity and low-production intensity to be associated, while high-production frequencies also favor high-production diversity ($X^2=4.97$, $p<0.05$, $Q=.62$). In terms of both analyses, production diversity and frequency are significantly related within the sample of potters.

This relationship, however, is not sustained when similar analyses are conducted on intra-community data (Table 20). In this case the only community of potters even

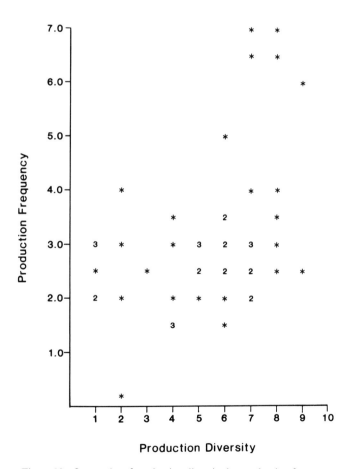

Figure 10   Scatterplot of production diversity by production frequency.

Table 19 *Contingency table of production frequency by production diversity*

	Production diversity	
Production frequency	Low	High
Low ≤3	27	10
High >3	5	8

$X^2=4.97$, $p<0.05$, d.f.$=1$, Yule's $Q=0.62$

closely approximating the regional value is San Isidro. Despite the fact that Sehualaca and Chuniapan de Abajo are significantly different with regard to both production variables, neither community exhibits a significant positive correlation between production frequency and production diversity.

The difference between the regional data and the community data is a function of outlier values from San Isidro. These values artificially inflate the significance of the regional statistic. Blalock (1972:381) has noted that the "effect of . . . extreme values is to produce a moderately high correlation where none exists among the remaining cases." Thus, the significant regional correlation between production diversity and production frequency is more apparent than real. This relationship is spurious and not reflected in the individual community data.

Vessel drying

Drying the ceramic vessels is perhaps the least technologically complex stage in Tuxtlas ceramic production. Drying requires little work on the part of the potter, save for physically moving the vessels and checking their progress over time. The Tuxtlas potters do not use drying racks and the majority of potters do not accelerate drying rates by exposing the vessels to low heat over the hearth, a practice found in other tropical areas (e.g. Arnold 1985:211–212; Reina and Hill 1978:63).

Despite the relative ease with which drying is conducted, these activities do have

Table 20 *Spearman's correlation coefficient for production diversity and frequency among Tuxtlas production communities*

Community	Median diversity	Median frequency	Spearman's r	Significance	N
San Isidro	6.50	3.00	0.43	$p>.07$	18
Bascascaltepec	1.50	1.62	1.00	—	2
Chuniapan de Abajo	4.00	2.00	−0.13	$p>.60$	17
Sehualaca	7.00	3.00	0.02	$p>.94$	13
Total	6.00	3.00	0.40	$p<.05$	50

important implications for the organization of production. After the vessel has been formed, it is set outside on the patio to dry. Potters begin working in the morning and vessels are left outside until dusk. Vessel drying, therefore, generally lasts between six and eight hours.

Pots in this *verde*, or green, state are fragile and can be easily damaged. During this period, therefore, the space occupied by the drying pots cannot be used for any other purpose. Children and animals are not permitted to get too close to the vessels, and even in other areas of the patio play is discouraged. The focus of attention thus shifts away from the vessels themselves to the area those vessels occupy.

Depending on the number of vessels to be dried, this stage of production can significantly affect the amount of available space within the houselot. In some cases more than 15 sq m of the patio is effectively removed from circulation during the six to eight hours of drying. This is a considerable area for some households. For example, a sample of twelve houselots from San Isidro produces a value of 12.36 sq m/person when the median patio area is divided by the median household population. If 15 sq m of patio space is "off limits," the area per individual drops to 9.63 sq m/person, a decrease of approximately 25 percent. Unlike drying the raw material, drying pottery does cause a substantial reduction in the amount of available patio space. Thus, while the technological demands of drying are minimal, the organizational ramifications may be considerable.

One indication of this pressure is the fact that the producers in San Isidro with smaller houselots will sometimes dry vessels on the roof of the house. This is not a preferred activity, because these roofs are usually constructed of thick, black tar paper and can become much hotter than the patio surface. Pots placed on the roof have a tendency to dry more quickly and unevenly, which increases the likelihood of cracking. The ceramics must be watched more closely and turned more frequently to avoid uneven drying. Potters place ceramics on the roof, however, to reduce the amount of patio area taken up by drying activities.

After the pots have dried, the solid clay base left over from *parado* formation must be removed and the vessel bottom shaved to the correct thickness. As noted earlier, potters perform this task with a piece of metal called a *raspador* which is frequently a recycled machete fragment or other piece of metal. In Chuniapan de Abajo, however, potters sometimes use a piece of *jicara* to conduct the same activity. Potters usually sit in the shade while thinning the vessels, staying either indoors or under a tree on the edge of the patio. The clay that is removed during this process is also recycled and used to make ceramics at a later time.

Vessel firing

Vessel firing is perhaps the most behaviorally complex stage in the Tuxtlas production sequence. From a technological standpoint firing is relatively unsophisticated; potters either fire in the open or use a simple updraft kiln. The interesting factor in this case is the distribution of these activities and the reasons behind that distribution. This section provides a descriptive account of the two firing procedures, including a section on vessel breakage and firing loss.

OPEN FIRING

Firing vessels without the use of a facility to partially control atmospheric conditions is commonly referred to as open firing (Rice 1987:153). Among the Tuxtlas potters, open firing is the most common procedure for baking ceramics, with almost two-thirds of the producers (N=32) firing in this fashion.

To fire in the open, the potter begins by covering the ground with a layer of wood. This bed (*cama*) of fuel actually serves three purposes: (a) it separates the pots from the wet ground, as the steam produced by heating the surface may break the ceramics; (b) it raises the pots off the ground so that air can circulate underneath, providing more complete oxidation; and (c) it serves to make the distribution of heat more even, by burning material both above and below the pottery. Other potters in Mesoamerica follow this procedure for similar reasons (e.g. Reina and Hill 1978:40, 76).

Once the bottom layer of fuel has been laid down, a support may be placed in the center of the fuel. In some cases a brick was used; other producers used a large portion of a broken *olla*, and one potter used a metal stake. Pots are then laid against this support in an overlapping manner, slowly increasing the number of vessels as the pile grows larger (Figure 11a). Producers will take great care to place the vessels properly, because if one of the interior vessels should shift or collapse, the entire pile might fall inward and a number of pots will break. Potters who are firing several different vessel types will always place the *comales* on last – these vessels serve as a form of insulation and help retain the heat. Between twenty and thirty *comales* are fired alone, or a group of five *ollas*, several *tecualones* and about twenty *comales* might be fired. Potters generally average about twenty-five vessels per open firing.

When the pots have been properly arranged, the producer will ignite the fuel on the bottom and then lay the remaining wood against the pile, producing a tipi-like structure (Figure 11b). If the potter waited until the pile was finished before lighting the fuel, the bottom would have less oxygen and burn more slowly, creating an uneven distribution of heat. When she is finished adding the fuel, the potter carefully watches the fire, occasionally adjusting the fuel or even adding a small piece or two (Figure 11c). After the firing is completed, the potter will spread out the ceramics and allow them to cool. The entire procedure usually takes less than two hours, with another hour before the ceramics are cool.

Pyrometric readings were not recorded for the Tuxtlas firings, but visual estimates do present a consistent range of temperatures. Flame color is a common method by which pre-industrial potters gauge firing temperatures (Foster 1955:11; Rice 1987:158), and a system for estimating temperatures from the color of the fire has been developed. According to Fournier (1973, cited in Lackey 1982:116), the correspondence of color to temperature is as follows: black heat – 400°C, dull red heat – 500°C, red heat – 700°C, orange-red heat – 850°C, yellow heat – 1100°C, and white heat – 1350°C. This system was verified by Lackey (1982) who, using a pyrometer, noted a close correspondence between these colors and temperatures during pottery firings in Acatlan, Mexico.

According to this chromatic system, the temperatures achieved during open firings in the Tuxtlas fall between 700°C and 850°C. Temperatures may have even been slightly higher during periods of wind gusts. These estimates compare favorably with other known open-firing temperatures. Colton (1951) noted temperatures between 720°C and 885°C among the Hopi, while Shepard (1956:83) reports temperatures up to 890°C for pottery fired by the Cochiti. These potters, however, were using fuels (such as sheep dung and cottonwood) that might burn hotter than the materials used in the Tuxtlas. In terms of fuel, comparable data are available from various New Guinea potters. Irwin (1977, cited in Rye 1981) recorded maximum temperatures between 840°C and 920°C for Mailu Island potters who were using coconut fronds and husks to fire unglazed cooking jars. It would thus appear that the estimates for the Tuxtlas producers fall comfortably within the range of temperatures documented for other potters firing under similar conditions (Rice 1987:156).

Figure 11a

Figure 11b

Figure 11c

Figure 11   Vessel firing in the open.

KILN FIRING

The use of kilns (*hornos*) has a limited distribution in the Tuxtlas. Only the potters of San Isidro use kilns, and kiln firing is the only form of vessel firing conducted in that community. *Hornos* are located adjacent to the house on the edge of the patio and each house averages one facility. In two instances this pattern did not occur. In one case the potter did not have a kiln and used a neighbor's *horno* to fire her ceramics. This woman stated that she did not work often enough to invest the time and effort into a kiln. In the second case there were two *hornos* in the household. The potter was in the process of moving the kiln closer to her house and had not yet dismantled the original facility. These two facilities were not used simultaneously, although the potter did fire in each of the kilns on separate occasions. When questioned about the continued use of the older kiln, the potter claimed that the new kiln was not quite ready.

Kilns are above-ground, updraft facilities that are constructed out of adobe, clay, and a few stones. Measurements are available for twelve of the kilns in San Isidro. The average diameter, including the walls, was 103.75 cm (s.d. = 8.26 cm), and the average interior diameter was 84.83 cm (s.d. = 6.76 cm). The average height from ground surface was 69.91 cm (s.d. = 13.11 cm).

Kilns are divided into an upper (firing chamber) and lower (firebox) section by pieces of scrap metal. These metal bars rest on a post in the center of the kiln. Pieces of metal were often taken from old cars, with chassis springs and leaf springs as the preferred parts. These metal bars rest on rocks that protrude from the interior wall of the *horno* and the pieces of metal extend from the sides to the center post. The use of a central post in this fashion is known from other parts of Mexico (Foster 1955), and archaeological data suggest it has considerable antiquity (Kneebone and Pool 1985; Santley et al. 1989; Winter and Payne 1976). In certain parts of Mexico this post is called the *macho* (Foster 1948, 1955:10) while in the Tuxtlas it is referred to as the *ombligo*. The firebox averages 27.16 cm in height (s.d. = 4.08 cm) while the firing chamber has an average height of 42.83 cm (s.d. = 11.66 cm). A small opening at the base of the kiln provides access to the firebox.

Prior to filling the kiln, the potter first removes any debris left over from the previous firing. This debris is often swept into the small streams adjacent to the households. The potter then rearranges the metal pieces, insuring that they are securely positioned and will allow the heat to circulate properly. The potter may even place large pieces of broken vessels atop the pieces of metal for extra support against the weight of the pottery to be fired. Finally, she begins placing the ceramics in the *horno* (Figure 12a). Larger items, such as *ollas* and *cazuelas* are the first vessels to be loaded. These ceramics are placed mouth downward, to insure that the interiors are fired as well as the exteriors. Smaller vessels, including *tecualones* and *maceteras* form the second layer of ceramics. In a procedure similar to open firing, the last items are the *comales*, again serving as a heat insulator. Large pieces of broken ceramics provide the final touch and an additional layer of insulation (Figure 12b).

The potter starts a small fire in the mouth of the firebox, often before the kiln is completely filled. This fire burns as the remaining vessels are loaded and slowly heats the contents of the *horno*. This initial heating is termed water smoking by ceramic technologists, and refers to a period during which the last remnants of water are driven out of the clay (Shepard 1956:81).

Kilns are fired for a period of about four hours. Pots are often left in the kiln overnight and are removed the following morning when the kiln has completely cooled. Temperatures for kiln firing are estimated to fall within a range similar to open firing, al·'iough the maximum temperature does not appear to greatly exceed 800°C. While it might seem unreasonable that kilns produce slightly lower temperatures than open firing, this assessment is also supported by ethnographic accounts of unglazed, utilitarian wares fired in simple updraft kilns. In Acatlan, potters fire to a temperature of between 750°C to 800°C using cactus and rubber as fuel (Lackey 1982:56–60). The potters of Jaba'a, Palestine, using rubber and dung, fire to temperatures in the low 700°C (Rye 1981). Diaz (1966) reports a temperature of 850°C for Tonala potters firing *loza de olor* ceramics and using wood and dung for fuel. Data from Highland Peru (Hagstrum 1989:Appendix E.2) indicate an average temperature of 857.5°C, firing with dung, shrubs, and straw. Finally, refiring experiments, currently being conducted by the Matacapan Archaeological Project, have been used to estimate firing temperatures for both archaeological and ethnographic ceramics. Using clays from several Tuxtlas sources, including San Isidro, the tests have indicated that oxidizing temperatures between 750°C and 800°C produce colors similar to that from kiln-fired archaeological materials.

Depending on the kinds of items being fired, a kiln load usually contains between thirty and fifty vessels. Potters fire about once a week, generally on Thursday or

Figure 12b

Figure 12a

Figure 12   Vessel firing in kilns

Friday, so that ceramics can be taken to the market over the weekend. In rare instances potters stockpile small quantities of vessels, especially at the end of the dry season. Producers say they are able to obtain a higher price per pot as wet-season production falls sharply and fewer ceramics can be found in the market.

BREAKAGE RATES

The percentage of vessels that break during a firing, or the "firing loss" (Rye 1981:118), is an important tool for comparing production efficiency among various potters. Consistent patterns of breakage may indicate problems in manufacture, as suggested in Guthe's (1925) observation that the entire base of vessels produced by the San Ildefonso potters often breaks off during firing. Evidence for a lack of atmospheric control while firing is manifested in bloating, warping, spalling, and dunting cracks (Rye 1981; Shepard 1956). Finally, the occurrence of misfired sherds is of interest to archaeologists wishing to reconstruct levels of production frequency and intensity (e.g. Feinman 1985; Redmond 1979; Santley et al. 1989).

Firing loss is primarily a function of manufacturing errors and firing control. In addition to vessel malformation, manufacturing errors include using raw materials that are not sufficiently processed and employing an improper ratio of clay to temper. Inadequate firing control will include heating the ceramics too rapidly, maintaining an excessive temperature, creating an uneven distribution of heat, and cooling the vessels too quickly.

There is a distinct difference between breakage rates for kiln and open firing in the Tuxtlas (Table 21). Pottery fired in the open is more likely to suffer damage than ceramics fired in kilns. Two factors are primarily responsible for this difference. The first is the relationship between temperature and time – open-air firing achieves a slightly higher temperature in about half the time and the pots cool more quickly. As noted above, Tuxtlas potters using kilns also water smoke their vessels, while potters firing in the open do not. The comparatively rapid heating and cooling associated with open firing certainly contributes to higher rates of breakage.

Production frequency may also affect breakage rates. Thus, the assumption might be that potters working more frequently are more skilled and this should be reflected in firing loss. The best way to examine this possibility is to compare breakage rates while holding firing type constant (Figure 13). A Spearman's correlation was performed to investigate this relationship for open-air firing but failed to produce a significant statistic ($r_s = -0.343$, $p > 0.05$). An additional factor, however, may be the producer's

Table 21 *Comparison of firing loss for kiln and open firing in the Tuxtlas*

| Community | Firing loss | | Production frequency[1] | | Firing | |
	Mean	Median	Manufacturing	Firing	Temperature	Length[2]
Kilns	21.0%	20.0%	3.00	1.00	700 – 800	4.00
Open firing	31.5%	27.0%	2.50	1.00	750 – 850	2.09

[1] Median days per week
[2] Median hours

age. Older potters work less frequently, but also have more production experience. These senior potters are thus represented at lower frequencies, while at the same time they lose fewer vessels during firing. This situation is known to have occurred in two of the "aberrant" cases. If these two cases are removed from the calculation, a stronger, significant correlation coefficient is produced ($r_s = -0.55$, $p < 0.05$). Unfortunately it was extremely difficult to collect consistent data on the potter's age. Conclusive evidence for this possible association must await further research.

FIRING VARIABILITY

One of the most interesting aspects of pottery making in the Sierra de los Tuxtlas is the occurrence of both open firing and kiln firing. Such juxtaposition of techniques is relatively rare, especially in the absence of any additional evidence for producer specialization (i.e. potter's wheel, levigation tanks). Among Mesoamerican potters, kilns are often associated with larger scale and/or intensive production entities (Diaz 1966; Foster 1955:10; Papousek 1974, 1981; Stark 1984; Thompson 1958). The use of kilns has also been included as evidence for increasing prehistoric producer specialization (e.g. Rice 1984b; van der Leeuw 1977). Kilns may also mitigate the effects of climate and/or pressure on fuel resources (Arnold 1985:213; Diaz 1966; Reina and Hill 1978:106). The occurrence of kilns in the study region provides an excellent opportunity to investigate some of these relationships.

This discussion examines open and kiln firing, as reflected in the production activities of San Isidro and Sehualaca. As noted previously, these two communities are

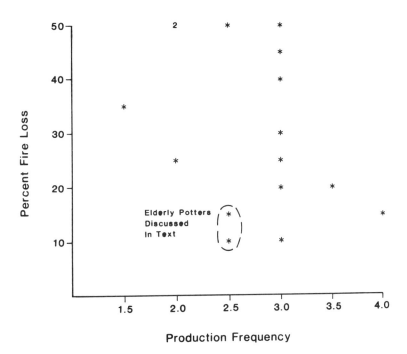

Figure 13   Scatterplot of production frequency by percent fire loss for potters firing in the open.

characterized by similar patterns of production frequency, household size and composition, formation techniques, and production diversity. In spite of these similarities, the potters of both communities employ different firing methods. Obviously, these similarities cannot be responsible for the different firing strategies. In order to understand this difference, attention must be focused on other components of the pottery system. These communities thus provide an excellent database for assessing the contribution of other factors to firing variability.

Precipitation

In one of the most thorough works on the forces affecting ceramic production systems, Dean Arnold (1985) has noted the importance of weather and climate conditions for pottery manufacture. In addition to the variability introduced into drying times and formation cycles, the firing of ceramics can be adversely impacted by climate, especially rainfall:

> firing success may be . . . reduced significantly during rainy weather in three ways: (1) rainfall prevents fuel from drying prior to firing and thus increases the probability of firing failure; (2) rainfall reduces firing temperature . . . by dampening fuel, flame, pottery and kilns; and (3) during firing, rainfall or other moisture may cause breakage, blackening and uneven heating resulting in a defective and low quality product.
> (Arnold 1985:70–71)

For potters who must fire during wet periods, it is necessary to control the limiting effects of rainfall as much as possible.

A primary means by which wet-season firing is controlled is through the use of kilns. For example, potters in India utilize a subterranean vertical kiln during the rainy season, but during the dry season pottery is fired in the open (Saraswati and Behura 1966, cited in Arnold 1985:213–214). In addition, there appears to be a close relationship between the predominance of kiln firing and rainfall intensities throughout the Indian continent (Arnold 1985:215). Finally, the elaborate kiln technology of Japan may have appeared in response to patterns of inclement weather (e.g. Rhodes 1970, cited in Arnold 1985:218). These kilns can achieve surprisingly hot temperatures and also provide the potter with a dry area to store fuel (Arnold 1985:218).

How does firing technology in the Tuxtlas compare with patterns in rainfall? As noted in Chapter 2, the Sierra de los Tuxtlas is characterized by significant differences in rainfall. The differences between the communities of San Isidro and Sehualaca, however, are not as dramatic. Both communities fall within the annual rainfall range of 2000–2500 mm, suggesting that differences in yearly precipitation are not a contributing factor to firing variability. Nor does the distribution of rain on a seasonal basis appear to differ significantly. Rainfall data are available for the towns of San Andres Tuxtla and Santiago Tuxtla, which contain the closest weather stations to San Isidro and Sehualaca, respectively (Table 22). These data indicate comparable patterns of rainfall during the dry season; if anything, the community of Sehualaca might receive

Table 22 *Dry-season rainfall data from weather stations at San Andres Tuxtla and Santiago Tuxtla*[1]

| | Mean precipitation | | |
Community	Monthly	Seasonal	Years reporting
San Andres Tuxtla	40.30	201.50	50
Santiago Tuxtla	54.44	272.20	28

[1] In millimeters (SPP 1981)

more precipitation than San Isidro. In view of these data, climatic patterns do not appear to make a major contribution to the differences in firing technology.

Fuel availability

The availability of fuel is a second factor that can determine the kind of firing technique employed by ceramic producers. Kilns have been characterized as providing improved insular capacities and greater atmospheric control (Rice 1987:158–163). A by-product of these features is a more efficient use of fuel. Potters faced with increased fuel shortages may experiment with different fuels or may alter the production technology to fire the same number of goods with less fuel. By providing greater fuel efficiency, kiln firing may be selected during periods of fuel shortages.

In one of the few studies in which data were collected on fuel consumption and firing behavior, Rye and Evans (1976:165) discuss the importance of kilns for efficient fuel consumption. They observed some suggestive patterns in the ratio of vessel weight to fuel weight for various firing practices. Pakistani potters firing unglazed wares used proportionately less fuel as the amount of atmospheric control was increased, moving from open firing to kiln firing (Rye and Evans 1976:165). While it is not clear if potters adopted kiln firing in response to resource pressure, Rye and Evans (1976:167) do note that preferred fuels are sometimes unavailable.

The use of kilns in Mesoamerica is also frequently associated with a stress on the available fuel supply (e.g. Diaz 1966; Lackey 1982; Papousek 1981). Reina and Hill (1978:106) describe the potters of Chianatla, in northwestern Guatemala, who were forced to experiment with different firing techniques as a result of fuel shortages. The potters originally practiced open firing, but the increased scarcities of kindling forced them to seek more efficient firing procedures. After experimenting with large lime kilns, the ceramic producers settled on a smaller facility that provided improved control, better heat retention, and enabled the potters to fire more vessels at a single time. All of these characteristics make kilns an efficient means of firing when fuel shortages occur.

Given the advantage of fuel efficiency associated with controlled firing, the use of kilns by the potters of San Isidro is a predictable response to a situation of increased pressure on fuel resources. As noted in the section on raw-material acquisition, only three of the seventeen San Isidro potters who fire their own ceramics actually collect their own fuel. These few producers were forced to make half-day trips to find the material, because of deforestation and the distance involved in acquiring wood. The vast majority of potters must purchase fuel and use approximately one *carga* per firing. Potters in San Isidro average one firing per week during the dry season, so the cost of wood is an important concern.

In comparison, the ceramic producers of Sehualaca were not confronted with a shortage of fuels. These potters made use of several materials including wood, palm-fronds, and cow dung. None of the Sehualaca potters were forced to purchase their fuel, nor is the 2.5 km distance to the resource especially excessive. It would consequently appear that the ceramic producers of Sehualaca face less stress in terms of fuel procurement. Under these conditions, it is doubtful if a more efficient use of fuel would be required.

Fuel availability does provide a contrast between the potters of San Isidro and Sehualaca. But kilns may not be as thermally efficient as they would seem. Rice (1987:162) suggests that a "large proportion of the energy produced is used just to heat the kiln structure itself; small kilns have a particularly unfavorable ratio of heat distribution with respect to pots versus structures." Moreover, kilns may produce a thermal gradient, whereby different areas of the kiln achieve and maintain different firing temperatures resulting in differentially fired vessels. In addition, kilns also require an initial investment of labor and must be maintained. During one observed firing in San Isidro, for example, the side of a poorly maintained kiln ruptured, ruining a load of pottery. The relationship between fuel availability and kiln use among San Isidro potters remains ambiguous.

Summary
While archaeological expectations of production behavior take certain relationships for granted, the data presented here suggest that those assumptions should be re-evaluated. Despite that fact that potters are operating within a similar domestic production mode, pottery making in Los Tuxtlas is marked by a surprising amount of intra-modal variation. Differences in production intensity, diversity, and technology are pronounced. Furthermore, this variability is often inconsistent with conventional expectations about potters and production techniques.

For example, two different methods of vessel formation were noted. However, there is no significant relationship between these methods and differences in production frequency. Nor is the number of vessel types produced associated with the amount of time devoted to production. Most startling is the distinction between open firing and kiln firing. When comparing Sehualaca potters who fire in the open with the kiln users at San Isidro, there is no difference in either the frequency of production or the diversity of the finished product. Moreover, explanations based on environmental variability are inconclusive at best.

These data suggest that the production characteristics displayed by a given group of potters should not become simplistic analogies for the past. The range of production behaviors within this sample of seasonal potters is startling. Models of pottery making that ignore this degree of variability may provide very narrow interpretations of the past. Finally, differences of this type are not confined to ceramic production. As we will see in the next chapter, ceramic consumption may also present some unconventional patterning.

4

Ceramic consumption in Los Tuxtlas

Matson's definition of ceramic ecology included an emphasis on "the functions in [the potter's] culture of the products [the potter] fashions" (1965:203). The suite of possible product functions will not be considered here. The ceramics produced in the Tuxtlas are primarily used for cooking and serving; this discussion presents information on the use and use-lives of this utilitarian pottery.

This section begins by considering variability in the frequency and proportion of ceramic vessels within the sample of fifty households. Differences in these measures are the result of two regulating forces. Assemblage diversity, or the occurrence of different pottery forms, is strongly associated with the techniques of food preparation practiced in the household (also Nelson 1985; Rice 1984a:245–246). Within households whose corn is ground mechanically, the containers used to boil corn are more likely to be metal. Those households processing corn by hand (using *manos* and *metates*) are more likely to have specific pottery vessels used in corn preparation.

A second factor conditioning assemblage size is access to replacement vessels. Access comprises several variables; among them are the number of potters within the community making the vessel type, the distance to the market, and the price of the vessel. Access to ceramics is used to investigate the interaction between household populations and assemblage size. The ethnoarchaeological literature suggests a poor correlation between the number of persons within the household and the frequency of pots within the assemblage (e.g. Kramer 1985:91–92). Within the Tuxtlas sample, however, communities exhibiting greater access also display a significant correlation between household population and assemblage size. In these cases, vessel access alleviates some of the pressure to stockpile pots, thus bringing assemblage size more in line with the everyday needs of the household.

The second portion of this chapter is devoted to assessing vessel use life. Ceramic longevity in the Tuxtlas sample is primarily affected in three ways. First, the frequency of vessel use provides a negative influence on the life span of ceramics. This finding is similar to that observed among other pottery-using societies (e.g. DeBoer 1985:348; Kramer 1985:89–90). Second, the cost of replacing a pot contributes to its longevity. Some variables used to determine cost are production time, amount of raw material used in production, producer skill, and intra-community availability. High replacement costs are associated with higher vessel use lives. Finally, the data indicate a tendency for longer-than-average life spans when a vessel type is *not* widely used in the community. This relationship, albeit tentative, is attributed to a cultural "tenacity" in which households adhering to more traditional behaviors (at least as reflected in pottery consumption) are more likely to curate their ceramic vessels.

Household ceramic assemblages in Los Tuxtlas

Six vessel forms constitute the overwhelming majority of types encountered within the traditional Tuxtlas household. These types include a bowl used for eating (*tecualon*), and five forms used for cooking – two for toasting (*comal, tostador*), one for frying (*cazuela*) and two for prolonged soaking and boiling (*olla de maiz* and *olla de frijol*). A description of their formal and functional properties was provided in the preceding chapter. This discussion concentrates on the number of vessels that occur within the household assemblage, the proportion in which these forms are encountered, and possible reasons for this variability.

VESSEL FREQUENCIES

The number of vessels within the household assemblage of Tuxtlas potters is relatively consistent from one community to the next. Among the fifty inventoried households the average number of vessels is 6.58 with a median of 6.00 (Table 23). Households in Sehualaca display the highest overall mean number of vessels (7.53), while Bascascal-tepec households contain the lowest average number of vessels (4.50). The figure for Bascascaltepec cannot be totally attributed to sample size; it appears that households in

Table 23 *Ceramic assemblage frequencies from sampled Tuxtlas households*

| | | | Community | | |
Vessel type	San Isidro (N=18)	Bascascaltepec (N=2)	Chuniapan de Abajo (N=17)	Sehualaca (N=13)	Total (N=50)
Comal					
Mean	2.11	1.50	1.82	1.69	1.88
Median	2.00	1.50	2.00	2.00	2.00
Tecualon					
Mean	1.55	2.00	2.11	1.38	1.72
Median	2.00	2.00	2.00	1.00	2.00
Cazuela					
Mean	1.00	—	0.64	2.15	1.14
Median	1.00		0.00	2.00	1.00
Olla de Frijol					
Mean	1.22	0.50	0.76	1.23	1.04
Median	1.00	0.50	1.00	1.00	1.00
Olla de Maiz					
Mean	0.38	—	0.41	0.92	0.52
Median	0.00		0.00	1.00	0.00
Tostador					
Mean	0.22	0.50	0.41	0.16	0.28
Median	0.00	0.50	0.00	0.00	0.00
Total					
Mean	6.50	4.50	6.17	7.53	6.58
Median	6.50	4.50	6.00	7.00	6.00

this community are replacing a portion of their ceramic assemblage with plastic or metal alternatives (see below). The data from Sehualaca, on the other hand, include one household that contained thirteen persons and a total of nineteen vessels. If this outlier is omitted and the Sehualaca average is recalculated, the mean number of vessels becomes 6.58 with a median of 6.00.

The patterning in assemblage characteristics underscores several important components of the relationship between vessel occurrence (i.e. presence or absence) and frequency (i.e. total number): (a) the vessel's role in food preparation; (b) the multipurpose nature of the vessel; (c) the number of servings that a single vessel can provide; and (d) the existence of nonceramic alternatives to replace a specific vessel. These variables work individually and in concert to shape the assemblage profile of any given community.

Comales are the most common pottery form in the sample, averaging just under two vessels per household. The frequency of *comales* is primarily a consequence of factors (a), (c), and (d) noted above. *Comales* are used to prepare *tortillas*, a flat corn cake that is common fare at every meal. An adult will often consume between three and six *tortillas* per sitting, and a single *comal* can be used to prepare about 4 *tortillas* at a time. It is necessary, therefore, to have more than one *comal* on hand. Moreover, there are few available alternatives that suit the purposes of the clay griddle. Metal replacements are a possibility (e.g. Arnold 1985:143), but as Krotser (1974:132) has noted, the people of Veracruz feel that metal griddles heat too rapidly and scorch the *tortilla*. Because of its role in food preparation, the number of individuals supplied by a single vessel, and the absence of acceptable replacements, the *comal* is the most ubiquitous pottery form in the assemblage.

The *tecualon* is the second most common vessel form, averaging 1.72 vessels per house with a median of two. *Tecualon* frequency is due to their multipurpose nature and their size. These vessels are used as serving/eating bowls, as small storage containers, as lids for *ollas*, and as bowls for grinding small amounts of herbs and spices. While the *chimolera* is specifically designed for grinding, *tecualones* are frequently used in their place. In addition, when employed as serving vessels these bowls are primarily single-serving containers. *Tecualones* thus appear to be a common item for two primary reasons. As serving vessels, they are used by only one person at a time, so households using bowls for this purpose generally have more than one. Second, even in those instances in which mass-produced dishes are replacing the *tecualon*, these bowls continue to be valued for their functional diversity.

The third most frequent ceramic type in the Tuxtlas assemblage is the *cazuela*; a cooking vessel that is similar to the *tecualon* in terms of its multi-use properties. *Cazuelas* are used for frying, making soup, cooking rice, and sometimes steaming. Each of the studied households has an average of 1.14 vessels, with a median of one. *Cazuelas* are large vessels that can be used to prepare sufficient food for up to approximately six persons, the median family size within the sampled households (see Chapter 2). In addition, the *cazuela* serves a variety of cooking functions. There is little necessity, therefore, to have more than one *cazuela* per household. It is important to note however, that the *cazuela* is the most common large cooking vessel, in part the result of its multi-functional qualities.

Ollas de frijol rank number four in terms of average number of vessels per type. There is a mean of 1.04 such vessels within the inventoried households, with a median of one vessel per house. The frequency of bean jars in the assemblage is apparently a function of the number of individuals served per vessel and the importance of beans in the *campesino* diet. *Ollas de frijol* are large enough to contain sufficient food for several persons, thus most households require only one vessel.

Ollas de maiz are the fifth most common vessel form in the Tuxtlas sample. Both the mean number of these vessels per household and the proportion of households containing these *ollas* is comparatively low. Given the importance of corn in the *campesino* diet, one might expect the same situation as that noted for bean jars – that each house would have at least one jar for cooking corn. The average household has only 0.52 of these vessels, however; stated another way, only about half of the households in the sample contain *ollas de maiz*. The actual number is twenty-three households, with three of the houses containing two such vessels and the remaining twenty houses possessing one *olla* each. Of these twenty-three houses, eleven were located in Sehualaca, six occurred in Chuniapan de Abajo, and the remaining six were encountered in San Isidro. In other words, not only are maize jars represented in less than half the total households, but almost half of these vessels were found in a single community.

The numerical differences between bean and corn *ollas* becomes more understandable when considering the technological system of food preparation. Food-preparation technology may contribute to the number of vessel forms within the assemblage and the frequency of vessels within those forms (e.g. Arnold 1985:127–144). Nelson (1985) provides an account of the corn-preparation technology in three Highland Maya communities and compares that with the Tarahumara of Chihuahua, Mexico. The Highland Maya employ a strategy in which the corn is soaked, boiled, ground while wet, and finally boiled again. The Tarahumara, on the other hand, parch their corn, grind it in a dry state, and then boil it. Nelson (1985) concludes that the intensive wet-grinding technology of the Highland Maya is more demanding in terms of assemblage size and diversity than the primarily dry-grinding carried out in the Tarahumara area.

In comparison to corn, beans require less intensive preparation. Beans are usually washed, soaked overnight, and then boiled for several hours. When ready, beans are eaten whole or mashed. Corn, on the other hand, is first soaked in a lime solution, boiled, and then ground. The process of grinding corn is especially arduous and time consuming. Among one Zapotecan community in Oaxaca, for example, corn grinding is said to take between six to eight "woman-hours" per day for the average household (Chinas 1973, cited in Isaac 1986:16). Data from other areas of Mexico likewise underscore the time-consuming nature of corn grinding (Foster 1967; Vogt 1970). Grinding corn by hand is conducted within the more traditional Tuxtlas households; more common, however, is the reliance on local, mechanized grinding mills (*molinos*). The soaked and boiled corn is brought to these shops early in the morning, where it is ground into a corn dough. The women then return to the houses where they make *tortillas* from this dough.

The technological simplicity of bean preparation suggests that the number of vessels associated with their use, and the frequency of those vessels, would be minimized. There is no technological reason to have more than one vessel (soaking and boiling are conducted with the same vessel), nor is there a behavioral reason (everyone is served from the same jar). When coupled with the widespread belief that food prepared in ceramics tastes superior to that prepared in metal containers (e.g. Arnold 1985:139; Rice 1984a:245), these facts would indicate a lack of incentive to alter the *status quo* food-preparation technology. As a consequence, the frequency of vessels associated with bean preparation is likely to be small and is not expected to vary markedly from community to community.

In contrast, there appears to be an inverse relationship between the frequency of *ollas de maiz* and the patronage of *molinos*. This pattern is certainly the case at San Isidro where two-thirds of the visited households do not use ceramics for boiling corn and do not grind the corn by hand. A similar relationship was also indicated in Chunia- pan de Abajo. In both these communities metal pots are used in place of ceramics to boil corn. Because the corn is ground after it is cooked, it is not subject to the same culinary restrictions that surround the consumption of beans. In other words, concerns with the texture and color of cooked maize are considerably less important than for beans because the corn is further processed after boiling. Under these circumstances, the use of metal pots is apparently more acceptable. It is interesting to note that a few informants mentioned that the taste of corn ground by machine was inferior to that of corn ground by hand. Viewed in light of the present discussion, however, it may not be the use of the machine that affects the flavor as much as the use of metal pots to boil the corn. Despite their pronouncement, most of these same individuals feel that the differ- ence in taste is not particularly significant.

The *tostador* is the least common vessel type encountered among the Tuxtlas house- holds. The average household in the Tuxtlas sample contained 0.28 vessels, with a median value of 0.00. In reality, only thirteen houses contained these vessels, which are primarily used for roasting coffee or, less frequently, corn. *Tostadores* occur most fre- quently in Bascascaltepec and Chuniapan de Abajo. An emphasis on household-level coffee production in these communities is partially a function of access to local markets. As noted earlier, both these communities are located a considerable distance from markets and have poor access in terms of transportation. The majority of Tuxtlas households prefer to purchase coffee at the market where they can obtain ground beans mixed with sugar, a favorite drink throughout the region. Those households with limited access to the market, however, are more likely to engage in producing their own coffee for consumption. It is not surprising, therefore, that the percentage of houses with *tostadores* is almost twice as high in Chuniapan and Bascascaltepec than in San Isidro and Sehualaca (36.84 percent vs. 19.35 percent), even though about the same percentage of houses produce the form in both groups (52.63 percent vs. 51.61 percent).

CERAMIC ACCESS
Thus far there has been only scattered mention of how the Tuxtlas household assem- blages compare with other documented groups. This section provides a more systematic comparison. These data are also used to substantiate the generally low correlation

between household population and assemblage size noted in the literature. A similar pattern holds true for the entire Tuxtlas sample but significant relationships are present among certain communities. The section argues that access to pottery is an important variable conditioning the relationship between ceramic assemblages and household populations.

The following comparison of the Tuxtlas assemblage with other groups focuses on New World ceramic producers. New World households are chosen because, as noted above, variations in diet and food-processing technology are relevant factors in the formal and numeric variability within a ceramic assemblage. Thus, a valid comparison should include dietary similarity among examples. Such is not the case for groups in Cameroon, who cultivate sorghum and groundnuts (David and Hennig 1972:3). Nor are the Kalinga (Philippine) data comparable, given their dependence on rice (Longacre 1981, 1985). In addition, more "anecdotal" censuses (N<10 households) are not considered.

The sampled Tuxtlas households exhibit a smaller average assemblage (6.58) than most of their New World counterparts (Table 24; also see Rice 1987:Table 9.4). The Highland Maya in Chiapas, Mexico, and Huehuetenango, Guatemala, possess the largest average household assemblages, hovering around sixty vessels (Deal 1983: Table 1; Nelson 1981:115, 1985). The "middle ground" is reflected among the Shipibo-Conibo, whose average household assemblage is 15.1 (DeBoer and Lathrap 1979:122–123). The Tarahumara of northern Mexico exhibit an inventory ranging between nine and twelve vessels (Pastron 1974:108–109). The only study to date that approximates the Tuxtlas values has been conducted in the Montaro Valley of Highland Peru (Hagstrum 1987, 1989:284). Households in eighteen different communities averaged 8.4 vessels in their assemblage.

The broad range of variability that characterizes these assemblage frequencies denotes a complex relationship between number of vessels, number of individuals, and access to ceramics (e.g. Rice 1987:294–295). One of the more common questions concerning assemblage size is the relationship between the number of vessels within a household and the number of individuals using those ceramics (e.g. DeBoer and Lathrap 1979; Kramer 1985:90–91). Nelson (1985) demonstrates that, despite the

Table 24 *Ceramic census data from select New World groups*

Area/group/community	Household sample	Assemblage mean	Reference
Chanal	51	62.9	Deal 1983: Table 1
San Mateo Ixtatan	53	57.0	Nelson 1981:115, 1985
Shipibo	18	15.1	DeBoer and Lathrap 1979:122–123
Tarahumara	10	9–12	Pastron 1974:108–109
Montaro Valley, Peru	199	8.4	Hagstrum 1987, 1989:284
Tuxtlas	50	6.5	

Table 25 *Contingency table of assemblage size by household population*

	Household population	
Assemblage size	Low	High
Low ≤ 6	18	10
High >6	7	15

$X^2=5.19$, $p<0.05$, d.f.$=1$, Yule's $Q=0.59$

overall difference in assemblage frequencies found within ethnographic examples, figures for household populations are relatively consistent from one group to the next. Variability in assemblage size is not matched by variability in average population figures from the studied communities.

A Spearman's correlation of household population and assemblage size in the Tuxtlas also produces an insignificant statistic ($r_s=0.26$, $p>0.05$). But when San Isidro and Sehualaca are evaluated as a group, there is a significant positive relationship between household population and assemblage size ($r_s=0.54$, $p<0.01$, N$=31$). This relationship was not present in the group containing Chuniapan de Abajo and Bascascaltepec ($r_s=-.012$, $p>0.05$, N$=19$).

The possibility that household size and number of ceramic vessels are somehow related is further suggested by a chi-square analysis of the two variables (Table 25). Households with populations below the median are more likely to have fewer vessels than large household populations ($X^2=5.19$, $p<0.05$, $Q=.58$).

These analyses indicate that, despite the low overall correlation between household size and ceramic assemblage for the entire sample, important inter-community relationships between these two variables do exist. However, the analyses suggest that it is only when certain conditions are met that a significant relationship can be expected.

Access to ceramics appears to be one factor influencing the population/assemblage relationship (Arnold 1988). Access includes such factors as distance to market, price of the vessel, and the number of potters within the community who make the vessel. One symptom of limited access would be seen in an increased stockpiling, defined by Nelson (1985) as "the accumulation of new vessels for eventual use." Stockpiling is the means for controlling the availability of an irregular supply.

According to Nelson (1985) the households of San Mateo Ixtatan rely heavily on ceramic stockpiles. Pottery is not made in the majority of households and ceramics must be obtained on a market day, usually with cash. The probability of available cash, a market day, and a vendor with the right product all occurring in conjunction is low. At the same time, vessel use lives are low and pots need to be seasoned before they are brought into service. Under these circumstances, vessel frequencies vary not as a direct function of immediate demand, but as a function of anticipated demand viewed in terms of probable access.

But stockpiling is not limited to non-pottery-producing households. In these circumstances access is a function of producer output. And output can be minimized because of annual or seasonal production or production technology. Among the Shipibo-Conibo, for example:

> the frequency of ceramic vessels is not directly governed by immediate households needs. In the Conibo village of Iparia ... fully half of the complete vessels were stored in the rafters as future replacements for broken vessels or as "special occasion" ware immediately available for serving guests. (DeBoer and Lathrap 1979:124)

The reason that these potters might wish to store half of the assemblage is in part a response to the specific cultural tradition of these Indians – their custom of serving household visitors beer in a newly-made ceramic mug. This possibility, however, only accounts for a small portion of the household assemblage. In fact, beer mugs constitute only about 10.5 percent of the complete vessels within the domestic Shipibo-Conibo ceramic inventory (DeBoer and Lathrap 1979:Table 4.3). Another possible reason for stockpiling is the comparatively low production output of the Shipibo-Conibo potter. According to DeBoer and Lathrap (1979:Table 4.2), a single vessel may require a week's worth of effort. Moreover, these potters often fire vessels individually (DeBoer and Lathrap 1979:120–121). Consequently, considerable "down time" would result should a vessel break without an available replacement. Under these circumstances, households would be more likely to build up an inventory of pottery. Thus, although the Shipibo-Conibo households contain potters, their low production output encourages stockpiling and inflates the household assemblage.

In contrast to these "stockpiling" strategies, the Peruvian households studied by Hagstrum (1985a, 1987, 1989) do not maintain large ceramic inventories. Rather, they would appear to have greater access to vessels. Hagstrum (1985a) considers ceramic production in these villages to be an example of village-level specialization, in that over 20 percent of the households manufacture pottery. Production output is also comparatively high; during one period from April through September, *olla* producers averaged over 140 pots per month (Hagstrum 1987). Recall that, despite this output, the average assemblage size is only 8.4 ceramic vessels. It would appear that these production communities have reasonably good access to ceramics and face less pressure to build a stockpile of pottery. A lower stockpile would bring assemblage size more in line with the immediate needs of the household.

If this relationship also characterizes the Tuxtlas potters, then San Isidro and Sehualaca, the communities exhibiting a significant association between household population and assemblage size, should have better access to pottery than the group of Chuniapan de Abajo and Bascascaltepec. As indicated in Chapter 3, potters in the former group operate at significantly higher levels of production frequency than potters in the latter group. Thus, households in San Isidro and Sehualaca produce goods more frequently and can obtain new ceramics with considerably more ease than those of the other communities. In addition, San Isidro and Sehualaca enjoy a more favorable position to major markets. This position is a function of both linear distance and available transportation networks.

There are also significant differences when we consider the percentage of households producing the six main vessel forms (Figure 14). In all cases, the percentage of households producing a given type in San Isidro and Sehualaca is at or above the percentage for households in Chuniapan de Abajo and Bascascaltepec. This difference is most striking for the production of *tecualones*, *cazuelas*, and *ollas de frijol*. For example, 87 percent of the sampled households in San Isidro and Sehualaca manufacture *cazuelas*, as compared with 21 percent of the households in Chuniapan de Abajo and Bascascaltepec. These differences suggest greater access to a range of ceramics within the former group.

In addition, we should consider the number of households that use a given pottery type but do not manufacture that type. It is meaningless to argue for differences in access if households *only* use those vessels they are producing. If this were the case, then all households would have the same relative access to ceramics. The difference between household production and household consumption is another facet of pottery access.

Since all households make and use their own *comales*, that vessel type is not affected by differential "access." Among the remaining vessel forms, however, intergroup differences are in evidence (Figure 15). Less than five percent of the San Isidro and

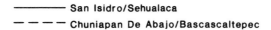

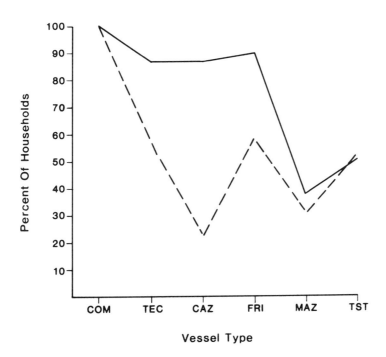

Figure 14   Percentage of producer households manufacturing six main vessel forms.

Sehualaca potters who have *tecualones* must purchase these vessels, while more than forty percent of *tecualon*-using households in Chuniapan de Abajo and Bascascaltepec do not manufacture bowls. Similarly, access to *cazuelas* in San Isidro and Sehualaca is considerably greater than for households in Chuniapan de Abajo and Bascascaltepec. Only when maize jars are considered is this pattern reversed. Of the six households in Chuniapan de Abajo and Bascascaltepec using *ollas de maiz*, all produced this vessel type. In four of the six main vessel types, households in San Isidro and Sehualaca can replace a given ceramic form with greater ease than the producers in Chuniapan de Abajo and Bascascaltepec.

Thus, access to pottery is higher in San Isidro and Sehualaca. Broken vessels are more likely to be replaced from a recently fired load of pottery than a "stockpile" of ceramics. Consequently, the household assemblage frequency is determined to a greater degree by immediate needs of the family. As a result, there is a significant relationship between household size and household assemblages within these communities.

In Chuniapan de Abajo and Bascascaltepec, where access is reduced, there is no relationship between household size and assemblage frequency. Unlike other New World households, however, this lack of a relationship is not a function of stockpiles.

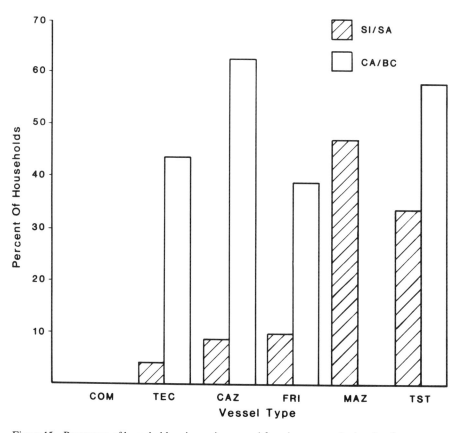

Figure 15   Percentage of households using a given vessel form but not producing that form.

In the case of Chuniapan de Abajo and Bascascaltepec there is a tendency for these households to contain even fewer ceramic vessels. Because of the difficulty involved in acquiring some of the vessel types (e.g. *cazuelas, ollas de frijol*), these households are beginning to adopt nonceramic alternatives. Many of these potters feel that this is a more cost-effective strategy, and even though these modern wares cost more, they usually last longer (cf. Hagstrum 1989:284–286). In contrast to the Highland Maya and Shipibo-Conibo, the households in Chuniapan de Abajo and Bascascaltepec are "streamlining" their assemblage rather than "stockpiling."

If streamlining is taking place, one would expect that the most expensive vessels would be de-emphasized, resulting in proportionally more inexpensive ceramics within the assemblage. This possibility can be tested by determining the proportional contribution of each pottery type to the assemblage. In instances of streamlining, the less expensive pottery should constitute a proportionally larger segment of the assemblage. If streamlining is not occurring, then costlier ceramics should make up a larger proportion of the assemblage.

A Kolmogorov-Smirnov (K-S) test was conducted in order to assess this possibility. A K-S test measures each variable's proportional contribution to the total, controlling for sample size (Blalock 1972). The null hypothesis of this test is that independent random samples have been drawn from the same population.

The results of this analysis indicate that a significant difference is present between the San Isidro and Sehualaca households on one hand and the Chuniapan de Abajo and Bascascaltepec potters on the other (Table 26). Moreover, the data indicate that the summed proportion of *comales* and *tecualones* (the least expensive pottery) is significantly higher in Chuniapan de Abajo and Bascascaltepec than in San Isidro and Sehualaca ($Z=-2.706$, $p<0.01$). This result suggests that price is differentially influencing the ceramic assemblages of these two groups. This variability is in keeping with expectations derived from our discussion of access to ceramics.

The fact that assemblage size is conditioned by a number of variables has important implications for the archaeological identification of production areas (Chapter 5). For example, Becker (1973:339) uses differences in vessel frequency and type diversity to differentiate between production and nonproduction households at the site of Tikal.

Table 26 *Cumulative proportions of vessel types within group assemblages*

Vessel type	N	San Isidro/ Sehualaca	N	Chuniapan de Abajo/ Bascascaltepec
Comal	60	.27907	34	.28928
Tecualon	46	.49302	40	.64912
Cazuela	46	.70698	11	.74561
Olla de frijol	38	.88372	14	.86842
Olla de maiz	19	.97209	7	.92982
Tostador	6	1.00000	8	1.00000
Total	215		114	

Similarly, Krotser (1974) suggests that sherds from a number of vessels of a single type might indicate to the archaeologist that a potter lived and worked in a given structure. This pattern is anticipated because a "potter keeps her unsold vessels in or close to the house" (Krotser 1974:136). If the patterning noted above is any indication, such a conclusion would be premature. In fact, households may contain large numbers of vessels specifically because they did *not* produce ceramics, or their production techniques limit vessel output (cf. Deal 1988:129). Archaeological ceramic assemblages are conditioned by a variety of factors, including a household's access to replacement vessels.

Vessel use life
Another variable conditioning the archaeological ceramic assemblage is the longevity of a vessel. Two main forces affect vessel use life at the intra-assemblage level: (a) use frequency and (b) replacement cost. The more often a vessel is subject to use, the shorter its average life span. On the other hand, the costlier a vessel is to replace, the longer it tends to last. Use-life variability between assemblages is a function of differences in raw materials. In San Isidro, the sand and quartz temper used by potters has an adverse impact on the life span of cooking vessels in that community.

In the following discussion, use life refers only to the time during which a vessel serves its primary function. Obviously, recycling activities and "provisional discard" could significantly increase the total life span of a given vessel (Deal 1983:193–196, 1985:253–259). Rigorous studies designed to collect information on the complete life cycle of ceramic vessels are only now beginning (e.g. Longacre 1981, 1985). Given the difficulty in collecting this information and the lack of a comparable data base, this discussion will focus on primary use life only.

An understanding of vessel longevity and the factors conditioning life spans are important archaeological concerns (e.g. Foster 1960a; Kramer 1985:89). For example, ceramic use life has obvious implications for pottery seriations, where the rate of a change in vessel attributes could well be a function of the relative longevity of a given vessel type (e.g. David 1972; DeBoer 1974). Different chronological scales are thus likely to be developed, depending upon which vessel form is employed to create the temporal sequence. As a result of this possibility, recent studies have suggested that ceramic seriations emphasize those vessels that prove to have the shortest life spans (David 1972; Longacre 1981).

Studies have also attempted to construct general relationships between the physical attributes of vessel forms and use life (Foster 1960b; DeBoer 1974, 1985). For example, DeBoer (1985) has recently proposed that procurement costs, manufacturing costs, and vessel weight are positively correlated with the life span of ceramics, while the use frequency (an admittedly composite measure) is negatively correlated with vessel longevity. The value of these propositions is their implications for the process of site formation, especially in terms of identifying activity areas and maintenance systems (e.g. Deal 1985, 1987; DeBoer 1985; Mills 1989). Data from the Tuxtlas provide an opportunity to address some of these variables from both the ethnographic and archaeological perspective.

INTRA-ASSEMBLAGE VARIABILITY

Pottery vessels are used in a number of diverse ways and are exposed to a variety of different conditions. Ceramics that are moved frequently run a higher risk of being dropped and broken than vessels remaining in out-of-the-way corners. Pottery used in cooking will suffer the effects of thermal stress, while vessels used for serving or dry/wet storage are rarely exposed to high temperatures. The way in which ceramics function within the behavioral system, therefore, is a critical element in the life span of a given vessel form.

Given the different functions of ceramics within an assemblage, one would expect to encounter a good deal of intra-assemblage use-life variability (i.e. differences among the vessel forms within the overall assemblage). Such variability is very much in evidence within the Tuxtlas sample (Table 27). Certain vessel types are characterized by a relatively short use life, while other forms last a considerably longer period. *Comales* exhibit the shortest average life span, lasting for little more than two and one-half months. *Tecualones* have the second shortest longevity, with an average use

Table 27 *Use-life values for six main vessel types within sampled Tuxtlas household assemblages*[1]

			Community		
Vessel type	San Isidro (N=18)	Bascascaltepec (N=2)	Chuniapan de Abajo (N=13)	Sehualaca (N=17)	Total (N=50)
Comal					
Mean	1.89	2.00	3.37	2.76	2.61
Median	1.75	2.00	3.00	2.50	2.50
Tecualon					
Mean	4.01	2.45	14.78	4.50	8.09
Median	2.50	2.45	6.00	4.50	4.50
Cazuela					
Mean	7.69	—	22.06	20.60	15.56
Median	7.00		18.00	12.00	12.00
Olla de Frijol					
Mean	9.58	12.00	19.66	20.00	15.83
Median	8.00	12.00	12.00	12.00	12.00
Olla de Maiz					
Mean	8.85	—	33.00	19.09	19.97
Median	10.00		33.00	12.00	12.00
Tostador					
Mean	9.25	4.00	23.33	30.00	18.53
Median	11.00	4.00	18.00	30.00	12.00
Total					
Mean	6.01	3.48	14.54	14.55	11.03
Median	6.31	3.48	13.40	10.20	7.90

[1] Use-life figures are presented in months

life of just over eight months. The four large cooking vessels all display considerably longer life spans. *Cazuelas* have a mean longevity of 15.56 months, followed closely by the *olla de frijol* with a use life of 15.83 months. The fifth longest life span is displayed by the *tostador*, with an average of just over one and one-half years. The final vessel type is the *olla de maiz* whose mean use life is almost twenty months. Overall, vessel forms in the sampled Tuxtlas households range from a low of seven weeks for *comales* in San Isidro to a high of two and three-quarter years for *ollas de maiz* in Chuniapan de Abajo.

In order to understand this wide variability in the life span of vessel forms, one must consider the various factors affecting ceramic breakage and curation. One of the most important of these conditions is use frequency (e.g. DeBoer 1985; Longacre 1981). As the term implies, use frequency is a general measure of the number of times a vessel is employed in task performance. And, as discussed by DeBoer (1985:348–349), use frequency is intimately related to the movement of a vessel. In this sense, passive systems, such as water storage, would result in low values when determining use frequency, while active systems, such as water transport, would produce high use-frequency values. Overall, an inverse relationship is expected between use life and use frequency (DeBoer 1985:Figure 14.1; Foster 1960b; Longacre 1981).

For the purposes of this discussion, use frequency will be based on the average number of times per week the vessel is utilized. Use was monitored in this fashion because the function of certain vessels is tied into the agricultural cycle, resulting in short periods of intensive use. Averaging was deemed to be a valid method for "smoothing" this variation.

The second consideration involved in vessel use life is replacement cost, a combination of several variables including procurement cost and manufacturing cost (e.g. DeBoer 1985). Replacement cost, as used here, is based on five characteristics: (a) production time, the amount of time required to manufacture the item; (b) producer skill, the experience and expertise necessary to successfully produce a vessel type; (c) raw material, the amount of clay and temper (by weight) used to make a single vessel; (d) access restriction, the percentage of producers within the sample who do not make the vessel type; and (e) price, based on the average cost of the item according to the producer. A positive relationship is expected between replacement costs and vessel longevity.

Overall, the Tuxtlas data are in keeping with these expectations (Table 28).[1] Use frequency ranks are negatively related to the ranks of mean vessel use life while procurement cost ranks exhibit a positive relationship with average vessel use life (Figure 16a–b). Moreover, ranks of use frequency are negatively associated with replacement costs (Figure 16c). *Comales*, with the shortest use life, are characterized by the highest use frequency and the lowest replacement costs. *Tecualones* have the second shortest longevity, are ranked second in replacement cost and fifth in use frequency. Some variability occurs beginning with *tostadores* (rank 5). This divergence

[1] Final rankings for replacement cost are derived by averaging the ranks for each category and then ranking the averages. In cases where there was significant overlap among the values for a given category the ranked scores were tied.

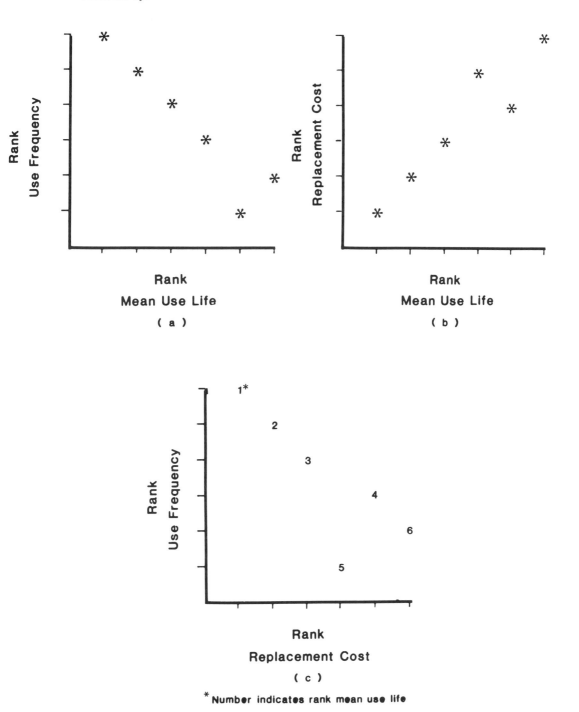

Figure 16   Relationships between use frequency, replacement costs, and use life for six main vessel forms.

Table 28 *Rankings of vessel acquisition for six main vessel types in sampled Tuxtlas household assemblages*

Category	Comal	Tecualon	Cazuela	Olla Frijol	Olla Maiz	Tostador
Use frequency						
rank	6	5	4	3	2	1
REPLACEMENT COST						
Production time	1	2	4	5.5	5.5	3
Production skill	1	2	4	5.5	5.5	3
Raw material	1	2	4	5.5	5.5	3
Availability	1	3	4	2	6	5
Price	1	2	3	4.5	4.5	6
REPLACEMENT COST						
RANK	1	2	3	5	6	4

is not severe, however, especially given that the median use-lives of the four vessels ranked 3–6 are exactly the same for the entire sample.

An additional factor that might influence average assemblage use life is production frequency. One might argue that potters working more frequently would be more skilled and are thus likely to produce longer-lasting vessels. Within the Tuxtlas data, however, there is no significant relationship between production frequency and assemblage use life, taken either as a whole or considered on a community by community basis (Figure 17).[2] At least in this sample, production frequency is not significantly affecting the durability of the finished product.

INTER-ASSEMBLAGE VARIABILITY

In contrast to the intra-assemblage patterning, the Tuxtlas use-life data display considerable inter-assemblage variability (differences for the same vessel type between communities). In other words, communities using the same vessel type are exhibiting significant variability in the life spans of those ceramics. Obviously, these differences should not be the result of functional variability, in as much as the vessel forms are used consistently from community to community. It would seem, therefore, that in addition to the variables noted above, vessel use life also varies as a function of conditions that are specific to the communities themselves.

Two factors appear to be influencing inter-assemblage differences within the Tuxtlas sample. The first is production variability, especially in terms of the raw materials used to manufacture the pottery. This distinction accounts for the wide differences between vessel use life in San Isidro as compared with that from Sehualaca and Chuniapan de Abajo. The second factor is curation, which is apparently a function of product accessibility. Communities that display low access to a given pottery type exhibit higher use lives for that vessel. This influence is represented in the different vessel life

[2] The Spearman's correlation coefficient for the entire sample is -0.108, indicating a weak negative relationship. The values for San Isidro actually covary in a positive manner ($r=0.167$), while the correlation for the remaining communities is negative ($r=0.014$).

spans between Sehualaca and Chuniapan de Abajo. Because of its small sample size Bascascaltepec is omitted from the following discussion.

Data for average household assemblage use lives can be divided into two groups: one containing values for San Isidro (6.01 months) and the other including pottery use-life data from Sehualaca and Chuniapan de Abajo (14.55 and 14.54 months, respectively). Upon closer inspection, however, not all vessel types fit comfortably into this grouping. *Comales*, for example, exhibit a life span that is relatively consistent from community to community. *Tecualones*, on the other hand, have similar patterns of longevity between San Isidro and Sehualaca, but average use life values are considerably higher in Chuniapan de Abajo. Finally, the life span of larger cooking vessels, including *cazuelas*, both *olla* forms, and the *tostador*, is much higher in Sehualaca and Chuniapan de Abajo than in San Isidro. The data suggest a complex pattern with larger cooking vessels making the largest contribution to overall variability, although additional differences are indicated.

Production variability
Variability in vessel use lives is also conditioned by the raw material available (Chapter 2). The Tuxtlas potters have access to the same relative quality clay: a fine-grain

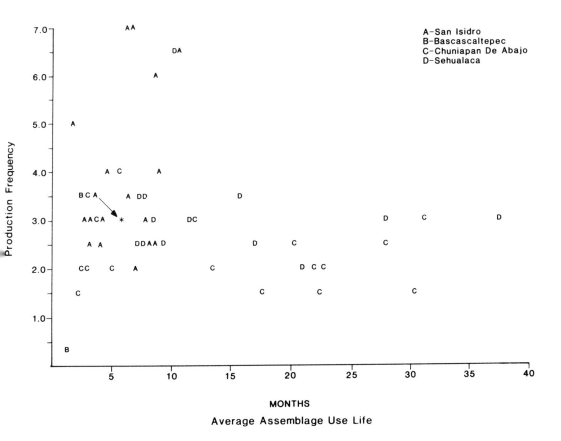

Figure 17   Scatterplot of production frequency by vessel use life for production communities.

kaolinite with minor differences in iron content and organic matter. Temper resources, however, do vary. While most potters use volcanic ash, the potters in San Isidro use a quartz-bearing sand temper. The use of this temper appears to be a major factor in reducing the use lives of San Isidro cooking vessels.

Differences in temper are especially crucial for cooking vessels since these ceramics are susceptible to thermal stress. Therman stress refers to the negative effects of heat on the fired clay body and is produced in two ways: (a) thermal expansion, the volumetric increase in size of the various paste constituents; and (b) thermal shock, the reduction in tensile strength as a function of unequal temperature increases along different portions of the vessel (Rice 1987:105; Steponaitis 1984:95–97). All things being equal, the greater the similarity between the thermal expansion characteristics of the temper and the fired clay matrix, the greater the vessel's resistance to thermal shock (Arnold 1985:24; Rye 1981).

According to Rye (1976), quartz, a mineral found in the temper deposits used in San Isidro, has a much higher rate of thermal expansion than minerals associated with volcanic activity, such as plagioclase and olivine. In other words, a reliance on quartz-bearing temper would be more likely to produce ceramics with lower resistance to thermal shock than pottery manufactured with temper such as volcanic ash.

The temper chosen by the San Isidro potters is thus expected to significantly affect the durability and use life of their product. Mann Witney U tests, comparing the difference in vessel longevity between San Isidro (by itself) and Sehualaca and Chuniapan de Abajo (as a group) produced significant results for all but two ceramic types. *Comales*, *cazuelas*, and both bean and maize *ollas* were all significantly different ($U=389.5$, $Z=2.54$, $p<0.05$; $U=236.5$, $Z=3.19$, $p<0.05$; $U=316.5$, $Z=2.66$, $p<0.05$; and $U=198$, $Z=3.64$, $p<0.05$, respectively). A comparison of *tostadores* failed to produce a significant difference ($U=24$, $Z=1.27$, $p>0.05$), quite possibly a consequence of the small sample size ($N=4$ and $N=8$, respectively). *Tecualones* were also not significantly different ($U=203$, $Z=1.86$, $p>0.05$).

These results are certainly in keeping with the expectations derived from the discussion of tempering materials. It appears that the presence of quartz in the temper of San Isidro pottery is strongly associated with comparatively low use-life values. The inclusion of quartz in the clay body is more likely to have a detrimental effect when vessel function involves cooking, an expectation supported by the fact that four of the five cooking vessels differed significantly between the two groups. The small sample size, when comparing *tostadores*, makes that comparison equivocal. The *tecualon*, the only non-cooking vessel, did not differ in a significant fashion.

Curation

The use-life data also suggest an interesting, yet somewhat perplexing, difference between use-life values in Sehualaca and Chuniapan de Abajo. When a certain vessel type is rare within a community, it usually exhibits a considerably higher use-life value then when the vessel is relatively common. This distinction may involve a more tenacious adherence to traditional habits in the face of changing community perceptions.

This relationship is best exemplified by *tostadores* and *ollas de maiz*. Just over 1 percent of the households in Sehualaca use the *tostador* while 41 percent of the households in Chuniapan de Abajo used this vessel. Comparing the longevity of this vessel type, we find the mean life span in Sehualaca is 30 months, but Chuniapan de Abajo has an average use life of 23.33 months. Approximately 35 percent of the households in Chuniapan de Abajo use *ollas de maiz* and these vessels have a mean life span of 33 months. In comparison, almost 85 percent of the Sehualaca households make use of this same pottery form, but it lasts an average of 19 months.

When the percentage of households using a given ceramic type is relatively large, however, dramatic variability in vessel life spans do not occur. For example, 76 percent of households in Chuniapan de Abajo use *ollas de frijol* compared with 100 percent of the sampled residences in Sehualaca. The life span of these ceramics averages 19.66 months in the former community, while the mean use life is 20 months in the latter. The overall pattern, therefore, suggests that when a relatively small percentage of households uses a given vessel, these households will display the highest use life for that ceramic type. This relationship does not appear to be a function of the kind of vessel; rather it is apparently associated with a resistance to, or inability to afford, metal vessels. Unfortunately, neither possibility can be fully explored without collecting additional information.

PART 2

Ceramic production and spatial organization

5

Archaeological approaches to ceramic production

The preceding section has placed the Tuxtlas potters in an ecological context. Information on the producer environment, coupled with data on pottery production and consumption, has exposed the dynamic nature of production-related activities. It is now time to consider how such a system might be approached from an archaeological perspective.

This chapter explores some of the fundamental issues involved in the identification and interpretation of pottery production. The first section considers how archaeologists establish the existence of production areas. Both epistemological and empirical issues are raised. This discussion argues that confusion in these two arenas presently hampers our inferential approach to ceramic production. Through an examination of these issues the stage is set for addressing models of production organization.

The second section focuses on these models and critically evaluates their utility. These approaches are shown to be overly static with only a limited applicability to many archaeological goals. This discussion underscores the need for a more rigorous approach to investigating production activities.

A frame of reference

After many years studying ceramics at the regional and inter-regional level, Mesoamerican archaeologists have recently begun investigating the actual location of ceramic production activities. This new emphasis on "microprovenience" studies (Rice 1981:219) is an outgrowth of research questions that seek a more detailed understanding of the producer's socioeconomic environment (e.g. Deal 1988:113; Feinman 1985; Santley et al. 1989; Stark 1985:158–160). Research into the scale of a production system is conducted more effectively when the actual production entities can be identified and their characteristics evaluated. Questions regarding political or economic control over manufacturing are likewise aided by investigations aimed at the location of production activities. Finally, studies of diachronic variation in pottery manufacture can benefit significantly from data derived from specific production areas (Arnold 1989; Rice 1984a:244–245).

This research focus challenges archaeological perceptions of ceramic production. In response, archaeologists and ethnoarchaeologists are increasingly taking stock of the methods by which production areas and activities are analyzed (e.g. Benco 1987; Deal 1983, 1988; Hagstrum 1989; Kramer 1985; Stark 1984). Stark (1985) has recently reviewed this issue using Mesoamerican data and assessed the reliability of identification procedures with special attention to domestic production. Her review reaffirms what other scholars have noted, namely that inordinate attention is often placed on the "overt categories of evidence," while other avenues of research are overlooked (Stark 1985:159–160, 172). The consequence has been the "infrequent" and "elusive" identification of production areas.

Much of this interpretational ambiguity can be traced to a lack of information stipulating the relationships between pottery manufacture and the archaeological record. The ethnographic record describing Mesoamerican pottery production is enormous (see Rice and Saffer 1982), but for the most part it will not answer questions raised by archaeological research. As cogently observed by Krause (1985:2), ethnographic information is best used to frame archaeological propositions; it should not be used to assess the results of fieldwork. Archaeologists cannot turn to ethnographies for answers, but they can use modern-day production to formulate methods for linking contemporary and prehistoric pottery making. Archaeologists interested in ceramic production must become increasingly involved in theory building (e.g. Arnold 1985; Rice 1984b:239; van der Leeuw 1984).

Archaeological inquiry

A preliminary goal of archaeological inquiry is to establish patterning in the arrangement of objects; in other words, to make statements about "what the world is like" (Binford 1982b:160). In order to achieve this goal, the archaeologist must first determine what attributes will be used to denote patterning. Obviously, patterning may be exhibited in a variety of different forms and in a number of different ways. The archaeologist must decide which attributes to monitor and how the item will be characterized (e.g. Dunnell 1971). Researchers *describe* the material; that is, they make statements concerning the physical properties of the objects in question and their relationships to one another in space. Given the static and contemporary nature of the material record, a description of the artifacts must precede the remaining levels of archaeological inquiry (e.g. Binford 1981, 1982a). All subsequent interpretations of the material record are a function of the initial description.

Archaeological description is restricted to contemporary phenomena; it cannot apply to the past. Thus, archaeologists must eventually move from a description (conducted with reference to the present) to an identification (conducted with reference to the past). Archaeological identification is the attempt to give meaning to material patterning in terms of what the world was thought to have been like. Archaeologists are engaged in a strategy designed to represent dynamic, past behavior as a function of the static, contemporary record. This inferential process cannot be accomplished through a simple presentation of material patterning. At some point the researcher must translate the described phenomena into identified phenomena. This translation involves a shift from the realm of observation to the realm of inference. It is through this process that the archaeologist attempts to give meaning to the past in terms of our present knowledge. Archaeological identification is an inferential strategy that necessarily assumes more than the empirical facts of the archaeological record. The methods employed in identification, therefore, constitute a crucial element in both inference generation and substantiating arguments of relevance (Binford 1977, 1981, 1982a).

Identification, however, is not the final stage of archaeological inquiry. Once the identifications have been made, the question arises as to what caused these patterns; that is, why do they exist? Archaeologists are not merely concerned with reconstructing the original material patterns, they are interested in understanding the behavior that produced those patterns. Moreover, researchers want to know how those patterns reflect the operation of the cultural system. These questions are addressed through archaeological interpretation.

According to Kaplan (1964) interpretation consists of two levels of specification: (a) giving meaning to acts, and (b) giving meaning to actions. An act refers to a "succession of biophysical events"; the meaning of the act "lies in the actor's purpose, or in the goal to which the actor is directed" (Kaplan 1964:139). An action, on the other hand, is "an act considered in the perspective in which it has meaning for the actor" (Kaplan 1964:139), and action meaning is "that [meaning] provided by the perspective of a particular theory or explanation of the action" (Kaplan 1964:359). In other words, acts are mechanical, without inherent meaning, while actions are acts with a specific act meaning. According to Kaplan: "A particular act may have a variety of different meanings, and so constitute different actions ... a variety of acts may have the same meaning and so constitute the same action" (1964:139). The distinction between act meaning and action meaning, therefore, could be generally construed as the more anthropologically familiar difference between "emic" and "etic" (e.g. Harris 1968:571, 575; Kaplan 1964:32).

The relevance of Kaplan's two-level approach for archaeological interpretation derives from the data used by archaeologists and the kinds of knowledge they pursue. Archaeologists do not witness the acts, they have no "informants" to clarify actions or act meanings, and they currently lack a well-developed theory for understanding action meaning. Do these limitations suggest that archaeologists do not engage in interpretation or, worse, that they should not attempt to do so?

Despite this apparent dilemma, archaeologists do engage in some degree of interpretation as discussed by Kaplan (1964). In fact, archaeological identification is actually the process of inferring actions based on a relationship between the material record (i.e. the described phenomena) and certain assumed acts (the biophysical performance). For example, the archaeological *identification* of an expedient lithic technology is actually an *interpretation* of some unseen action in the past. The acts, in this case, involve assumptions about certain biophysical tasks of raw-material introduction, reduction, and consumption at a site. The identification of these acts as expedient, however, requires an inference that the behavior is not conditioned by the actor's perception of future needs. This perception is the *act meaning*; it involves the purpose of the actor or the goal to which the actor is directed. In this instance the actor's purpose is to perform an activity (i.e. creation and use of a lithic implement) quickly and in terms of some immediate return. As such, the archaeological identification of expedient lithic reduction is a consideration of an *action*; that is, it is an inferred act coupled with the inferred meaning of that act for the actor. The consideration of an action in these terms constitutes an interpretation, as defined above.

Action meaning in archaeological interpretation occurs when the researcher gives meaning to an action as derived from a particular theory or explanation. In the above example, the meaning of the action might be provided by a theory regarding the logistical organization of mobile groups and the economic orientation of the group as a function of mobility. The action meaning is not used to create the theory; rather, the theory is used to generate the action meaning (Kaplan 1964:140). Archaeological interpretation, therefore, always subsumes some theory, some belief about the operation of the world, regardless of whether or not that theory has been formalized and explicated.

Given this characterization, the reader may feel that archaeological interpretation is a rather subjective process, especially considering the static nature of the available data. Thus, some individuals would suggest that archaeology is not "scientific" and that a pursuit of a scientific approach is a sterile endeavor (e.g. Bayard 1969). The subjectivity of archaeological interpretation is an accurate, but somewhat irrelevant, observation. Regardless of methodological sophistication, a case can always be made that any science, be it "hard" or "soft," includes an element of subjectivity (e.g. Kaplan 1964:387; Nagel 1961:473–475). One can never be sure that the observations made by one individual are exactly the same as the observations made by another. The issue is not whether subjectivity is involved in interpretation; giving meaning to past acts or actions is necessarily a subjective endeavor. The critical issue concerns the procedures employed to evaluate these interpretations. The scientific method is not a cookbook for obtaining and interpreting information. The purpose of the scientific method is to establish groundrules for the evaluation of propositions. Verification is the end and the scientific method provides the means toward that end. It is at this level that objectivity becomes an integral aspect of archaeological inquiry.

Archaeologists deal with patterns in material things, not with act meanings. *Anything* apart from those material arrangements must be inferred. Thus, it is not necessary to understand an act in terms of the actor's interpretation of that act (cf. Hodder 1982, 1987). The crucial fact for the archaeologist is that the actor, regardless of the meaning, behaves in a consistent fashion as a function of that meaning. For example, it may not be important that a culture associates the color red with "outside" while white is associated with "inside" (Hodder 1987:444). Of archaeological importance, however, is the degree to which interior activities are consistently and repeatedly different from exterior activities. Consistency in behavior produces regular patterning in the material record. The action (as defined above) does not produce the archaeological record. It is act repetition that generates the material patterning. Archaeological data is produced by culturally repetitive behavior, regardless of its inherent meaning to the actor.

A final comment should be made regarding the relationship between act and action interpretation. Some archaeologists, unaware that they are confusing the two levels, may become entangled in a tautology referred to as *the circle of interpretation*: "act meanings are inferred from actions and are then used in the explanation of the actions, or actions are construed from the acts and then used to explain the acts" (Kaplan 1964:362). Archaeologists might find themselves confronted with either situation. For example, consider the proposition that high concentrations of material constitute a production locale or workshop (e.g. Becker 1973; Spence 1981). The acts of manufacturing are assumed to result in higher than average material densities; thus, the occurrence of such densities is thought to indicate the action of production. When production areas are archaeologically identified (i.e. presented as actions), however, the archaec'ogist is using the inferred action (production behavior) to explain the material patterns, even though the material patterns were required to indicate the action. In the absence of some independent means of justification, this interpretation could never be falsified and the researcher would learn very little about production behavior in the past.

Act meaning may also be derived from an inferred action, and then be used to validate that inferred action. Researchers have suggested that production of new or more elaborate ceramic forms often results from increased economic competition (e.g. Feinman, Kowalewski, and Blanton 1984:229; Foster 1965:52–55). The observation of new attributes is used to establish the production of new pottery forms which are then used to propose economic competition. Competition, in turn, is presented to account for the occurrence of the new attributes. The difficulty is that these attributes were used to infer the action of new production strategies. Again we see a tautology and no evaluation of the validity of the assumed relationship.

It is no simple task, therefore, to move from a description of the archaeological record to a justifiable identification of production behavior. It is extremely easy to confuse levels of inquiry and engage in tautological reasoning. But this distinction is not merely an exercise in terminology. A clear distinction between description, identification, and interpretation is essential to rigorous archaeological inquiry.

Identifying production areas
Archaeologists rely on three main classes of data to identify production locations. The first set of criteria reflects the potter's control over the production process. Archaeologically, this control is displayed in the tools and facilities used to manufacture ceramics. The occurrence of these implements, therefore, is considered as one class of production activity diagnostics.

The second category of evidence results from the traditional potter's frequent inability to perfectly control production. Despite a producer's skill, some manufacturing errors will usually occur. These mistakes, or production residues, constitute another means by which archaeologists may detect production activities. Not all errors are the same, and the frequency of individual errors and the ratio of different errors can provide information on the intensity and organization of production as well as the location of production (e.g. Redmond 1979; Rye 1981).

The finished product provides the third category of information for evaluating production activities. The way in which the ceramic vessel was made, the effort in execution and decoration, and the routinization of production yield evidence of producer specialization and production efficiency. Because not all producers manufacture for the same market (e.g. Brumfiel and Earle 1987; Earle 1987), an analysis of the finished product can generate data on patterns of distribution and characteristics of the consumer population (e.g. Feinman 1980; Fry 1981).

PRODUCTION IMPLEMENTS

Production implements refer to the tools and facilities employed in ceramic manufacture. Implements may be as simple as a piece of gourd or as elaborate as sophisticated kilns. Between these extremes lie a number of different tools and techniques, all reflecting diverse processing, forming, and firing behaviors. These differences make production implements a category sensitive to production variability. Moreover, given the materialist emphasis in archaeology, it is not surprising that archaeologists would rely on production implements to locate areas of pottery making (Stark 1985:160).

Production implements are used in all phases of the production sequence and may represent the entire range of production activities. Implements play an especially important role in vessel formation, decoration, and firing. Thus, archaeologists may cite such items as molds, polishing stones, grinding implements, and kilns as evidence of production activities. While there is little doubt that, when correctly identified, these implements indicate pottery manufacture, it is the process of identification that remains problematic.

Production implements are not self-evident. As noted above, identification is necessarily an inferential process. The identification of vessel molds is a case in point. Debate during the 1960s centered on the function of so-called "mushroom stones." Some archaeologists suggested that these forms represented actual effigy objects, used in association with the consumption of hallucinogenic fungi (Borhegyi 1961). Other Mesoamericanists, however, believed that these objects were employed as molds for ceramic manufacture, similar to ethnographically documented molds used in various areas of Mesoamerica (Kohler 1976). Obviously, the resolution of this question requires independent contextual evidence. To what degree are the "stones" associated with residential debris or architecture? Are there associations and/or correlations between the assemblage frequency and these items? And if used as molds, how well do the dimensions of these "stones" mirror the dimensions of the recovered pottery?

Larger features such as kilns are also subject to ambiguity. Recent excavations in North Africa exposed an archaeological feature first thought to represent a hearth (Redman and Myers 1981). The excavators later entertained the possibility that the feature was actually a kiln. Debate over the identification of kilns has also occurred in areas of Mesoamerica (e.g. Bordaz 1964; Stone and Turnbull 1941).

The differential preservation of production implements must also be considered. In many instances, smaller implements are made from organic materials and are not well preserved. Forming tools are frequently generated from plant material including gourds, pieces of large seed coverings, and pieces of wood (Arnold 1985:37; Foster 1955:4; Krotser 1980:132; Thompson 1958). Seeds are sometimes used as polishing implements (Reina and Hill 1978:159–160), while vessel molds can be made of wood or basketry (Rice 1987:125). Even if all recovered production implements have been identified correctly, there is a host of potential information that may not be preserved in the material record. Archaeologists, consequently, obtain a very incomplete picture of pottery manufacture if they rely too heavily on production implements to identify production areas.

PRODUCTION RESIDUES

Despite a potter's attempts to improve control over production, vessel firing often remains an inexact process. The concern exhibited by potters prior to vessel firing has frequently been noted in the literature (e.g. Foster 1965:50; Papousek 1981; Reina and Hill 1978:68–69). Many traditional potters do not have the control over material quality and production technology that would insure successful production. As a result, ceramics may spall, melt, or even explode during the firing process (Rice 1987:104–107; Rye 1981). These production residues constitute the second class of evidence in the archaeological record.

Production residues refer to the unintentional results of ceramic manufacture. Because these residues are unintentional, and often undesirable, the factors conditioning their archaeological occurrence may be quite different from those factors affecting the deposition of other production indicators, such as production implements or even "stockpiles" of finished products (e.g. DeBoer and Lathrap 1979; Krotser 1974; Nicklin 1979). The disposal of production residue may come about in two main ways: (a) material may be recycled so that its function and even its form may be altered; or (b) the material may be physically relocated to reduce its interference with other activities (e.g. Deal 1983:193–196). In the context of this discussion, recycling could include re-use of misfired sherds as grog (temper) (Rice 1987:411–412; Shepard 1956:25) or assigning new functions to the items depending on their size. For example, many potters reuse misfired sherds as aids in the firing process (Kramer 1985:81). When firing in the open, production residue may be placed on the ground to separate the "green" ceramics from the steam produced by heating the ground surface (Arnold 1985:71; Reina and Hill 1978:76). If kilns are employed, large sherds are frequently placed atop the kiln to provide a layer of insulation to maintain temperatures (e.g. Rye and Evans 1976:164; also Chapter 3). Smaller sherds are also used to separate pots from one another within the kiln (especially if pots have been decorated prior to firing) or to partially enclose vessels in order to alter the firing atmosphere (i.e. reduce the amount of oxygen available for combustion) (Lackey 1982; Rye 1981). Of course, the decision to use misfired sherds in these different ways is primarily a function of their size and availability. Large sherds, which cover more area, are more suitable for use as kiln covers while only the smaller sherds would be placed within the kilns themselves.

First, the point must be made that sherd concentrations associated with vessel firing do not always contain obvious production defects. Stark (1984) provides a contemporary Mexican example of a sherd dump associated with kiln firing in which no evidence for severe overfiring or other production errors is exhibited. Open-air firing locations in New Guinea have also failed to produce evidence for deformed or waster sherds (Lauer 1974). Winter and Payne (1976:39) have extended this observation to the archaeological record. In their excavations of a prehispanic kiln at Monte Alban, these archaeologists encountered no defective sherds. Minimal quantities of misfired sherds have been observed in other archaeological contexts. For example, waster sherds constituted only 1 percent of the survey material from TS 73 in Tehuacan, despite the fact that ceramic production is characterized as a "highly specialized operation . . . carried out in a workshop by a group of full-time laborers" (Redmond 1979:124).

Although defective sherds do associate with production in some contexts, they certainly do not in all contexts. More information on disposal and other maintenance-related activities is required from contemporary production activities. This additional data would help establish the circumstances under which residue might not be expected to occur "on site."

In addition to the absence of residue, recovered debris may have little to do with ceramic manufacture. For example, production areas are sometimes identified by a ceramic assemblage exhibiting an emphasis on a certain vessel form or ware. Other activities, however, could also be responsible for such a pattern. In some cases salt is produced by placing saline water in ceramic vessels and then allowing the water to evaporate. These basin-like containers frequently break, resulting in large ceramic assemblages dominated by a single vessel form (e.g. Muller 1984; Sanders et al. 1979:172–175). Consequently, archaeologists must always demonstrate that pottery making is the most likely conclusion to be drawn from inferred production residues (e.g. Stark 1985).

PRODUCTION RESULTS

The final line of production evidence focuses on the successfully manufactured ceramics. This evidence, termed production results, encompasses a variety of physico-chemical analyses and enables archaeologists to characterize pottery manufacture based on such attributes as degrees of product standardization (Rathje 1975:415; Sinopoli 1988; Wright and Johnson 1975), design elaboration (Rice 1981, 1984b), and overall amounts of energy investment per vessel (Feinman et al. 1981; Kolb 1981).

Provenience analyses using production results are often conducted from a regional perspective (Rice 1981:219, 1987:413–425). Questions focus on the potter's access to raw materials and the distribution of the finished product. Paste compositional analyses, for example, can be used to distinguish between locally made ceramics and imported vessels (e.g. Bishop and Rands 1982). Production results have also been used to infer the overall scale and organization of production activities, as well as providing evidence for market orientation (Feinman 1985, 1986).

One of the most frequently cited lines of evidence for this purpose is vessel standardization. Archaeologists have proposed that the formal similarity of vessels can be used as a relative measure of producer specialization. In most cases, standardization is linked to increasing administrative control over production and/or economies of scale:

> High degrees of standardization in a class of goods are expected to result from large-scale production and political and/or social emphasis and enforcement of uniformity . . . On the other hand, if demonstrable differences can be identified between the products of individual workshops, and/or vessels found in localized areas of the city, then a noncentralized mode of ceramic production can be argued for.
> (Sinopoli 1988:587)

In addition to formal regularity, standardization may also be exhibited in paste characteristics and repetitive or simplified design elements.

Some of the limitations to this assumption are addressed in the following section. But it should be noted that potters are quite capable of producing surprisingly uniform vessels without production regulations and administrative overseers (e.g. Hodder 1981). Routinization does promote standardization, but even seasonal potters can be extremely adept at producing consistent vessel forms. Moreover, formal standardization can result as much from vessel function as producer specialization. Dean Arnold (1985:147–149) notes how motor habit patterns, associated with vessel use, select for consistent regional varieties in pottery. Finally, one must also consider the possibility of specialists producing relatively *unique* vessels, as is the case for some Maya polychrome (Rice 1985). These points highlight some of the limitations in overemphasizing implements, residues, or results when making identifications of ceramic production loci.

Interpreting production activities

The identification of production areas is ultimately used to make statements about the characteristics of past socioeconomic systems. In order to achieve this goal, archaeologists attempt to establish the scale of production. Production scale refers to the size and complexity of the production system, including determinations of workforce size, input/output quantities, and technological capabilities (e.g. Rice 1987:180–181).

Archaeologists usually establish production scale according to a typological scheme of pottery manufacture. A number of similar production typologies have been generated; these schemes present manufacturing variability as series of discrete production "states" or "modes," ordered from part-time manufacture to full-time producer specialization (Balfet 1965; Myers 1984; Peacock 1981:8–11, 1982; Rice 1987:184; Stark 1985; van der Leeuw 1976:392–398, 1977, 1984). Each of these modes has different material implications for the archaeological record.

Despite various degrees of specificity, these typologies emphasize two central aspects of the economic system. The first is production output, or the number of items manufactured over a given period. Production output is scaled in general terms from low to high. The level of output is primarily based on four variables: (a) the number of individuals engaged in production activities; (b) the amount of time devoted to production activities; (c) the available technology; and (d) the cost of raw materials in terms of labor, time, and/or money.

The second component of the economic system is market demand. Market demand is generally conditioned by the number of consumers, their preference for a given item, and the relationship between their income and the price of that item. Price, in turn, is primarily determined by production costs. Production efficiency is a relative measure of these expenses. Generally speaking, the greater the production efficiency, the lower the cost of producing a given item. As indicated in the following discussion, this typological approach attempts to translate variability in production output and the market demand into archaeological expectations concerning the technology used in production, the amount of residue that should result from manufacturing, and the quality and appearance of the finished product (Feinman 1980; Myers 1984; Peacock 1982; van der Leeuw 1976, 1984).

HOUSEHOLD PRODUCTION

The first mode in models of ceramic production is usually termed household or domestic production (Peacock 1982:8; Rice 1987:184; Stark 1985:160; van der Leeuw 1984:748–750). Household production is characterized by part-time activities aimed at maintaining the domestic assemblage; it is not geared toward generating additional revenue. Household production may occur once every several years or it may be integrated within the seasonal activities of the household (David and Hennig 1972:4; Fontana et al. 1962). Potters engaged in household production are almost invariably female and must organize production in accordance with other domestic chores (Balfet 1965:162).

Household potters devote little time to manufacture and do not employ specialized production techniques. Activities are usually arranged in a serial fashion with a single individual responsible for performing all manufacturing stages. Consequently, production output is quite low. Moreover, because these potters are providing for their own needs, they are not influenced by market demands. Decisions concerning the formal and stylistic attributes of their vessels are personal choices and are not determined by economic competition with other producers (e.g. Balfet 1965:165–166).

The archaeological consequences of household production are thought to include low densities of manufacturing residues and expedient production tools. In addition, the formal composition of the archaeological assemblage should mimic the normal household inventory since production is directed towards maintaining the household ceramic inventory (Krotser 1974:132; Stark 1985:160). The lack of resources and the low incentive to invest in production technology is also expected to be mirrored in the relatively poor technical quality of the finished product. Some ethnographic accounts, however, have noted that an emphasis on decoration often occurs at this level, perhaps to partially mask irregularities in the paste or defects caused by poor firing (e.g. Balfet 1965:165–166).

HOUSEHOLD INDUSTRY

As the term implies, a household industry is characterized by higher levels of output than household production (Peacock 1982:8; Rice 1987:184; van der Leeuw 1984:751–752). Like household production, the household industry potter operates at a part-time level and the majority of these producers continue to be women. The major difference is that household industry production is conducted more frequently and is directed toward a larger consumer market.

An increase in production output requires an additional investment in manufacturing activities. As noted earlier, production output can increase through more efficient production techniques, the involvement of more producers, and/or more time devoted to production. Technological development may require added expenditures that the household industry potters cannot afford. Consequently, production output is usually increased by allocating additional time and labor to ceramic manufacture. Production becomes more regularized and is generally conducted on a seasonal basis. The majority of activities continue to be performed serially, but the increased output may result in "bottlenecks" during certain phases of production. During these periods additional labor may be required. Children may provide much of this assistance, such as setting pots out to dry, fetching tools for the producer, and helping to move vessels to the firing locale. Spouses may also help by collecting fuel or other raw materials. These tasks are not specific to individuals, however, and anyone may be asked to temporarily assist in the production process.

Like household production, the archaeological appearance of the household industry would be difficult to establish. Pottery making is still conducted within the domestic compound and production residues are expected to be mixed with other domestic debris. An increase in production output may result in higher ceramic densities, reflecting those vessels that were broken during manufacture. The same suite of products may be manufactured, however, so the number of different vessel forms entering the archaeological record should not be significantly different. Production technology will usually remain comparatively simple, but more discarded tools might be expected as a result of the increased number of individuals involved in production activities.

WORKSHOP INDUSTRY
According to the models of ceramic production, the workshop industry is characterized by full-time ceramic specialists (van der Leeuw 1984:753–754). Revenues from workshop industry products constitute the main source of income for these potters (Peacock 1982:9). Full-time specialists are most commonly male, but all family members may assist with various stages of production.

Workshop industries are designed to supply goods to a large number of consumers. This increase in the production output may also be associated with a desire to improve the operational efficiency of manufacturing activities. Operational efficiency may be especially important for the changed incentives of a "profit motive." One means of achieving this goal is by the reorganization of production activities (e.g. Diaz 1966). Rather than performing tasks in a serial fashion, several producers may perform activities simultaneously. Simultaneity may be simple (several producers conducting a single task together, such as loading a kiln) or complex (each producer performing a different production task) (e.g. Wilk and Rathje 1982). Task specialization and improved activity scheduling can thus contribute to more efficient production activities. The need to produce larger amounts of output may also select for new tools and facilities. For example, the use of molds or a potter's wheel can increase the speed of production while a kiln can reduce the amount of breakage during firing (Arnold 1985:202–214). Through these capital investments the producer is able to extend the potential output of the production system.

The workshop industry, then, may be characterized by an increasing dependence on revenues coupled with an increased reinvestment of those revenues into the production system. In order to meet a larger market demand, the potter will attempt to increase operational efficiency and may even begin to specialize in the production of a narrow range of goods. From an archaeological standpoint, this specialization may alter the appearance of the ceramic assemblage associated with these workshop locations (e.g. Krotser and Rattray 1980; Redmond 1979). These assemblages are expected to become skewed toward the occurrence of specific forms and/or wares, making them noticeably different from the residues of part-time, household producers (e.g. Stark 1985:Table 7.1).

NUCLEATED WORKSHOPS AND MANUFACTORY

The most complex preindustrial organization of ceramic production is called the nucleated workshop or manufactory (Peacock 1982:9–10; Rice 1987:184). These two production types are quite similar; the major difference is size, with the manufactory exhibiting a somewhat larger workforce than the nucleated industry (Peacock 1982:9). Both forms of production emphasize high volumes of output with the finished products destined for a supra-regional market. Thus, these levels of production operate at a significantly greater scale in terms of both production output and market demand.

Production at this larger scale often restricts the possible location of manufacturing activities (e.g. Nicklin 1979). Nucleated workshops and manufactories are generally situated away from the major concentrations of population, often because they produce noxious by-products and waste materials (Peacock 1982:38). Another factor conditioning the location of ceramic production may be transportation requirements. Large amounts of raw materials must be brought into the production area and large quantities of finished products must be shipped out. The difficulties in achieving both goals will help determine where the industry is located in terms of raw materials and prospective markets (Nicklin 1979; Santley et al. 1989:127; Weatherill 1971).

The emphasis on large-scale production will increase the number of individuals involved in manufacturing activities. As noted above, a larger work force requires additional activity scheduling in order to make operations more efficient. New tools and production techniques such as levigating tanks, processing pits, and massive kilns may also be adopted (Benco 1987; Myers 1984; Peacock 1982:43–46). Given the increased number of producers and the size of the production facilities, the spatial requirements of this level of production can be quite extensive. These characteristics should be reflected archaeologically in extremely high densities of production residues, remnants of large production facilities, and the size of the production area.

ATTACHED OR TETHERED SPECIALIST

The attached specialist is a producer who manufactures craft items on demand, either for an individual or single family unit (e.g. Brumfiel and Earle 1987:5; Hagstrum 1985b, 1989:277). These producers are usually highly skilled artisans who can command large payment for their services. The attached specialist may produce comparatively few items but at the same time may require a more complex production technology. Such a potter may be "charged with the production of objects that correspond to badges of rank or prestige for the elite patrons and therefore are items not in general or widespread use and which may even be unique in their occurrence" (Gero 1983:42, cited in Clark 1986:44). Rather than manufacturing the same item for a number of different consumers, the attached specialist is more likely to produce a number of different items for the same consumer.

This form of production has been ethnographically documented for several African and Asian cultural systems (e.g. Leuzinger 1960; Sahlins 1958). In addition, it would not be surprising if attached specialists also operated in the prehispanic Mesoamerican cultures (e.g. D'Altroy and Earle 1985; Earle 1987; Santley et al. 1989:120). The archaeological identification of these producers, however, can be difficult. Given the skill of the attached specialist, minimal quantities of debris may be generated. Thus, while the craftsmanship and skill reflected in a product could signal the existence of a tethered specialist, it can be more difficult to establish the location of that activity. The association of production facilities with elite residences merits further consideration in this regard (e.g. Santley et al. 1984, 1985).

Specialization and the production model

The preceding discussion has outlined the common procedure by which patterning in the archaeological record is transformed into statements about prehistoric ceramic manufacture; that is, how we move from description to identification to interpretation. Archaeologists employ a typological system to determine what manner of production is reflected by the archaeological material. Both the typology and the archaeological implications have been generated from ethnographic accounts of pottery making.

A main component of the production model is its emphasis on the time and energy investment in pottery making. Potters are often dichotomized into "part-time" or "full-time" specialists (e.g. Arnold 1985:18; Kramer 1985:80; Rice 1987:189; Stark 1985:162). Part-time producers are commonly female, make pottery on a seasonal or even annual cycle, and do not rely on ceramic production as an important source of revenue (Balfet 1965:162–163). Full-time specialists, on the other hand, are most often male and ceramic production is their primary means of livelihood (Rice 1987:189–190).

How do archaeologists identify (i.e. infer) producer specialization? In many cases identification is achieved through arguments concerning production efficiency. This argument may take two forms: (a) a positive association between production efficiency and vessel standardization; and (b) a positive relationship between market competition and energy investment in the product. The degree to which these relationships are justified is critiqued below. Not only are the assumptions unwarranted but their material implications remain ambiguous. Current arguments associating producer specialization with the archaeological record provide an unsatisfactory foundation for identifying specialization in the archaeological record.

VESSEL STANDARDIZATION

The degree of vessel standardization within a given assemblage has been used to suggest a number of characteristics about the prehistoric socioeconomic system. These characteristics include increased centralization and/or administrative control over production (e.g. Feinman, Blanton, and Kowalewski 1984:164; Sinopoli 1988:586–587; Wright and Johnson 1975) and overall growth in the production-distribution system (e.g. Rathje 1975:415; Rice 1981). Both of these scenarios imply increased production intensity and a positive relationship between vessel standardization and production industry scale.

While increases in production efficiency and ceramic specialization can certainly result in vessel standardization, additional factors may also contribute to a more standardized ceramic assemblage. For example, one could conceive of a situation where the *infrequency* of production would select for vessel standardization. Archaeologists have often noted that ceramic producers are generally opposed to technological change (e.g. Foster 1965; Nicklin 1971; Reina 1963, 1966). One reason for this unwillingness to "experiment" is said to be the unpredictable nature of production and the potential loss if production fails (cf. Papousek 1981). Under conditions of infrequent production, potters may attempt to replicate, as much as possible, every production step in order to minimize potential failure. Most of these products are utilitarian; thus, their functional requirement may also serve to control the amount of acceptable product variability (Arnold 1985:144–151). The emphasis on replication, both formal and technological, would be exhibited in the relative standardization of the finished products.

The use of molds presents another impetus for formal standardization. Unfortunately, a reliance on these implements is not restricted to high-intensity production activities. An example of this situation is the use of already existing vessels as molds. The Papago Indians of the Southwest make ceramics sporadically and often use the base of a previous vessel as a mold for a new pot (Fontana et al. 1962). Such a procedure would obviously create similarity in form and size of vessels. A similar procedure is also practiced by the part-time Fulani and Gisiga potters (David and Hennig 1972:5). The fact that standardization may be achieved in both low-intensity and high-intensity production contexts suggests that vessel standardization may be a capricious index of increasing specialization.

COMPETITION

A positive association between economic competition and assemblage variability has been noted by several researchers (e.g. Feinman, Kowalewski, and Blanton 1984:299; Foster 1965:52–53; Hendry 1957:235). Researchers argue that competition among potters for a portion of the market encourages producer experimentation. Such experimentation, in turn, should be archaeologically visible through the introduction of new product designs. Moreover, these new forms are often more costly in terms of energy investment than the vessels manufactured previously:

> potters will decrease the amount of energy that they will expend in the preparation of a single ceramic vessel when the competition between these potters is diminished. Alternatively, increased competition between potters has been shown to result most frequently in the production of a wide variety of ceramic vessels that often require a large expenditure of energy to produce. (Feinman 1985:197)

Energy investment per vessel is thus expected to be greatest when producers are competing for consumers.

Unfortunately, this claim contradicts other expectations regarding production efficiency in a market system (e.g. Benco 1987). Given a competitive situation, more efficient production techniques (i.e. standardization) will lower unit cost, resulting in a cheaper and more competitive product. Diverting resources to the development of new products, or investing *more* energy in the manufacture of each product, will increase unit costs and make the product *less* competitive. The belief that a producer necessarily becomes more competitive by increasing production costs is unjustified.

Balfet's (1965, 1984) ethnographic work among the Maghreb potters in North Africa is quite revealing in this regard. Balfet noted that producers operating at low levels of output invest more energy in production than more specialized potters. According to Balfet, the greatest energy investment, especially in the area of vessel decoration, is displayed at the household level of production. In these situations, the greatest variability in production:

> is found in the *finishing and decoration* of the pottery. Among the
> non-specialist women potters, these variations are so great from one region to
> another that it would be irrelevant to give an account of them here . . .
> Finishing is always carefully done, and pottery objects . . . pass again and
> again through the hands of the part time potter who devotes hours to
> polishing the slip to get a uniform smooth and brilliant finish . . . Moreover,
> they show great freedom in the choice of decorative compositions
> (Balfet 1965:165–166, original emphasis).

These findings are certainly at odds with the idea that competition is the reason for energy investment. According to Balfet's (1965) study, *energy investment may be highest when potters are primarily producing for their own needs, not for a competitive market.*

What could be the reason for this ambiguity? When the problem is studied more closely, it becomes apparent that those individuals citing competition as a causal variable in assemblage elaboration and energy investment are discussing situations in which there is either a disruption of the traditional market or the establishment of a nontraditional market (e.g. Cook 1984; Reina and Hill 1978:262–264). These new markets include pottery consumers with different formal and stylistic tastes. The demand of this new clientele supports an elaboration of vessel forms (Rice 1984a:248–249). "Competition" in this sense is a *symptom* of new consumer demands; it is not a cause of production variety. Producer competition without a subsequent formal elaboration in the ceramic assemblage is quite possible, especially if there are prescribed cultural norms concerning the appearance of an item (e.g. Hill 1985; Reina 1966; Reina and Hill 1978).

Competition implies a range of product acceptability and as that acceptance range expands, so too will the diversity of products. Most archaeological approaches to this question have thus far emphasized the producer. We must also consider the consumer. In a market system, competition is not necessarily the cause of energy investment and design elaboration; rather, *energy investment and design elaboration are the result of differential consumer demands.*

An emphasis on efficiency arguments, be they from the perspective of competition, vessel standardization, or some other measure, are only valid when the necessary relationships between production and consumption have been established. Moreover, production models that focus on the amount of time invested in the production strategy must be readjusted to incorporate measures that are more amenable to the archaeo-logical record. These assumptions and procedures are some of the major difficulties involved in current approaches to interpreting ceramic production in the archaeo-logical record.

Summary

This chapter has provided a critical assessment of the state of the art in ceramic-production studies. Specifically, the focus has been on the criteria used to identify production locations and interpret variability in manufacturing activities. This dis-cussion has demonstrated that many of the current procedures used to investigate activities are too ambiguous to provide reliable interpretations.

The problem of ambiguity results from an inability to securely link the organization of pottery manufacture to archaeological patterns. The difficulty is not that current methods for monitoring production are necessarily *wrong*; rather, the problem is that our current understanding does not allow us to predict when they will be *right*. The same ethnographic record that supplies the basis for identifying production locations and establishing production modes clearly demonstrates the range of variability in production activities. The value of middle-range research is its emphasis on documen-ting and understanding the specific conditions under which production decisions are made. By establishing these situational factors we begin to construct a theory of ceramic production that allows us to *anticipate* archaeological patterning.

6

Spatial organization and ceramic production

The relationship between production activities and material residue is neither simple nor self-evident. Linking the two requires research conducted in a contemporary setting. These connections cannot be established directly from the archaeological evidence; those material patterns are the very phenomena we are attempting to decipher. Analyses of production decisions, and their material implications, must be established through research that controls for both behavior and the material record.

At the same time, archaeologists cannot simply rely on ethnographic anecdotes and interpretations through analogy. As noted previously, there is a distinction between learning by experience and learning from experience. The discussion in Chapter 5 suggested that inordinate emphasis has gone toward the former. This section considers how pottery making within Los Tuxtlas may assist with the latter.

This chapter explores ways to link variability in the organization of ceramic production with the material patterns of manufacturing activities. The emphasis on both the material technology and behavioral components of production allows the archaeologist to begin considering the potential contribution of these factors to the archaeological consequences of production. This perspective represents a first step toward developing a middle-range theory of ceramic manufacture.

This discussion makes the point that the material technology associated with a given production system can be as much a function of internal conditions as external variability. In addition to such considerations as the natural environment and/or market demand, the potter must also select production techniques that are suited to the specific characteristics of the context of manufacture. Manufacturing context refers to those forces operating on the producer as a function of the specific setting of vessel production. As the following discussion argues, the manufacturing context will regulate the *archaeological* appearance of production every bit as much as climate or competition.

Finally, the emphasis in this discussion is on vessel firing. In terms of identifying production loci, other production stages may not leave the kinds of debris that will be recovered archaeologically. Firing, on the other hand, is more likely to produce the material patterning that can be observed in the material record. Moreover, the unexpected variability in firing activities within the Tuxtlas provides an excellent set of data for investigating organizational variability in pottery manufacture.

Ceramic production organization
The organization of ceramic production has traditionally been presented as a series of discrete modes or states. As argued previously, this conceptualization has encouraged a

static view of production; that is, manufacturing is seen less as a combination of individual activities and more as a technological totality. Activity organization is viewed as the dependent variable, to be altered when the appropriate manufacturing techniques are required. Production change is thus perceived as pronounced differences in the tools and techniques of pottery manufacture.

This perspective places very little emphasis on production activities *per se*. Activities within a production scale or mode are held constant while attention is more often focused on differences between system states. And while considerations of production scale may be common in the literature (e.g. Feinman, Kowalewski, and Blanton 1984:299; Rice 1981:222–223; Stark 1984; van der Leeuw 1977), this term is primarily intuitive and scale may imply significantly different degrees of input and output across systems (Kramer 1985:80–81; Rice 1987:180–181).

MATERIAL TECHNOLOGY AND ORGANIZATIONAL STRUCTURE

The organizational structure of production both conditions and is conditioned by the tools and techniques used in manufacture. Organizational structure refers to the spatio-temporal scheduling and execution of a task as a function of the differential requirements of that activity. Production technology in this context is a double-edged sword; the potter is free to chose from the array of available techniques, but there are specific consequences resulting from those choices. These decisions can result in the differential character and structure of production, even among producers operating at similar levels of intensity (Arnold 1987).

The way in which material technology may limit production is reflected in the organizational structure of pottery making. Ceramic production may be organized as either a flexible activity or one that assumes a more restricted, rigid structure. This characterization is represented by a continuum of production activities, with spatially flexible tasks at one end and spatially restrictive behaviors at the other (Arnold 1987:235). These end points of the production continuum reflect the extremes of potential behavior; obviously the majority of activities will fall somewhere along this line. Nonetheless, the characterization of production activities as spatially flexible and spatially restrictive is a useful heuristic device for investigating organizational variability within production systems.

Spatially flexible activities are not confined to a specific location; rather, they may be moved from location to location as space becomes available. The elastic nature of these tasks usually means that they are finished relatively quickly and produce low-bulk material (see below, also Anderson 1982). This is not to say that spatially flexible activities are necessarily expedient, although many expedient tasks could be characterized this way. On the contrary, spatially flexible activities may be part of the daily cycle of behavior and may even occur at scheduled intervals. Unpredictability is not a necessary condition of these activities. It is the ability to interrupt and relocate an activity with relative ease, rather than temporal uncertainty, that characterizes the spatially flexible behaviors.

Spatially flexible activities will select for tools and techniques that do not hinder potential task relocation. The spatially opportunistic nature of these activities would tend to encourage smaller, portable implements and discourage larger, less manageable tools. Ceramic production tools associated with this kind of behavior include such items as polishing stones, small molds, and cutting implements. These tools may be used in any location and are easily moved about as the conditions affecting the use of space change (e.g. sunlight, wind direction, location of children). In situations of spatially flexible activities, therefore, material technology does not condition the location of tasks; rather, the need to maintain a degree of locational flexibility exerts pressure on the kinds of tools that can be successfully utilized.

Vessel thinning in Los Tuxtlas is one example of a spatially flexible activity. Two implements are required for this task: (a) a thin strip of metal or knife, and (b) a container to hold excess clay. These tools are readily transported to any location within the compound and, if initiated outdoors, the activity may be quickly relocated if the weather becomes threatening. The demands on material technology necessary for this flexible use of space require tools that are portable and simple, reducing set-up time prior to the activity and dismantling time following the production task.

In comparison, spatially restrictive activities are associated with a different material technology. These tasks must be conducted at a given location, often due to a reliance on some facility or procedure. In comparison to flexible activities, restrictive behaviors usually take longer to complete and tend to generate more bulk residue. In addition, the need to conduct these tasks at a given location increases the importance of activity scheduling. Increased spatial and temporal planning improves the likelihood that a specific area will be available for the restrictive task.

Examples of spatially restrictive activities in ceramic-production behaviors include the reliance on such facilities as the potter's wheel, kilns, levigation tanks, and permanent grinding devices. These facilities require that certain activities are conducted in a specific area. For example, with the exception of itinerant potters (e.g. Donnan 1971; Voyatzoglou 1974), producers seldom relocate their wheels or kilns on a regular basis. Even the use of metates for grinding raw materials such as temper (Deal 1988:121; Guthe 1925) can restrict the amount of locational flexibility exhibited by producers. Activities are located as a function of these more permanent facilities; these implements serve as structuring elements for the organization of production.

It should be noted that activity restriction can occur without a reliance on immobile facilities. Processing foodstuffs such as corn might be conducted on the outskirts of the houselot and can require portable implements such as knives and baskets. The location of these activities is a function of their spatial demands and the residue produced (see below). In terms of causality, spatially restrictive activities are a necessary consequence of permanent facilities. The presence of an immobile facility implies the occurrence of an activity organized in a spatially restrictive fashion. When encountered in the archaeological record, immobile facilities may provide a uniformitarian anchor (e.g. Binford 1981:28) for modeling the technological organization of past manufacturing activities.

Given the sedentary context of most ethnographically documented ceramic producers (e.g. Arnold 1985:125), it is easy to imagine the different effects of production organization on the use of space. For example, at the level of household production it would be advantageous to utilize a technological system that afforded the greatest flexibility in spatial demands. The irregular fashion in which production usually occurs in these contexts, coupled with the variety of additional domestic chores required of female producers, would select for a material technology that was organized in an unrestricted manner. Potters could thus adapt their production activities to whatever conditions existed at the moment. In more intensive production environments, where concerns with efficiency and output are paramount, it would be advantageous to have production activities located in specific areas. The demands of domestic production thus select for a flexible system of technology, while the pressures of more intensive ceramic manufacture are better served by a more restrictive technology.

Other considerations may also impinge on production organization. These factors include the amount of area available for production activities, the size of the labor force, and the sequence of production tasks. Production scale, therefore, need not be the primary force conditioning the technological decisions made by the producer. Producers will adopt those techniques that best conform to the context of manufacture.

Consideration must also be given to the distinctive character of Old World and New World ceramic production. The different technological systems employed by these potters would have required a significantly different approach to supplying consumer populations in the respective regions (e.g. Arnold 1986). The use of the potter's wheel and wheeled transportation in the Old World would have created a production organization – and thus an archaeological record – very different from that in the Americas. While kilns are known to have occurred in prehispanic Mesoamerica (Winter and Payne 1976; Santley et al. 1989), no evidence for wheel-thrown pottery has yet been recovered. Producers apparently relied on mold-made pottery as the most efficient means of vessel formation. Consequently, the quantity of ceramics produced by a single New World specialist could have been far less than that for an Old World specialist, given the same production time. Distribution in Mesoamerica also occurred without pack animals, further circumscribing the movement of large volumes of ceramics (e.g. Sanders and Santley 1983). Given this distinction, claims for "specialized large-scale production techniques" (Feinman 1985:196) among pre-Columbian Mesoamerican potters must be viewed in context. Technological sophistication could well have played a comparatively minor role in prehispanic Mesoamerican ceramic production/distribution systems.

ACTIVITY ORGANIZATION

Archaeologists have noted that the conditions under which activities are organized have important implications for residue generation and the maintenance of activity locations (e.g. Binford 1978; Hayden and Cannon 1983; O'Connell 1987; Schiffer 1976). Material generation and loci maintenance, in turn, directly affect the material patterning, or the archaeological appearance of the activity area (Schiffer 1987). The organization of activities, therefore, is directly responsible for the occurrence and structure of the material record. By understanding the role of activity organization, researchers can begin to predict the situations under which different patterning should appear and be able to account for variability in that material distribution when encountered.

A primary task in understanding production organization is to separate and discuss the characteristics that regulate the production process. This discussion presents six components of activity structure that are shared by manufacturing activities. These components are: (a) frequency; (b) spatial requirements; (c) duration; (d) regularity; (e) residue intensity; and (f) participation. The importance of many of these conditions has been recognized elsewhere (e.g. Anderson 1982; Binford 1978; Kent 1984), but their role in understanding the organization of ceramic production has not been fully explored.

Activity frequency refers to the number of times a given activity is performed during a specified period of time (Anderson 1982:124). In terms of ceramic manufacture, for example, formation may occur three times a week, while gathering raw material may only occur once a week. Frequency is important because a positive relationship has been noted between the frequency of an activity and the designation of space for conducting that behavior (e.g. Anderson 1982:124; Binford 1978). In other words, activity frequency is one contributor to spatial restriction. All things being equal, an activity performed once a month has a lower likelihood of being conducted in the same location than an activity conducted on a daily basis.

The second element of activity organization is the amount of space needed to perform a task. Activities may be thought of as either requiring relatively large amounts of area or requiring relatively small amounts of space; that is, they are spatially extensive or spatially intensive. Factors conditioning spatial requirement include the number of persons involved in the activity, the amount of debris produced, and even the degree to which tasks are conducted in a seated or standing position (Binford 1978, 1983a:165).

In terms of the ceramic-production system, extensive activities include behaviors such as processing raw material and vessel drying, while vessel formation and vessel firing are more spatially intensive. In the Tuxtlas, vessel drying often requires considerable amounts of patio space in order to insure proper drying. Raw-material preparation, especially when mixing clay and temper with the feet, also requires large amounts of space. Vessel formation, on the other hand, is conducted in a relatively small area of the house, often by the front door or next to a window. Similarly, vessel firing occupies a comparatively small area.

Duration is the third component of task performance common to ceramic manufacturing activities. Duration refers to the amount of time required for successful task completion. Activity duration is inversely related to spatial flexibility; that is, the longer the activity episode, the greater the chance of it being conducted in the same place (Anderson 1982:124–126). This relationship is especially crucial for activities in which interruption and movement may reduce the progress at any given point. Forming a small bowl, for example, can be conducted relatively quickly, and it is even possible to relocate the activity once it has been initiated. Forming a large storage vessel, on the other hand, is more time consuming, and task relocation will increase the likelihood of undoing some of the progress that has been made. The duration of the task, coupled with the disruptive potential in movement, will select for a relatively permanent location for performance.

The fourth component of production is activity regularity, or the consistency in scheduling activity episodes. Activity regularity reflects the temporal patterning involved in activity performance. In other words, regularized behavior permits increased scheduling of activities in order to avoid potential task conflicts. As noted above, this kind of scheduling is important for spatially restrictive activities. As space is used in a more restrictive fashion, the need for scheduling other tasks increases. Activity regularity provides the temporal predictability that this scheduling would require.

The fifth consideration in the organization of the production system is the amount of residue generated by a specific activity. Archaeologists have noted that activities producing large amounts of bulk are often located on the perimeter of the residential zones (e.g. Binford 1983a:187; Nicklin 1979; Yellen 1977:92). The density of by-products actually reduces the amount of usable space at any given time. Residue generating activities, therefore, limit spatial availability, thus interfering with the execution of other activities.

As mentioned above, few ceramic-production activities generate considerable residue. In fact, only vessel firing in the Tuxtlas produces significant amounts of waste material. It is no surprise, therefore, that vessel firing is the only production activity in the Tuxtlas that consistently occurs outside the immediate patio area (see below). Of course, the potential danger of firing is an additional concern. Nonetheless, it does appear that the amount of debris generated from vessel firing, and thus a decrease in the space available for other activities, is a main concern in the location of firing activities.

The final component of activity structure is participation. Participation refers to the degree to which a performer is actually engaged in the task being conducted. Participation may be scaled along a continuum, with *high participatory* tasks referring to activites that cannot be completed without a participant's continuous presence, while *low participatory* activities do not require participants. This distinction has important implications for the scheduling of production behavior, specifically in terms of two activities being conducted at the same time.

In a non-industrial production system, high-participatory activities include such tasks as collecting raw material and vessel formation. In neither case will the end result be achieved without the individual's participation. The consequence of high-participatory activities is that other chores cannot be conducted while the participatory act is in progress.

Low-participatory behaviors, on the other hand, include those instances in which the producer is only indirectly responsible for the activity. Vessel drying and firing fall into this category. Although the producer may place the vessels in a certain location and even turn the vessels at various times, during most of this stage the producer is not directly involved in drying the vessel. And while the potter may watch over the firing, or occasionally add fuel, the pots are firing on their own. During kiln firing, which in the Tuxtlas may take several hours, the producer is able to conduct other tasks while firing is taking place. This flexibility is simply not possible with high-participatory activities.

An important element of this distinction concerns the locational requirements for low-participatory activities (e.g. Smyth 1989:118–121). Because the activity may not be continuously observed, low-participatory activities must be located so that potential interference is minimized. For example, drying vessels will be placed in an area relatively free from the destructive potential of children at play or domestic animals. If some physically inaccessible location is not convenient, then the producer must "section off" the space and not allow other activities to be conducted. Such partitioning does not always require physical barriers; the potter may simply instruct household members not to use that area for other purposes. Nonetheless, the space has been effectively removed from general household use. Thus, as a function of the low-participatory nature of the activity, and their extended duration, these behaviors can significantly curtail the amount of space available for other tasks. It is this exclusionary component that is important to the allocation of space, especially in a residential setting.

Production organization and the use of space
Now that the various components of the production system have been presented, it is time to consider their operation in terms of actual production activities. Several assumptions are explicated. First, ceramic production is being conducted in a relatively sedentary setting. This is not to say that mobile groups do not make pottery; some do (Arnold 1985: Table 5.1). The vast majority of ceramic production and its eventual intensification, however, is associated with sedentary communities.

The second assumption is that, through intensification, potters are attempting to increase both the output and efficiency of production. While arguments for "rationally economic individuals" may be considered teleological (e.g. Binford 1983a:221), this assumption is difficult to avoid when speaking of purposeful intensification. Although some ethnographic accounts of pottery manufacture have suggested that traditional producers do not always behave in the most efficient manner possible (e.g. Diaz 1966; Reina 1966), these comments, unlike the present discussion, do not appear to be directed toward the use of space. This assumption of efficiency, although debatable, remains explicit in the model.

The final assumption within the model is that "all things are equal." This general comparison will not account for all of the vagaries introduced by variability in family size, market accessibility, and resource acquisition. Previous chapters have noted that these differences can affect the characteristics of the production/consumption system. Following this discussion, the effects of spatial variability on ceramic firing will be considered.

SPATIAL MODEL
The ethnographic record has demonstrated that incipient ceramic production occurs intermittently on a seasonal or even annual basis (e.g. Balfet 1965; David and Hennig 1972; Kramer 1985). Production output is low, and the array of vessels mimics the

household inventory. Production is consistently in the hands of the females, and, while other household members might assist sporadically, the potter generally works alone.

In terms of the activity elements discussed above, production frequency, duration, and regularity would have comparatively low values. These three variables serve as a monitor of production intensity, which would also be low. Low intensity results in relatively limited amounts of output and residue, thus minimizing the spatial requirements of production activities. Low intensity would also reduce the number of items being dried and fired, thereby shortening the duration of low participatory tasks. The swift completion of these activities would limit their effect on the allocation of space within the domestic compound.

As noted above, low frequency, duration, and regularity would select for a technology that enables spatially flexible activities. At this level of production there should be little investment in production tools and almost no occurrence of immobile facilities. As a result, spatially demanding activities (such as vessel drying) and residue producing activities (such as firing) should also be located in a flexible fashion. Spatial flexibility is at a premium and pressure is exerted against intensive scheduling of tasks.

While not a given, it is assumed that production intensification is an outgrowth of this incipient level of ceramic manufacture. A producer may first increase the scale of production; that is, the actual number of goods manufactured at any one time. Obviously, a scalar change could be accomplished with little in the way of technological alteration. Producers may simply work more frequently or include more individuals in the production system. In either instance, production may be increased without investing in new material technology. In fact, given the expense of new tools and techniques (i.e. learning, investment, upkeep) it is doubtful if a new technology would be adopted before other organizational alternatives are exhausted.

With an increase in production frequency and duration, there will be pressure to begin locating the activity in a specified area. It is simply too disruptive for a frequent and lengthy activity to be continuously moved about. As the activity is conducted more frequently, it will likely be repeated in a given location. As noted earlier, however, activity restriction can occur without a technological change. In other words, technological development and behavioral reorganization both represent potential alternatives to a given set of production circumstances. The selection of either response thus reflects the situational conditions under which the potter is operating.

An increase in production output will also affect vessel drying and firing. The area devoted to vessel drying must expand, and the total production output will take longer to dry. Concomitant with this increase in space and time consumption, there should be a shift in the arrangement of other domestic activities so as not to interfere with drying. Portions of the houselot would be "sectioned off" for longer periods of time, effectively reducing the total available area of the residential compound. Firing either will have to occur more frequently, or more vessels will have to be fired at a single time. In other words, firing becomes either more temporally demanding or more spatially demanding. Given either scenario, pressure will be exerted to begin firing in the same location. An increase in frequency, as noted above, will select for increased locational permanence. More vessels fired at once will increase the spatial demand of the activity, also reducing the number of available locations for task performance.

A decrease in the locational flexibility of production tasks would seriously hinder the use of space in the houselot. As production activities become more frequent less space is available for conducting other tasks. At this point, a decision might be made to allocate a portion of the available area to be used exclusively for production activities. This exclusionary use of space alleviates some of the pressure on the compound area by grouping activities and their associated implements in one location. The designation of an exclusive production area thus mitigates the scheduling pressures on the remaining domestic area.

Once this specific work area has been established, further intensification would select for technological change rather than labor reorganization. In other words, technology will enable the maximization in output that otherwise would have been accomplished by increasing the number of individuals performing the same task and the amount of time invested in production. It is possible that technological developments are most desirable when other options have been eliminated and there is a limit on the amount of space that an activity can occupy.

This perspective views the organization of ceramic production as a function of alternatives presented by intra-systemic variables. The requirements of incipient production select for a manufacturing system based on spatial flexibility and little investment in material technology. As production intensifies, changes should occur first in terms of time investment and secondly along organizational lines. Activities will be located so as to limit the amount of interference and scheduling becomes more important. Organizational complexity is thus the first response to intensification.

If production demands continue, space will be used in a more restricted fashion, with certain tasks designated for certain areas. Because spatial flexibility is no longer an option, there will be less demand for a technological system that enables locationally flexible activities. Technological choices should thus begin to include more permanent facilities which reduces the option of spatial flexibility. Activities thus become entrenched within specific areas of the houselot.

Further intensification requires the movement of production to a location that is specifically devoted to ceramic manufacture. These workshop locations are only indirectly affected by domestic activities in terms of organization and potters are able to schedule tasks in a more efficient manner. The culmination of this process would be the manufactory, a totally separated entity away from the house and completely unaffected by the scheduling of domestic activities.

A CONSIDERATION OF FIRING ACTIVITIES
According to the above discussion, firing in the open would be considered a spatially flexible behavior. No permanent facilities are required so potters are free to locate firing in response to a number of situational conditions within the houselot. Such conditions include the number of activities simultaneously being conducted in the

houselot, the number of individuals on hand, and weather. In fact, potters firing in the open are often forced to move this activity in order to insure successful production (Arnold 1985:218–219; Shepard 1956:75). Because no permanent wind breaks are used, rapid changes in wind direction and intensity can cause unequal heating of the vessels or may cause the pot to come into contact with the fuel. At best, this problem may only produce fire clouds, or color blemishes on the finished product. At worst unequal firing and rapid temperature variability can result in vessel cracking and increased firing loss (Rice 1987:155–156).

In contrast to the negative consequences of wind, potters may also take advantage of wind variability to improve firing. A slight breeze can cause the fuel to burn more evenly and hotter, actually improving the quality of the finished product. In some instances the potter locates firing not to avoid wind but to exploit these conditions. For example, Tschopik (1950) noted that potters in Peru will often position their firing atop a knoll, in order to maximize firing conditions. Because of the difficulty involved in firing at such a high altitude, these potters take full advantage of all possible conditions. Potters in Highland Guatemala exploit the wind in a similar fashion (Reina and Hill 1978:40, 63).

The spatial flexibility exhibited in open firing can thus be viewed as a response to microenvironmental variability. Changes in the environment force potters to somehow mitigate these factors in terms of vessel firing. The simplest response under these circumstances is to move the activity location in order to reduce the threat of disruption. Changing activity location requires no additional technology and little additional investment in time. Thus, the flexibility in open firing is a locational, as opposed to technological, response to changing production conditions.

What happens, however, when this option is no longer viable? That is, what if firing cannot be so easily relocated? Under these circumstances the hazards to firing posed by microenvironmental variability are much greater. The potter cannot respond with locational flexibility, and thus faces an increased risk of production failure. Given this situation, the potter must respond with a non-locational method for improving control over the firing conditions. This response is frequently technological in nature.

A kiln is the logical technological choice when potters are unable to relocate vessel firing. One of the most simple kilns is the updraft variety, similar to those used by the San Isidro potters (Chapter 3). These kilns are separated into two chambers, a lower chamber for fuel and an upper firing chamber in which the vessels are placed. This design produces the equitable distribution of heat needed to reduce firing loss without requiring considerable capital and labor investment in construction.

In sum, open firing is less technologically demanding than kiln firing. In order to reduce microenvironmental variability in firing conditions, the potter firing in the open needs only to move the activity to a different location. The potter may even benefit from this mobility by taking advantage of certain weather conditions. The ability to relocate the firing activity provides the potter with the necessary control over firing atmosphere.

When the locational option has been eliminated, however, some other means for controlling firing atmosphere is required. Simple pits are one possibility, but they may result in significantly higher breakage rates than were originally obtained through open firing (e.g. Rye and Evans 1976:41, 62). The next option would be a simple updraft kiln, which provides a better control of firing atmosphere and can also produce the necessary conditions for thorough fuel combustion and sufficiently high temperature.

The decision to use kilns as opposed to open firing, therefore, is not necessarily a function of some desire to intensify production output. Rather, the reliance on a kiln may actually be imposed upon the potter because of a number of considerations including spatial pressure within the houselot. The amount of area available for production activities thus assumes a more prominent role in production organization than previously considered. Of course, space is certainly not the only, nor perhaps even the most important, factor affecting production activities. Nonetheless, the interplay between activities and the use of space has important implications for the organizational structure of ceramic production.

Spatial organization and vessel firing in Los Tuxtlas

This section analyzes three aspects of firing activities in Los Tuxtlas. First, firing variability is discussed in terms of houselot space and activity areas. The emphasis will be on the effective area available for firing activities within the compound. Next, the location of firing activities throughout the houselot is considered, first in terms of distance from structure and then according to direction from structure. The final section presents data on the material correlates of production areas. These data include frequency and weight information from individual excavation units placed in firing areas at four different houselots. Taken together, these data strongly support the proposition that producers using kilns are responding to spatial limitations within the houselot.

THE AVAILABILITY OF SPACE

The first point requiring consideration is the degree to which the spatial resources of the production communities might differ. The model presented above suggests that potters with less space are more likely to use kilns than producers with greater amounts of available area. Moreover, this hypothesis predicts that such variability should occur regardless of differences in production frequency and intensity.

For the purposes of this presentation, only the exterior area of the houselot is considered. Firing in Los Tuxtlas is conducted outdoors; thus areas not likely to be used for firing (i.e. the space within the structures) are excluded. This model will compare the amount of exterior space with patterning in firing activities.

The houselot areal data suggest that San Isidro is subject to much greater spatial stress than the remaining communities (Table 29). Not only does San Isidro display the smallest value for average exterior space, but this difference remains apparent even when controlling for household population. A similar pattern is indicated when the patio areas are compared. Even when population is held constant, the San Isidro values continue to be one-half to one-third the area of the remaining communities. It would appear, therefore, that San Isidro would be exposed to greater household population density and thus increased spatial pressure in terms of available area for conducting firing (and other) activities.

Table 29   *Areal data for sampled Tuxtlas houselots*[1]

Community	N	Mean exterior area	Mean exterior area/ person	Mean patio area	Mean patio area/ person
San Isidro	(13)	142.27	23.45	112.28	18.31
Bascascaltepec	(1)	477.93	119.48	148.46	37.11
Chuniapan de Abajo	(11)	344.26	60.39	306.00	60.57
Sehualaca	(5)	293.35	63.40	224.65	33.97
TOTAL	(30)	252.70	46.89	203.25	37.04

[1] Measured in square meters

Two statistical tests were performed to insure the significance of the difference. The first test compared exterior area per person in San Isidro with the remaining communities. As the data distribution in Table 29 suggests, the difference is significant ($U=356$, $Z=3.871$, $p<0.01$).

The second run compared exterior area per person in San Isidro only with that of Sehualaca. As noted above, the use of kilns was predicted despite similarities in production intensity. These differences were examined in Chapters 2 and 3, and it was suggested that both San Isidro and Sehualaca operated at similar levels of production, while Bascascaltepec and Chuniapan de Abajo were characterized by lower production levels. Thus, it is possible that the inclusion of these latter two communities in the calculation was inappropriate. In order to insure that the results were genuine it is necessary to control for production frequency. Despite this recalculation, a significant difference continues to be exhibited ($U=98$, $Z=2.512$, $p<0.02$).

It does appear, therefore, that the community using kilns is also characterized by significantly smaller exterior space, especially in terms of household population. This pattern conforms nicely to the model discussed previously. Potters confronted with a reduction in the available space are less likely to use behavioral organization to counter the effect of microenvironmental variability on vessel firing. Rather, these producers are forced to adopt a technological response to ensure successful task completion.

FIRING PLACEMENT WITHIN THE HOUSELOT
Now that the basic relationships between firing activities and available area have been established, it is time to consider the potential implications more closely. This section investigates the placement of firing activities within the houselot. Placement in this sense includes distance to activity from nearest structure, size of activity area, number of such areas, and the location of the activity.

The most striking difference in firing among the various communities is displayed in the average distance to firing areas (Table 30). In San Isidro this value has a mean of 5.67 m whereas the values for the remaining communities are approximately twice as high. The single Bascascaltepec observation produces a mean of 12.25 m. In

Table 30 *Locational data for firing activities in production communities*

Community	N	Average distance to firing areas[1]		Average size of firing areas[2]		Average firing areas/ houselot	
		Mean	Median	Mean	Median	Mean	Median
San Isidro	(13)	5.67	5.50	1.21	1.11	1.00	1.00
Bascascaltepec	(1)	12.25	12.25	2.49	2.49	2.00	2.00
Chuniapan de Abajo	(11)	11.65	11.25	1.85	1.18	1.40	1.00
Sehualaca	(5)	11.52	9.42	1.26	1.43	1.60	1.00
TOTAL	(30)	9.21	9.42	1.50	1.17	1.29	1.00

[1] In meters
[2] In square meters

Chuniapan de Abajo the average distance to firing areas is 11.65 m. The same value for Sehualaca is 11.52 m. The distance to firing in San Isidro is significantly less than the distance to firing in the remaining three communities ($U=294$, $Z=3.454$, $p<0.01$).

The inter-community variability indicated by mean size of firing area and even the average number of firing areas per houselot is not so remarkable. There is a tendency for San Isidro to exhibit slightly smaller firing areas, although this difference is not significant. Neither is the difference in the number of firing areas within the houselot. This category, however, merits further consideration. When firing in the open, the most obvious remnant is a patch of burnt area, usually with a small scattering of associated ceramics. Given the rapid re-vegetation that characterizes the Tuxtlas, this evidence may be rapidly covered over. Precisely because potters relocate open firing as the conditions permit, these areas are not re-used regularly and may be obscured. The number of open-air firing areas, therefore, most likely represents the firing activities immediately prior to the household visit. In other words, it is likely that, given equal visibility, the figure in this category would increase considerably for potters firing in the open.

When considered in light of the previous discussion, it is quite reasonable that the distance to firing should be the least in San Isidro. It has already been established that San Isidro houselots are significantly smaller. One would expect, therefore, that the distance to firing activities would decrease as the compound area decreases.

In addition to firing distance, a second question involves the actual location of that behavior. The model proposed that open firing should be characterized by locational flexibility, while kilns are not. Potters firing in the open should be placing their activity in a number of different areas as wind velocity and direction changes. Kiln potters, on the other hand, would be expected to display little overall variability in the location of firing activities.

As noted above, the frequency of firing areas was affected by visibility, so it was difficult to assess flexibility simply in terms of the number of different firing areas.

Consequently, information was collected on the direction of firing from the nearest domestic structure. If potters within a community emphasize a specific direction when firing it suggests that this task is not being moved around the compound. Should a number of different directions be noted, however, it would indicate that flexibility in firing location was taking place.

While the patterning is not conclusive, there are strong indications that potters are operating according to the above model (Figure 18). San Isidro production is marked by an overwhelming emphasis on locating kilns toward the southeast. The only other community exhibiting this degree of clustering is Bascascaltepec, but this pattern probably results from sample size. The producers in the remaining two communities, however, appear to be more flexible in locating firing activities. The potters in Chuniapan de Abajo make use of almost all directions for firing, with some favoritism indicated for firing to the west. Sehualaca also shows a tendency to locate firing in a number of different directions, with the frequency of those occurrences also distributed in an equitable fashion. Given the fact that these open firing areas represent only the

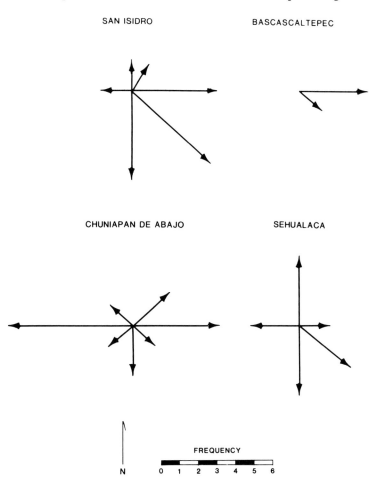

Figure 18   Directions and frequencies of firing activities.

more recent firing episodes, the data do suggest greater flexibility among those producers firing in the open.

Because San Isidro potters use permanent firing facilities, the prevailing wind direction regulates where those kilns are placed. In the Tuxtlas, the prevailing wind is usually from the north with some minor oscillate resulting from the topography (Garcia 1970). Since the threat of accidental burning can be significant, San Isidro potters make a conscious effort to keep firing activities down wind from the nearest structure. Because kiln users are unlikely to relocate firing, they position the kiln so that it will be down wind the majority of the time.

The fact that variability in wind direction does occur is reflected in the number of different directions used in the remaining communities. While more than three-quarters of the San Isidro potters use either the east, southeast, or south to fire ceramics, the producers in the remaining three communities located only about one-half of their activities in these same directions. These potters are not constrained by facility immobility and can alter their firing location as the situation demands. This flexibility is represented in a more equitable distribution of firing activities throughout the producers' houselots.

MATERIAL EVIDENCE OF FIRING AREAS

As part of the ethnoarchaeological research conducted in the Tuxtlas, a program of excavation was carried out at four production houselots (Arnold 1987). These excavations included 1 x 1 m units placed in and around firing loci. Two kiln locations in San Isidro were excavated as were two open firing areas in Sehualaca. This section uses these data to compare some of the material correlates of firing activities.

Two aspects of firing areas will be considered in this discussion. The first involves the amount of debris, particularly ceramics, encountered in open versus kiln firing. Due to the mobility that characterizes open air firing, there should be significantly less material build up associated with these areas. On the other hand, the reduced atmospheric control associated with open firing could also result in a greater firing loss and more production debris. This section will examine some of the variability exhibited by these differences in firing.

The second discussion centers on the formal composition of the ceramic assemblage associated with the firing activities. As part of the excavation program, all ceramics were categorized according to ware designation and rim sherds were further subject to formal classification. This section uses these formal data to characterize the ceramic assemblage recovered from the firing areas. The purpose of this analysis is to compare the differences between firing strategies, as well as generate some ideas concerning how to discriminate between these assemblages and nonproduction contexts.

Material residues

One of the most common assertions in the literature is that a high number of artifacts, especially sherds, is indicative of production areas (Feinman 1985; Krotser and Rattray 1980; Redmond 1979; Santley et al. 1989; Stark 1985). While this association is certainly reasonable, it has little archaeological utility when presented as a simple

Table 31   *Total assemblage data from excavated firing areas*

Excavation	Total number	Total weight[1]	Mean weight/item
San Isidro			
SI-01	4130	16,513.7	3.99
SI-17	3933	40,581.1	10.31
Sehualaca			
SC-06	572	2,063.8	3.60
SC-09	401	490.3	1.22

[1] In grams

comparative relationship. In other words, it can be difficult to operationalize the fact that production areas should have "considerably more" ceramics than nonproduction areas. As mundane as it may seem, archaeologists must begin to quantify these kinds of statements in order to make them archaeologically relevant.

One of the goals of the houselot excavations was to obtain data on the actual material appearance of firing areas (Table 31). These data indicate some interesting similarities and important differences both between firing strategies and within firing strategies. The most obvious difference is in the total number of artifacts. There are approximately 4000 items in both of the kiln areas, while the open firing zones exhibit approximately one-tenth the number of artifacts. The weight of this material, however, does vary within and between groups. The first kiln at SI-01 weighed in with 16.5 kg of material, for an average artifact size of almost 4 g/item. In comparison, the material from the other kiln area (SI-17) weighed 40.5 kg and contained an average artifact size of 10.31 g/item.

The open firing areas were characterized by much lower material weights but displayed some similarity in artifact sizes. The firing area at SC-06 produced slightly over 2 kg of material and a mean weight per artifact of 3.60 g. This average size is similar to the kiln area of SI-01. On the other hand, the recovered artifacts at SC-09 weighed less than 0.5 kg and averaged 1.22 g/item.

These patterns suggest that material frequencies and weights are much higher in kiln contexts than in open firing areas. The average size of items, however, displays a great deal more variability, both within and between areas. The highest value is 10.31 g/item for one kiln area and the lowest average weight per item is 1.22 g, recovered from an open firing area. The kiln at SI-01 and the open firing area of SC-06, however, are very similar in terms of average weight per item.

Ceramics and carbon materials constitute the two largest artifact classes in terms of assemblage proportion (Table 32). Material frequencies continue to be much higher for the kiln contexts than the open firing areas. There is less variability, however, when the size of artifacts is considered. For example, the average weight per sherd in the two firing contexts is not substantially different. When the figures for each firing type are combined, the San Isidro ceramics average 9.09 g/sherd while in Sehualaca the value is 6.98 g/sherd.

Table 32 *Ceramic and carbon artifacts from excavated firing areas*

| Excavation | Ceramics | | | | Carbon | | | |
	Number	Weight[1]	Mean weight/item	Percent weight	Number	Weight	Mean weight/item	Percent weight
San Isidro								
SI-01	2093	11,526.2	5.50	69.79	1016	2431.6	2.39	14.72
SI-17	2739	32,427.1	11.83	79.90	529	385.4	0.72	0.94
Sehualaca								
SC-06	172	1,257.7	7.31	32.79	96	32.0	0.33	30.00
SC-09	31	160.8	5.18	60.94	265	147.3	0.55	1.55

[1] In grams

With the exception of SI-01, the average weight of carbon material does not vary appreciably from area to area. In the case of SI-01 several very large pieces of carbon were recovered, somewhat inflating the overall average. Since these artifacts were weighed as a group, rather than individually, it is impossible to remove those individual outliers and recalculate the statistic.

Finally, ceramic and carbon materials make an important contribution to the total assemblage weight. In three of the four excavations ceramic artifacts constitute 60 percent or more of the total material weight. Only SC-06 has a considerably lower value with 32.79 percent. Conversely, the carbon remains make up a much smaller percentage of the total weight, with the firing areas from SI-01, SI-17, and SC-09 all exhibiting values under 15 percent. SC-06 is again the exception, with carbon constituting 30 percent of the assemblage weight.

In sum, these data indicate both differences and similarities between the firing contexts. The most apparent difference is in material frequencies and weights. The kilns in San Isidro produced much higher material quantities, a function of the singular location of firing activities. Open firing, on the other hand, is less likely to result in high material densities, primarily because the activity is not repeated in the same location. In this sense, expectations regarding the "higher" than normal quantities of material associated with firing activities are difficult to interpret. Certain firing activities do produce high values, but there is considerable variety even within similar production modes.

Along other lines, however, the patterning is not so different. The size of ceramic artifacts associated with firing areas is a case in point. In this instance the ceramics did not mirror the variability noted above nor were the proportions of ceramic and carbon material appreciably different. SC-06 was the consistent outlier in this regard. This pattern is difficult to explain; however, one possibility might be the fact that the potter at SC-06 operated at a lower production frequency than the remaining three potters. Whatever the reason, the results do indicate that measures such as average artifact weight and proportion of material may be better diagnostics of firing areas than simple frequency or even weight assessments alone.

Vessel forms

The most common form throughout the firing locations is the *comal*, which accounts for 75.18 percent of all rim forms recovered (Table 33). As discussed previously, the *comal* is the easiest vessel form to produce and is the only vessel made by all the interviewed potters. Moreover, the short use life of the *comal* would indicate that this form is in relatively high demand and thus should be manufactured more frequently than the remaining vessels.

An additional factor strongly conditions the occurrence of *comales*. These vessels also serve as a kind of "kiln furniture," in that broken *comales* are used to cover the ceramics during firing. This practice is especially common for kiln firing, in which there are literally hundreds of large *comal* fragments scattered around the kiln. Because of the different strategy involved in open firing, however, associated concentrations of *comales* are almost nonexistent. In these cases, the number of forms is less a function of repeated firing and aggregation than actual breakage per firing episode.

Table 33 *Frequency of vessel forms represented in excavated firing areas*

| | | Excavation | | |
Vessel form	SI-01	SI-17	SC-06	SC-09
Comal	273	525	5	–
Tecualon	15	11	1	–
Ashtray	215	1	–	–
Olla de Frijol	1	2	2	–
Cazuela	–	–	1	1
Vase	7	–	–	–
Vessel support	1	–	–	1
Unidentified	5	–	1	–
TOTAL	517	539	10	2

Apart from the *comal*, no other vessel type was represented in all four excavations. *Tecualon* rims were present in three of the firing areas, most notably in San Isidro. Ashtrays, a comparatively small item, were common at SI-01, but practically non-existent in any other excavation. As noted earlier, the potter at SI-01 has begun concentrating on making ashtrays to be used in the hotels and restaurants of the Tuxtlas region. The fact that ashtrays constitute 41.58 percent of the forms from the SI-01 excavation reflects this specialization. This high percentage of ashtrays also accounts for variability in the residue weight noted among the San Isidro potters.

The *olla de frijol* was also represented in three of the four excavations, but in extremely low numbers. Similarly, *cazuela* rims were encountered in both of the Sehualaca excavations, again in very small amounts. SI-01 produced seven sherds from a vase-like vessel used as a flowerpot. Nubbin supports were recovered from two of the excavations. These supports were originally part of a *chimolera*, or chile grinder. Finally, a total of six unidentifiable rim sherds were recovered from the excavations. These rims were very small fragments, so identification of the vessel type was impossible.

The difference in the total frequency of rims thus mimics the variability in overall assemblage size discussed above. The kiln is more likely to serve as a "collection point" for these artifacts, especially those forms repeatedly used as kiln furniture. This fact is indicated by the overwhelming frequency of *comal* rims recovered in the excavation. The difference indicated at SI-01 is primarily a function of the specialization in ashtrays at this household.

Open firing areas are characterized by considerably lower frequencies of rim forms. This difference, however, does not necessarily reflect lower production levels. Rather, the variability is a function of the manner in which the firing location is used. In comparison to kilns, open firing areas are subject to less intensive use episodes. In these cases, there is a reduced emphasis on kiln furniture and the recovered materials tend to provide a more accurate indication of the proportion of different vessel types fired at any one time. Thus, the most archaeologically obvious firing areas (i.e. kiln locations) could well be the least reliable in terms of interpreting production output. This possibility, however, requires a much larger sample and improved control over the number of forms and frequency of vessels being fired per individual episode.

Summary
Firing loci are not well represented in the ethnoarchaeological literature of ceramic production. This fact is unfortunate, in that assumptions regarding firing locations and their material residue are used to identify pottery making in the past. An understanding of how ceramic firing integrates with the remaining components of the pottery production system is desperately needed.

This discussion has approached vessel firing from two perspectives. First, consideration was given to how production activities are organized. Organization was discussed in terms of a technological component and a locational component. Interaction along these dimensions has critical implications for where production tasks are conducted and the kinds of material technology used in those tasks. Activities characterized as spatially flexible will select for portable tools and will include relatively low-intensity tasks, such as vessel thinning. Spatially restrictive activities, such as firing in a kiln or grinding temper, are often located in one area due to a reliance on some facility that cannot be readily moved. Spatially restrictive activities generally take longer to perform and generate larger quantities of debris. These tasks also require greater scheduling of space, since their locational alternatives are limited.

Various characteristics of activities were also mentioned, indicating how such things as frequency, duration, and output would determine where tasks were performed. The distinction was also made between activities that required constant attention and those that would take place irrespective of the potters' participation. The majority of tasks involving vessel forming would fall under the former category while such activities as kiln firing or levigating clay would more likely belong to the latter group.

The discussion then turned to how vessel firing could be construed in these terms and a model of firing behavior was presented. This model suggested that the amount of space available to producers could have a significant impact on the kinds of firing techniques conducted. Moreover, these decisions could be made, not as a consequence of consumer demand or exposure to new techniques, but rather in response to the specific context of manufacture. As spatial availability was reduced, open firing became circumscribed and could no longer mitigate the deleterious effects of microclimatic variability. Consequently, new firing techniques were required. Controlling the firing atmosphere, originally done by changing firing locations, now had to be achieved "artificially." Kiln use in San Isidro was attributed to this need to control firing conditions when the locational option was exhausted.

This discussion does not imply that kiln users everywhere are responding to spatial pressure. Nor does it suggest that all potters who fire in the open relocate that activity across space. The Tuxtlas potters have *not* been presented as an analog for all other ceramic producers. But the data suggest that spatial factors are affecting the organization of pottery making in Los Tuxtlas. The fact that potters throughout the world may not organize their activities in the same fashion should hardly be surprising. That same fact, however, does not invalidate the perspective adopted in this study – the selection of production tools and techniques limits the spatial options available to the potter. And one factor that influences that decision is the organizational context of production activities.

7

Disposal patterns within production houselots

The previous chapter established that firing variability correlates with differences in spatial pressure at the houselot level. As space becomes less available in sedentary settings there will be a need to restructure activity organization and begin intensifying the use of space within the compound. The process of activity restriction was presented in terms of the transition from open-air firing to kiln firing. As long as sufficient space was available, open firing would provide a locational response to microenvironmental variability. When spatial flexibility was no longer an option, a technological response to controlling firing conditions was observed.

If this relationship is accurate, then material patterns unrelated to ceramic production should be similarly affected. In other words, spatial constraints should be regulating a variety of activities, not just pottery manufacture. If comparable associations between areal availability and non-production organization are indicated, then the emphasis placed on space as a crucial resource in ceramic production would be supported.

This chapter discusses houselot maintenance in terms of spatial pressure and organization. When there is little pressure on spatial resources, maintenance is expected to be less intensive and the maintenance regime should display a broader, more extensive patterning in material distributions (e.g. Hayden and Cannon 1983:156). As areal pressure intensifies, however, activity areas should be maintained in a more intensive fashion (e.g. Schiffer 1987:59). By extending the behavioral expectations in this manner, this discussion provides additional corroboration for the organizational perspective adopted in this research.

Three distributional patterns are identified below. First, the size of discrete refuse areas in small houselots is significantly larger than refuse middens in larger compounds. One expectation of the preceding discussion is that spatial reduction will select for a more regularized use of specific facilities and areas. An outcome of more regularized use of a dumping area would be a larger midden. Second, material distributions throughout the houselot are more dispersed in the larger compounds than the smaller houselots. Less space should be associated with more intensive maintenance, all things being equal. The data suggest that larger compounds display a more dispersed distribution of material than smaller houselots. Third, artifact types, frequencies, and weights within the "maintained" patio area are strikingly different in the two residential contexts. Smaller, organic materials characterize the interior patio areas of small houselots, while larger, inorganic items are more equitably distributed across the patio surface in large compounds. Taken together, these data support the proposition that activities in sedentary settings are structured, at least in part, according to the available spatial resources. Moreover, this discussion demonstrates that, although these areas may be "maintained," archaeologically recognizable signature patterns are present and recoverable (e.g. Arnold 1987; Deal 1985; DeBoer 1983; Hayden and Cannon 1983; Killion 1987; Schiffer 1987).

Maintenance and disposal: An overview

Before beginning the discussion of refuse patterning, it is necessary to briefly consider the maintenance regime practiced in the study communities (also see Killion 1987). Refuse in the Tuxtlas is rarely buried; in fact, none of the households regularly dispose of refuse in this fashion. Sweeping was the most prevalent form of maintenance; interview participants stated that the house interior and the patio area were swept once in the morning and again in the afternoon. Personal observation, however, indicated that exterior sweeping was not as conscientiously performed as interior cleaning. Piles of resultant debris were often distributed around the periphery of the patio. When sufficient refuse had been collected these piles were usually burned.

At households located adjacent to large streams, refuse was often swept over the bank where the water would eventually remove it. The removal of refuse by sweeping it "over the edge" was common in many instances in which the houselot was higher than the surrounding area. In these cases rain would serve as the dominant mechanism by which the refuse was ultimately removed. Within the upslope communities of the northern zone (such as San Isidro), refuse could be seen within many of the small erosional channels that cut through the settlement.

Whether swept over the edge of the houselot or burned, an area of refuse was usually present around the patio fringe. This distribution has been termed the "toft" zone (Deal 1983, 1985; Hayden and Cannon 1983). Killion (1987), conducting research among Tuxtlas households practicing infield agriculture, noted a similar distributional pattern, in which the weight of material along the outskirts of the patio was much greater than that within the maintained zone, both in terms of surface and subsurface distributions. The presence of refuse, built up along the border of the patio, appears to be a common result of a maintenance system dominated by sweeping.

A number of disposal stages affect the ultimate deposition of refuse within the Tuxtlas houselots. The occurrence of "provisional" discard, recently identified by Deal (1983:193–196), is one such stage. Provisional discard involves the placement of worn-out or broken objects in out-of-the-way locations where they can be retrieved at a future time. These objects are thus removed from the active context but are not disposed of *per se*. Rather, they are located under beds, tables, and along walls within the house, or are placed outside the structure against the back or side walls. According to Deal (1983, 1985), provisional discard could account for a large portion of the potential archaeological assemblage, and may even have been mistaken as evidence for activities areas in the material record.

A process similar to provisional discard occurs among the sampled houselots in the Tuxtlas. Households often have a fair number of used items within the house or kitchen, stored for future use. These items include ceramic vessels, old metal containers, empty glass and plastic bottles, and worn metal tools, such as *machetes* or hoes. The positioning of objects around the exterior walls of the structures within the compound is also a common practice. Finally, these re-usable items may be placed in a refuse pile on the patio fringe. Thus, the domestic landscape is dotted with a number of objects in various stages of use and/or discard.

One class of refuse requires separate comment. Material that is potentially harmful, such as broken glass, is usually placed in a designated location a good distance (more than 20 m) from the patio (also Deal and Hayden 1987:285–290). These items are often deposited around the base of living trees or are placed in the cavities of a dead tree. In rarer instances these dangerous items are buried, again at some distance from the patio.

Of course, the fact that sweeping occurs does not insure that patio areas will be completely free of refuse or debris. As archaeologists have noted (e.g. Binford 1978; DeBoer 1983; Schiffer 1987:62–63), certain materials, especially smaller items, are often missed during maintenance episodes. In the Tuxtlas houselots, these small items are rapidly incorporated into a well-trampled patio matrix. In addition, children are notorious for reintroducing larger debris that was previously removed from cleared areas (Hammond and Hammond 1981; Killion 1987). Finally, activities such as dropping and tossing (Binford 1978:345, 1983a:156) will constantly introduce new materials onto the patio periphery. In other words, maintenance does not mean the complete absence of debris. Maintenance refers to the process, not the material consequence. The patterning produced by the consistent and repetitive operation of these activities produces the distribution of surface artifacts encountered in the Tuxtlas data.

Surface artifact patterning within the potters' houselots
The patterns discussed here were derived from two sets of data. First, maps were generated for thirty potters' houselots. Information was collected on the size, location, and distance from nearest structure of midden areas (Arnold 1987). Second, controlled surface collections at four houselots were completed. Two houselots were occupied by potters firing in kilns and exhibit smaller than average compound size. Open firing was practiced in the remaining houselots; these compounds are larger than average. Taken together, these complementary data sets demonstrate that spatial availability has a significant impact on activity organization.

DISCRETE REFUSE AREAS
The piles of debris produced by sweeping and related maintenance episodes constitute the most obvious refuse entities within the thirty sampled compounds. The size of these areas provides insight into the structure and organization of maintenance activities. These data can then be contrasted with information on more dispersed artifact distributions presented in the following sections.

Variability in the size of discrete refuse areas should be indicative of relative maintenance intensity – the overall size of the swept area, the frequency of cleaning, and the thoroughness of the maintenance. Assuming similar activity regimes, smaller patio areas will be used more intensively (i.e. activities per square meter) than their

Table 34   *Areal dimensions of discrete refuse piles among sampled Tuxtlas houselots[1]*

Community	N	Total refuse area/houselot		Average refuse area/houselot		Number of refuse areas/houselot	
		Mean	Median	Mean	Median	Mean	Median
San Isidro	(13)	5.67	5.51	3.91	3.89	1.54	1.00
Bascascaltepec	(1)	25.90	25.90	12.95	12.95	2.00	2.00
Chuniapan de Abajo	(11)	3.12	2.77	1.80	1.95	2.09	1.50
Sehualaca	(5)	3.65	2.63	3.37	2.63	1.20	1.00
TOTAL	(30)	5.07	4.08	3.35	2.75	1.70	1.50

[1] Measured in square meters

larger counterparts, simply because less space is available. As a consequence, refuse areas in smaller houselots are expected to be significantly larger than deposits found within the larger residential compounds.

Among the thirty houselots in which discrete disposal areas were present, these concentrations occupied an average total area of 5.07 sq m (Table 34). This average is obviously affected by the extremely high value from Bascascaltepec (25.90 sq m). This value represents the total of two refuse deposits within the compound of a single household. The adult woman residing in this household was partially crippled; consequently, there was a concerted effort among family members to place refuse in two specified areas. Although interesting in itself, this outlier is not representative of houselot maintenance activities. Omitting the Bascascaltepec observation from the total calculation produces an average value of 4.35 sq m (N=29).

The total refuse area/houselot figures in San Isidro are markedly higher than those of Sehualaca and Chuniapan de Abajo. Total refuse area/houselot reflects the sum of values; all discrete refuse areas within the compound are included in this figure. San Isidro's higher value, therefore, could be a function of two possibilities. Refuse concentrations in San Isidro may actually be larger than in other communities, or San Isidro houselots may contain more discrete refuse areas. Figures, therefore, were also generated for both the average size of refuse areas per houselot and the average number of refuse areas within the houselot.

When controlled in this manner, average refuse area/houselot continues to vary from community to community, while the number of refuse areas does not change dramatically. San Isidro displays a median value for average refuse area/houselot (3.89 sq m) that remains above those of Sehualaca (2.63 sq m) and Chuniapan de Abajo (1.95 sq m). On the other hand, the figures for number of refuse areas/houselot are relatively consistent at the intercommunity level. A statistical analysis, comparing average refuse area/houselot of San Isidro (N=13) against the Sehualaca and Chuniapan de Abajo values as a group (N=16), produced a significant result ($U=259.5, Z=2.82, p<0.01$). It would appear, therefore, that refuse concentrations in San Isidro houselots are significantly larger than in the other two communities.

One variable affecting the average size of refuse deposits appears to be the amount of clear space within the compound. The cleared area refers to that portion of the exterior compound most frequently used for activities: "[s]weeping and trampling from constant household foot traffic keep this area free of refuse, hard debris, and weeds ... sweeping and foot traffic maintain this area as a patch of clear bare earth" (Killion 1987:227). The clear area is periodically cleaned and produces a large portion of the debris encountered in the discrete refuse dumps.

One might expect that the larger the maintained area, the greater the average size of refuse piles. In other words, the more area there is being cleaned, the more material should be incorporated into midden locations. The Tuxtlas data, however, suggest the opposite relationship. Among the sample households there is actually a significant, negative relationship between average refuse area and the maintained patio area ($r_s=-0.525$, $p<0.01$).

This correlation is consistent with the relationship between spatial pressure and activity organization discussed above. Given similar activities, smaller patios are used more intensively. Intensive use requires more frequent periods of maintenance. At the same time, the small area is selecting for the creation of locationally specific dumping areas. In unison, these forces produce larger discrete middens associated with smaller patio areas.

LOW-DENSITY REFUSE ZONES
In reality, discrete refuse areas encapsulate a comparatively small portion of the discard behavior conducted within most houselots. Most debris occurs in a more dispersed distribution throughout the compound. This section presents comparative data on this second disposal pattern. Two examples of surface artifact distributions are discussed. The first houselot, from San Isidro (SI-06), represents the group of smaller com- pounds. The second houselot, from Chuniapan de Abajo (CH-15), is a member of the larger compound group. The following comparison suggests that differences in distribution of dispersed material also associate with houselot area.

CH-15 occupies almost four times the exterior area as the example from San Isidro SI-06 (Table 35). This difference is evident even when controlling for household population; calculated in this way CH-15 is still about four times greater than SI-06. The size of the patio area and the amount of patio area per person are also quite distinct – on the order of approximately eight times greater in CH-15. It was suggested above

Table 35 *Spatial information for piece-plotted map data*[1]

Houselot no.	Exterior area	Exterior area per person	Patio area	Patio area per person
SI-06	132.11	22.01	35.28	5.88
CH-15	511.09	85.18	257.47	42.91

[1] Measured in square meters

that San Isidro houselots differed from other communities in terms of the dimensions of discrete refuse dumps. The question to be considered here is to what degree differences are also indicated in the pattern of diffuse debris across the domestic compound.

A complete absence of debris characterizes SI-06 within the patio zone, with only a few items within the cleared footpath to the south (Figure 19). Material is present along the fringes of the swept area within the zone of vegetation to the south of the patio. SI-06 is an example of the "over-the-edge" maintenance strategy noted above. The houselot slopes downward from north to south and the patio area is raised approximately 20 cm above the area of vegetation to the south.

On the other hand, CH-15 does not have the cleared patio area that characterizes SI-06 (Figure 20). While the amount of refuse at CH-15 is certainly less in the patio area than the surrounding vegetation zone, the patio is by no means free of debris. The presence of this debris, however, does *not* imply that the patio undergoes no maintenance; rather, it exemplifies critical variability in the system of maintenance and refuse disposal.

A comparison of the frequency and percentage of items within the cleared and uncleared areas of these two houselots underscores this difference (Table 36). While

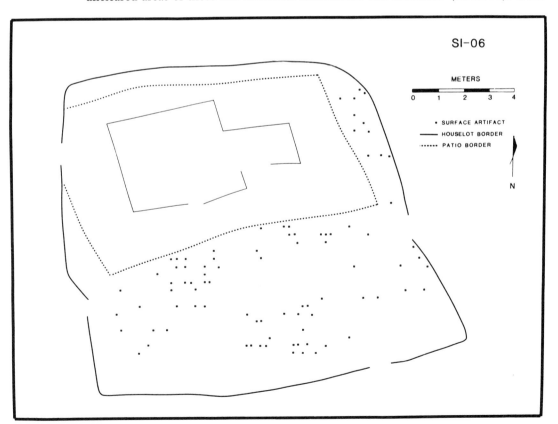

Figure 19   Surface material distributions at SI-06

Table 36   *Comparison of material distributions in cleared and uncleared contexts at SI-06 and CH-15*

Houselot	Artifact count			Artifact percentage	
	Cleared	Uncleared	Total	Cleared	Uncleared
SI-06	8	86	94	8.5	91.5
CH-15	82	171	253	32.4	67.6

only 8.5 percent of the artifacts at SI-06 occur within the patio context, at CH-15 this value is 32.4 percent. In addition, CH-15 is characterized by approximately 2.5 times the total number of artifacts on the surface. Household population size should not be contributing significantly to this difference because both households have identical population sizes (N=6). In fact, even though activities such as sweeping are delegated to the female members of the family, SI-06 has fewer female members (N=1) than CH-15 (N=5). Thus, neither population size nor composition is primarily responsible for the distribution of surface materials within the compound.

It would appear that fundamental differences in the organization of maintenance behavior are reflected in these two houselots. The smaller houselot of SI-06 is

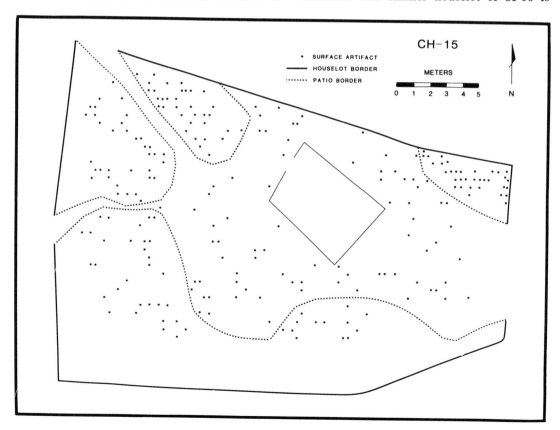

Figure 20.   Surface material distributions at CH-15.

characterized by a more rigorous pattern of sweeping, as indicated by the low proportion of surface material within the patio and the build up of debris along the patio border. The compound at CH-15, on the other hand, is apparently subject to less intensive maintenance. Materials are distributed throughout the compound, with almost one-third of those artifacts occurring within the "maintained" patio area. This pattern suggests an artifact distribution subject to less intensive waste management.

MATERIAL SIZE/TYPE DISTRIBUTIONS

The proposed association also has implications for the size and type of refuse occurring within the patio. Sweeping would be expected to deposit smaller items (those missed) near the residence, while larger items would be moved out toward the patio periphery (e.g. McKellar 1983; Schiffer 1987:62–63). Additionally, organic material should constitute the majority of the smaller items (being more susceptible to breakage) while inorganic debris should make up most of the larger items.

If maintenance is not being carried out as intensively, a different pattern would be expected. First, the average size of refuse should increase, since larger items are not being selectively removed by frequent sweeping. Furthermore, there should be a more equitable distribution of material types across the patio surface, not a distinct pattern of small organics near the residence and larger organic material toward the periphery. In other words, the material consequences of dropping and tossing behavior should be more pronounced within the less systematically maintained houselots.

Data to assess this possibility were obtained through a program of controlled, systematic surface collections within the maintained area of four houselots. Two compounds from San Isidro were selected to represent the small houselots. The remaining two examples were from Sehualaca and represent the larger compounds. The general suite of domestic activities, including the frequency and intensity of ceramic production, was comparable among the four households. Firing techniques, however, were different; the San Isidro households fire in kilns, while the Sehualaca households practice open firing. If kilns are a response to spatial pressures in the Tuxtlas sample, then artifact size and material type within the surface collections should reflect the pressure.

Within each houselot a transect originating at the central residence and continuing across the patio was established. Collections units 1 x 1 m in size and approximately 3 m apart, were then established along this transect (Figure 21). All visible artifacts within each unit were collected. These items were then grouped according to material type (i.e. ceramic, bone, glass), counted, and weighed.

For this discussion material types have been collapsed into three main groups. The first group is organic refuse, usually associated with food preparation and consumption. Items such as mango seeds, maize cobs, and banana peels are common within the Tuxtlas houselot. Additional organic materials include eggshell, chicken bone, and fresh-water mollusk.

Inorganic material constitutes the second group of debris. Ceramics, metal, and glass make up the main material types within this category. Ceramics are the most common single type, followed by metal items and glass artifacts. Collectively, inorganic refuse constitutes the largest portion of the recovered debris, both in frequencies and weights.

Carbon is the third material group discussed here. Carbon consists of all charred

Figure 21   Location of surface collections within patio area.

material, although wood certainly was the most prevalent form. Hearth maintenance and cleaning activities make the largest contribution to the amount of recovered carbon. In addition, piles of burnt refuse on the perimeter of the patio can also produce scatters of carbon and ash. Finally, Killion (1987) observes that periodic outdoor festivals may also result in concentrations of burnt material. According to household informants, however, these activities are very rare within the four compounds selected for analysis.

Collection units within each houselot were ranked according to distance from the residential structure (i.e. 1–4). These rankings are termed "zones" in the following discussion, with Zone 1 occurring closest to the residence and Zone 4 farthest from the residence. These data were then collapsed at the group level; thus, Zone 1 data from each San Isidro houselot were combined, as were the data from Zones 2–4. The same procedure was then performed on the Sehualaca surface collections. The product is a comparable set of data from each houselot group that maintains the locational and spatial integrity of the original collections.

San Isidro

Two distinct patterns are indicated in the San Isidro data (Figure 22). Artifact frequency (as a percentage of the total assemblage) is relatively constant through Zones 1 and 2, and then begins to drop off in the two remaining patio zones. This pattern indicates that artifacts within the patio are more likely to occur closer to the residential structure. The weight of artifacts (also as a percentage of the total assemblage), on the other hand, displays a different curve. Artifact weight initially decreases with distance from the structure, makes a significant jump in Zone 3, and then falls in the final collection. In contrast to artifact frequency, the weight data indicate that the single highest percentage of assemblage weight occurs farther away from structure.

The relationship between frequency and weight can be used as an index of artifact size. When frequency and weight display comparable percentage values, then artifacts are approaching mean assemblage weight or average size. When frequency exceeds weight, artifacts are generally below average assemblage weight and are smaller in size. When weight exceeds frequency then material is greater than average weight and tends to be larger in size.

Within the San Isidro data, artifacts within the zone closest to the house approximate the overall average of 1.86 g per item. The material from the next area, however, is smaller, as indicated by the higher frequency and lower weight. As the collections are placed farther away from the house, the size of individual material increases, with the weight value accounting for a higher percentage of the total than the frequency value. The size of items in the farthest zone returns to the overall average, as indicated by the similarity in both frequency and weight proportions.

In the San Isidro surface data most of the material is close to the house but that same material is relatively small compared to other items throughout the patio. As noted above, this pattern would be anticipated in a maintenance system dominated by frequent sweeping. Most refuse originates from the domestic structure and is introduced into the patio in three main ways: (a) it is swept out the door; (b) it is dumped by the doorside; and (c) it is tossed or dropped onto the patio from the doorway. The result of these disposal modes is a concentration of debris immediately outside the structure, with a scatter of heavier, tossed items farther away. Due to their size and the intensive foot traffic, the smaller items closest to the house are the most likely to be quickly trampled into the patio matrix (e.g. Schiffer 1987:62). Inorganic material that is not rapidly embedded within the maintained surface is subject to

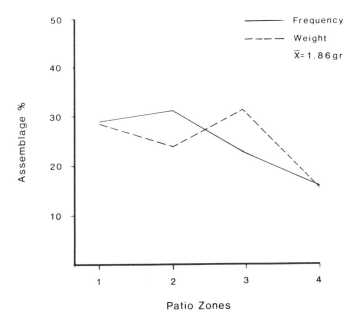

Figure 22   Total assemblage frequency and weight: San Isidro surface material.

relocation by sweeping, which moves items away from the structure and out onto the patio. This material tends to be larger, but it also constitutes a smaller percentage of the total. For example, an eggshell deposited outside the door will quickly become part of the patio surface and may break into several pieces during the process. A pottery sherd, on the other hand, will be moved toward the patio perimeter; it is much heavier but only constitutes a single item. The pattern of many small items near the house and fewer – but larger – items scattered across the patio should be indicative of an intensive maintenance system dominated by sweeping.

If this characterization is accurate, one should also find variability in the distributional patterns of the three material classes discussed above. Organic material and carbon should be more abundant close to the structure because these materials tend to be the smallest and are associated with indoor activities such as food preparation. Inorganic material, however, should occur at a greater distance from the structure; these items are heavier and are thus more likely to be tossed from the doorway or be transported by sweeping.

Data from the material grouping support this expectation (Table 37). There is a prominent peak in the frequency of carbon within Zone 2 followed by a steep drop and

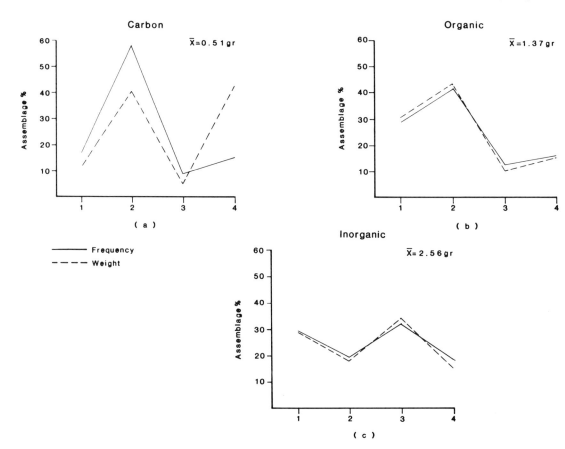

Figure 23.   San Isidro surface material by type.

Table 37 *Surface collection data from San Isidro houselots*

Patio zone	Organic			Inorganic			Carbon		
	Count	Weight[1]	Mean[2]	Count	Weight	Mean	Count	Weight	Mean
1	82	118.3	1.44	318	802.9	2.52	32	10.8	0.33
2	119	168.3	1.41	205	507.0	2.47	108	38.2	0.35
3	35	41.1	1.17	344	994.2	2.89	17	5.5	0.32
4	45	57.9	1.28	199	427.6	2.14	28	40.1	1.42
TOTAL	281	385.6	1.37	1066	2731.7	2.56	185	94.6	0.51

[1] In grams
[2] Mean weight per item

then a small increase (Figure 23a). Thus, the highest carbon densities are encountered in the first two patio zones. Moreover, the mean size of material in these loci is 0.35 g/item, about one-third smaller than the overall carbon average of 0.51 g/item. Considerably larger materials occur in the zone farthest from the residence. As noted above, this area is nearest the patio fringe, and is more likely to contain material produced by burning. Moreover, comparatively larger pieces of carbon may be tossed toward the patio perimeter when the hearth is cleaned.

As expected, organic material is similar to carbon in its overall distribution (Figure 23b). Organic debris are relatively small, with an assemblage mean of 1.37 g/item. The majority of organic debris is encountered in the Zones 1 and 2, with both frequency and weights falling sharply after this point. Unlike carbon, a larger portion of the organic material occurs immediately outside the main residence. As noted above, organic debris is often swept outside, while carbon tends to be carried and dumped. The difference in relative distance indicated by these two groups is probably a function of this maintenance variability.

According to expectations, the frequency and weight of inorganic material should decrease away from the main structure, but then increase toward the patio periphery. This pattern is exhibited by the inorganic data (Figure 23c). The frequency of material drops off as one moves away from the residence and then picks up in the third patio zone. Moreover, the largest items are present in this zone, as indicated by the highest average weight per item (2.89 g/item). Material counts and sizes decrease toward the outskirts of the patio; based on the research conducted by Killion (1987) these values are expected to pick up again immediately off the patio in the "toft" zone. The surface pattern for inorganic material is consistent with a pattern produced by sweeping and some tossing of these larger items.

Sehualaca

The distribution of surface material in Sehualaca is very different from that in San Isidro (Figure 24). The patterning indicates a similar jump in both frequencies and weights as one moves away from the main residence; artifact size is relatively constant in these first two cases. A steep drop in weight occurs in Zone 3 and while artifact frequency also decreases it is not as severe. Surface materials in this zone are therefore smaller than average. Although artifact weight increases in Zone 4, the frequency value continues to decrease. This pattern indicates an increase in artifact size above the assemblage mean for this final zone.

The Sehualaca surface material denotes an activity area that is maintained less intensively. Overall, the average weight per item in Sehualaca (2.14 g) is greater than the value in San Isidro (1.86 g). Furthermore, the size of items in Zone 2 does not decrease as it does in the San Isidro sample. In fact, the debris in Zone 2 exhibits a mean weight per item that is slightly above the overall average. Artifact size drops as the deposit moves away from the patio center, but material of above-average size is found again in Zone 4.

Both the frequency and weight of surface debris in the Sehualaca group increase immediately away from the residence. Comparatively smaller artifacts occur in Zone 3, and larger items are found farthest from the structure. This distribution results from limited sweeping, but is produced primarily through dropping, tossing, and dumping of certain artifact groups.

The quantity of material within the Sehualaca sample is considerably less than artifact frequencies from San Isidro (Table 38). This difference is primarily the consequence of variations in household population between the two groups; the combined household population from the two San Isidro compounds is twenty-one, compared with a figure of five from the Sehualaca households. When artifact frequencies are presented as quantity of material per person, however, surprisingly similar values are generated. The San Isidro houselots produce a value of 84.57 collected artifacts per individual, while the Sehualaca compounds contained 88.4 artifacts per person. Differences in artifact frequency, therefore, are more apparent than real. When controlling for household population, and thus the number of individuals producing the refuse, material quantities differ little between the groups.

Carbon materials were almost nonexistent in Zone 1, but their frequency increases through the third zone, in which approximately half of the entire number of carbon items were recovered (Figure 25a). Carbon frequency then declines in the final zone. Carbon weights also increase throughout the first two zones. Weight actually exceeds number in Zone 2, suggesting larger than average items. Weight then drops in Zone 3 (below average size) and finally increases in Zone 4, surpassing item frequency and again indicating larger than average items.

Some small carbon items do occur near the residence, but the majority of this material (and some of the largest items) are located away from the structure. This pattern is consistent with dumping ash away from the doorside toward the outer area of

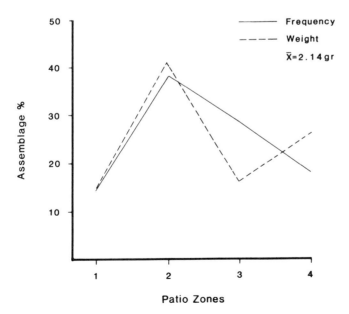

Figure 24 Total assemblage frequency and weight: Sehualaca surface material.

Table 38 *Surface collection data from Sehualaca houselots*

Patio Zone	Carbon			Organic			Inorganic		
	Count	Weight[1]	Mean[2]	Count	Weight	Mean	Count	Weight	Mean
1	3	0.4	0.13	16	24.5	1.53	39	109.9	2.81
2	36	24.7	0.68	30	36.4	1.21	97	322.3	3.32
3	64	19.6	0.30	5	2.0	0.40	55	158.6	2.88
4	22	29.5	1.34	1	0.3	0.30	57	239.2	4.19
TOTAL	125	74.2	0.59	52	63.2	1.21	248	830.0	3.46

[1] In grams
[2] Mean weight per item

the patio. Refuse build up through dumping is expected when areas are not swept or otherwise cleared as intensively. In low-intensity maintenance regimes, the amount of debris that accumulates on the patio can interfere with task performance (e.g. Schiffer 1987:53). An initial effort is thus made to locate this refuse farther away from the central activity area, thereby reducing the potential for task interference. The pattern produced in Zone 3 probably results from such dumping activities. The larger than average items located in Zone 4 are most likely produced through the migration of larger materials toward the patio perimeter, in addition to tossing and refuse burning as noted for San Isidro.

The distribution of both the organic and inorganic items also supports this interpretation. The organic material is most common immediately around the house-lot; in Zone 1 items are above average in size (Figure 25b). Material frequency and weight falls considerably as one moves out into the patio area. Inorganic items display a similar, albeit less pronounced distribution (Figure 25c). Material frequency increases in the first two patio zones, falls in Zone 3 and then levels off. Material weights are comparable; however, in this case the larger than average items are located the farthest from the central structure.

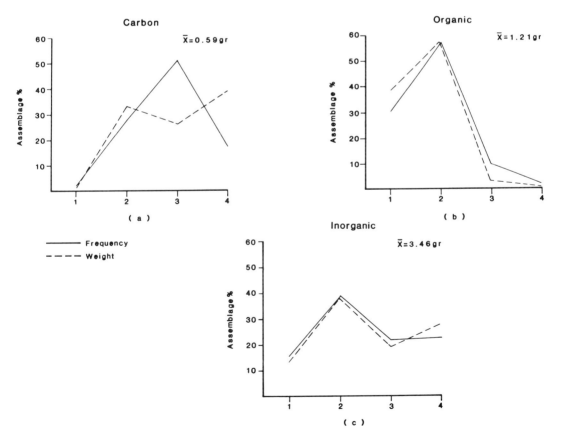

Figure 25 Sehualaca surface material by type.

The variability displayed in these two samples results from different intensities of, maintenance. Although similar disposal activities introduce material onto the patio (i.e. dumping, tossing, sweeping), these activities apparently differ with respect to available houselot area. In San Isidro, where houselots are smaller, a more thorough pattern of maintenance, dominated by sweeping, is indicated. In Sehualaca, where pressure on available space is minimized, compounds are swept less often and refuse accumulates through a conscious effort.

A comparison of the average weight per surface item for these two groups underscores this distinction (Figure 26). The patterns are almost mirror images, suggesting that significant differences in houselot maintenance do exist. In Sehualaca items are comparatively larger around the immediate residence while in San Isidro material sizes increase farther out onto the patio. Surface refuse is apparently being swept away from the domestic structure in San Isidro, resulting in the high weight per item value in Zone 3. At Sehualaca these areas are not swept as intensively so their size is comparatively greater in the immediate vicinity of the residence. The increased size of artifacts in Zone 4 at Sehualaca indicates that items are being tossed toward the patio fringe. Tossing is necessary, since reduced sweeping would eventually produce an unwanted clutter of items close to the house.

Summary
The amount of space within the Tuxtlas houselot sample affects the distribution of debris within the compound. The size of discrete refuse piles, the quantity of material throughout the compound, and the average weight and type of debris are significantly different among the two houselot groups. Within the sample, smaller houselots

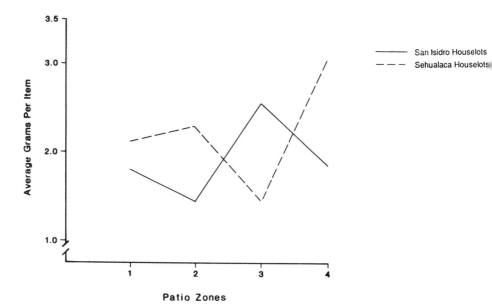

Figure 26   Average weight per item: San Isidro and Sehualaca surface material.

contained larger discrete middens and exhibited lower debris frequencies across the residential compound. These patterns are attributable to more intensive maintenance regimes within the smaller compounds.

This variability also has implications for the type and average weight of patio refuse as a function of available activity area. In the Tuxtlas, sweeping is a major component of an intensified maintenance regime. Sweeping usually begins within the residence and material is eventually moved through the door, onto the patio, and toward the patio periphery. Since sweeping may miss smaller (usually organic) refuse, these materials are over-represented closest to the residence while larger, inorganic items "captured" by sweeping are more prominent toward the patio edge. In larger houselots, where more activity space is available, maintenance is less intensive and the effects of sweeping are less noticeable. Larger items (both organic and inorganic) are distributed more equitably across the patio.

The proposition that spatial variability may have a significant impact on production and non-production activities is supported by these data. Both San Isidro houselots use kilns; if kilns are at least partially a response to greater spatial stress then that stress should also be indicated in the overall system of houselot maintenance. In Sehualaca, open firing is associated with larger compounds. The need to use space as efficiently in this context is less pronounced. These houselots, therefore should be characterized by less intensive maintenance. That these expectations are met in both cases supports the important role of spatial availability in regulating the organizational character of ceramic production activities.

PART 3

Application and implication

8

Ceramic production organization in archaeological perspective

Actualistic studies can be notoriously difficult to apply archaeologically. In most cases, the need for middle-range research evolved out of ambiguity in archaeological material that had already been recovered. Since the results of middle-range research have usually followed on the heels of archaeological fieldwork, it is hardly surprising to find that potentially pertinent archaeological data may not have been collected, or the collection procedures were not congruent with the findings of actualistic studies.

This fact, however, should not dampen the applicability of middle-range research to archaeological material. In addition to identifying new methods for conceptualizing and retrieving information, actualistic studies must be sufficiently flexible to expand the information potential of a pre-existing archaeological data base. The possible information inherent in archaeological remains already recovered cannot be overlooked.

This chapter applies some of the spatial concepts developed in this study to a recently documented Mesoamerican ceramic production system. To be useful, a concern with the spatial organization of pottery making should contribute at two levels of analysis. First, this focus should be able to differentiate between various production entities and supply information on the character of ceramic manufacture. Second, the principles of organizational structure should enable the archaeologists to monitor variability within a given production mode. As noted previously, a static approach to organization is one of the main weaknesses in the conventional model of pottery production (Rice 1984a:233; van der Leeuw 1984:720). This chapter demonstrates that an emphasis on the organizational structure of production can augment conclusions derived from previously collected data.

First, synchronic variability within pottery making is considered. Evidence for a large-scale production industry is discussed in light of organizational variability. Data on the spatial arrangement and association of production facilities accord well with research conclusions derived from more conventional archaeological indices. This analysis demonstrates the value of emphasizing space as a complementary approach in researching ceramic production systems.

An emphasis on spatial organization also provides benefits when investigating diachronic production variability. In this example, significant temporal changes in production organization are identified, despite the overall similarity in production activities through time. The ability to monitor within-group change diachronically contributes to an improved understanding of social, economic, and political forces operating on the manufacture of pottery in the past.

The following discussion utilizes archaeological data from the site of Matacapan, Veracruz, Mexico (Arnold 1987:340–369; Pool 1990; Santley et al. 1984, 1985, 1989). Matacapan is located within the same area of the Tuxtlas in which the present study was conducted. This exercise, however, is *not* intended as a direct historical analogy, or any form of analogy (e.g. Ascher 1961; Wylie 1982). Contemporary Tuxtlas potters are not presented as cultural analogs for the ceramic producers at Matacapan.

Rather, the use of the Matacapan data is based on two factors. First, the natural production environment has already been established. Similarities in the ceramic ecology of the region help reduce some of the potential variability that might otherwise be brought about through differences in raw materials and climatic regimes. Arnold (1985:231–232) notes that this approach "can provide a basis for modeling the past and developing inferences about social, political, and economic structure independently of direct historical connections of the ancient and modern societies and apart from ethnographic analogy."

In addition, surface collection procedures at Matacapan also permit spatial and quantitative analyses of material distributions. Unlike "grab sample" techniques (e.g. Santley et al. 1989:112), in which collection unit size and recovered artifact densities are not specified, surface materials at Matacapan were obtained in a controlled, systematic fashion. The exact provenience of each collection is know. Spatial variability in the distribution of artifacts and features across the site can be monitored with confidence.

Ceramic production at Matacapan

Matacapan is a large urban center, with a central habitation zone approximately 12.5 sq km in area and containing over 100 mounded residential and public structures (Arnold 1989; Santley et al. 1989). The central area consists of a complex of temples and other platform architecture surrounded by a more dispersed suburban occupation. The site dates primarily to the Middle Classic Period (*c.* A.D. 300–800), but earlier and later components have also been encountered (Pool 1990; Santley et al. 1984, 1985). Based on ceramic seriation and corrected radiocarbon dates, the Middle Classic has been partially subdivided into Phase D/E (A.D. 450–650) and Phase F (A.D. 650–800) (Santley and Ortiz n.d.).

Available evidence suggests that Matacapan was situated along a major transportation and communication route linking the central Mexican Highlands and the Maya Lowlands. Matacapan is especially noteworthy for the amount of Teotihuacan-related material recovered from surface and subsurface contexts, including talud-tablero architecture, green obsidian from the Pachuca mines of Central Mexico, and figurines and ceramics that mimic Teotihuacan stylistic attributes (Santley et al. 1984, 1985; Valenzuela 1945). These data have been used to suggest strong economic interaction between Matacapan and other areas of Mesoamerica (Santley et al. 1984, 1985, 1989).

Research into the prehispanic economy of Matacapan has focused on several crafts, including cloth (Hall 1989), lithics (Kerley 1989; Santley et al. 1986), and figurines (Kann 1989). To date, ceramic manufacture has received the most attention (Knee-

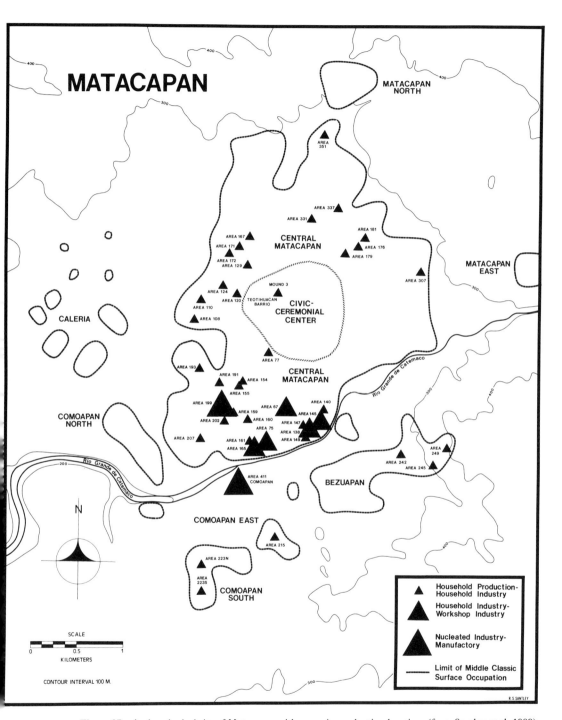

Figure 27 Archaeological site of Matacapan with ceramic production locations (from Santley et al. 1989).

bone and Pool 1985; Pool 1990; Santley et al. 1989). Based on surface collections, more than forty specific areas of the site have been grouped into three general ceramic production modes: household production/household industry; household industry/ workshop industry; and nucleated industry/manufactory (Figure 27). These modes were established using some of the conventional techniques discussed in Chapter 5 (Santley et al. 1989:115–121). The goal of the present discussion is to determine the degree to which information on spatial organization of production may amplify our current understanding of these entities.

EVIDENCE FOR INTENSIVE PRODUCTION

One of the production areas identified at Matacapan is situated about 2 km south of the site's central urban zone in the present-day community of Comoapan (Kneebone and

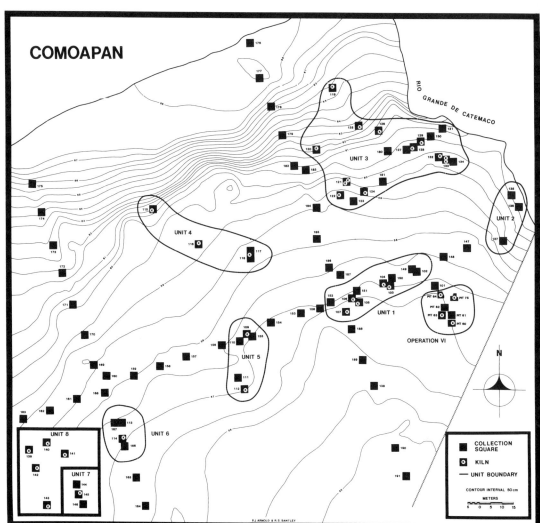

Figure 28   Survey and excavation squares at Comoapan (from Santley et al. 1989).

Pool 1985; Santley and Arnold 1986; Santley et al. 1989). Although modern occupation has covered much of the site, surface data indicated a complex of partially destroyed kilns and localized high densities of misfired pottery. A total of 100 3×3 m surface collections were obtained in an area approximately 4 ha in size (Figure 28). Of these collections, forty-six were placed over kilns and atop possible production dumps that were visible on the surface. The remaining fifty-four units were arranged in a systematic fashion to sample lower-density areas. This strategy was followed to sample the range of ceramic forms and wares that were manufactured and the extent of their distribution across the site's surface.

In addition to the surface collections, nine excavations were completed. Six excavations were located in Operation VI, a 150 sq m area containing the remains of four kilns and a large midden of ceramics debris (Figure 29). The remaining three excavations were placed within firing facilities in other parts of the site to obtain comparable information on kiln morphology and firing activities.

The prehispanic kilns encountered in these excavations are surprisingly similar to the modern kilns used in San Isidro. The ancient kilns are circular, updraft facilities with a maximum diameter of 150 cm. These facilities are constructed of planoconvex adobe bricks and conform to the two-chamber design discussed previously. The firing chamber (upper portion) is separated from the fire box by means of adobe arches (*arcos*) that radiate from the interior walls to the center of the kiln. These arches rest upon a central supporting post (*ombligo*) also made of adobe. Spaces between the *arcos* allow the heat from the fire box to circulate into the firing chamber. Access to the fire box was through an opening at the base of the kiln which could be covered to alter the firing atmosphere from oxidizing to reducing. This opening was always situated on the downslope side of the kiln, probably to minimize interior flooding caused by the heavy rains of the region. This pattern also occurs at San Isidro. In all cases the upper walls of the firing chamber have been destroyed, but the complete structure is estimated to have stood approximately 1.5 m tall. The precise use life of each kiln is unknown, but given their impressive state of preservation in excavated contexts, it is likely that they functioned for a minimum of several years.

Based on patterning in the recovered assemblage from Comoapan, this area was tentatively identified as an intensive production industry. A surprising lack of manufacturing tools and an apparent emphasis on firing certain ware/form combinations suggested that Comoapan was a specialized production location, perhaps one in which only firing took place (Santley et al. 1989:119–120).

Despite these observations, some doubts about the character of the Comoapan complex may be entertained. For example, only two pieces of ground stone and no identifiable manufacturing tools were recovered from an assemblage of more than 63,000 artifacts, an observation inconsistent with archaeological expectations of pottery-making loci (e.g. Deal 1988:117–121; Stark 1985:159–160). Moreover, a pattern of 36 kilns located over an area of 4 ha could conceivably result from a situation analogous to modern-day San Isidro, where nonspecialist households fire ceramics on a seasonal basis. The archaeological record might also reflect the activities of a small number of production episodes extended over the course of several generations. These possibilities are difficult to assess in terms of the number and frequency of items. Information on the spatial arrangement of facilities and activity areas at Comoapan, however, can assist in resolving this issue.

In a nonspecialist context such as San Isidro, the majority of manufacturing tasks occur within the house or on the patio, with vessel firing usually located on the periphery of the patio. The small amount of debris generated by raw-material processing and vessel forming (e.g. exhausted manufacturing tools) is generally mixed

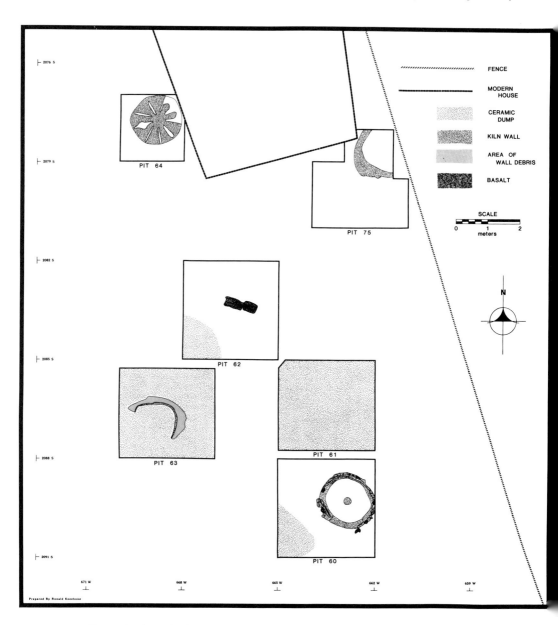

Figure 29   Operation VI excavations in Comoapan (from Santley et al. 1985).

with the additional domestic refuse, which is either incorporated into the patio surface or swept into discrete refuse piles. The majority of firing residue, on the other hand, is piled directly adjacent to the kiln. This material is kept from spilling out onto the patio and at the same time creates a provisional discard pile to be used for kiln furniture or other expedient activities. The production debris that does enter the maintained area also finds its way into the patio matrix or the domestic refuse pile.

Considering production from an organizational perspective, larger-scale manufacture would select for a much different use of space. Intensified manufacturing activities usually move out of the residential setting, reducing the amount of interference and distraction of domestic tasks (e.g. Nicklin 1979). Manufacturing steps such as vessel forming, raw-material processing, and firing may become increasingly segregated and production chores may become more specialized.

With more vessels being fired, potters using kilns have two alternatives: either increase the size of the kiln or build more of them. In either situation the production of more items results in larger amounts of debris. As the amount of this material increases, so will efforts to keep the firing area relatively clear. While some material will inevitably remain next to the kiln(s), the majority of this debris will be placed in a separate area. A dump need not be located at a great distance, however. Maintenance can thus be conducted continuously, minimizing the need for regularized clearing and further activity interruption.

The spatial organization of production evidence at Comoapan is in keeping with these expectations of a more intensive production industry. At San Isidro, for example, each kiln is associated with a single adjacent waster dump. In Comoapan, however, the ratio of kilns to dumps is approximately 3:1. At Comoapan, therefore, middens tend to be localized with several kilns apparently contributing to the same dump. The localization and more intensive use of middens associates with a need to use space more effectively. Efficient spatial organization is essential in larger-scale production entities, since disorganization and unscheduled activities may interrupt production tasks and reduce output levels.

The possibility that more intensive production is contributing to the Comoapan middens can be evaluated by comparing material densities in Operation VI excavations with artifact densities obtained from excavations adjacent to the kiln in San Isidro (SI-17). Operation VI excavations produced a total of 44,278 sherds. Almost 80 percent of this material originated from 7 cu m of fill in a ceramic dump located about 7 m from the kilns in units 64 and 75. This dump contained approximately 5000 sherds per cu m. In comparison, the ceramic totals adjacent to the SI-17 kiln constitute 1166 sherds per cu m. The Comoapan dumps are not situated adjacent to kilns and the volume of their contents is four times that found in San Isidro. This patterning indicates that pottery manufacture at Comoapan was organized much differently, and probably more intensively, than household production at San Isidro.

Additional support for this conclusion derives from the overall absence of residential debris within the Comoapan complex (Santley et al. 1989:119). In a domestic production context space use is often multipurpose, a fact reflected in houselot refuse. Shallow excavations conducted in San Isidro houselots (Arnold 1987:329–331) encountered both residential debris and several discarded production tools. In more intensive industries, however, activity segregation becomes the rule. The lack of domestic refuse in Comoapan indicates that production has moved outside the residential context. The fact that this intensive production industry is located outside of Matacapan's central urban core and is situated next the main river flowing out of the Tuxtlas is also significant (e.g. Kramer 1985:81; Nicklin 1979; Santley et al. 1989:127).

In combination, these data support the identification of Comoapan as an intensive production locus. The absence of certain artifacts results from the specialization and segregation of tasks common within large-scale production entities (e.g. Peacock 1982:38–43; Rice 1987:184). Specialization and segregation is further indicated by the spatial distribution of archaeological material. Comoapan kilns tend to occur in clusters of two to four facilities with a single associated midden. This organizational arrangement is not exhibited in the Tuxtlas houselot sample, nor would it be anticipated given a domestic mode of production. Finally, the location of Comoapan on the outskirts of Matacapan and adjacent to a potential transportation artery also implies intensive pottery-making. In sum, conventional observations on artifact densities, the frequency of production tools, and the occurrence of firing areas at Comoapan are certainly suggestive. By considering the spatial organization of production activities we can eliminate potential ambiguity and broaden our understanding of pottery manufacture at this prehispanic complex.

CHANGES IN PRODUCTION ORGANIZATION

As discussed above, a weakness of the conventional methodology for classifying production systems is the de-emphasis on variability, while those attributes meeting the definitional requirement for class membership are stressed. An analytical approach of this type makes it very difficult to chart diachronic change, especially if differences are not sufficient to warrant a re-evaluation of class membership.

An emphasis on the organizational structure of production can help alleviate this difficulty. The following discussion uses survey data from west-central Matacapan to monitor variability in the organization of pottery making from Phase D/E through Phase F. Using conventional techniques, this area was characterized as exemplifying pottery making at the household production/household industry level (Santley et al. 1989:117–118). Further analyses of this material, however, suggest internal reorganization of these production entities through time. Thus, while the mode of production may not vary notably, intensifications in production organization are taking place. This reorganization is also in keeping with independent evidence for a changing socio-economic climate at Matacapan during the latter portion of the Middle Classic. An emphasis on the spatial organization of manufacturing activities permits us to observe this variability.

Comparisons of surface material densities provide the first clues as to the dynamic nature of pottery making at this time (Table 39). During Phase D/E there are 21 discrete concentrations of production debris that contain more than 100 sherds per collection unit. In contrast, during Phase F this number decreases by approximately 20 percent to 17 concentrations. Moreover, the total number of collections units

Table 39 *Production evidence from west-central Matacapan surface survey*

Phase	No. of squares	No. of waster squares	No. of kiln debris squares
DE	267	11 (4.11%)	15 (5.61%)
F	204	9 (4.41%)	29 (14.21%)

Phase		Total Wasters	Total Kiln Debris
DE		14	24
F		61	34

Phase	No. of wasters/ waster square	No. of kiln debris/ kiln debris square	Percentage of squares with wasters and kiln debris
DE	1.27	1.60	9.73
F	6.77	1.17	18.62

containing production evidence decreases from 267 in Phase D/E to 204 in Phase F. Finally, the number of collections containing firing errors also decreases. The fact that these indices are decreasing through time might suggest that ceramic production, at least in this portion of the site, is become less intensive toward the end of the Middle Classic.

An analysis focusing on the spatial organization of production disputes that suggestion. In fact, from this organizational perspective a strong argument can be advanced that pottery manufacture is actually beginning to intensify during this time period. The data suggest that production is becoming more centralized and that potters may have been working together, despite the comparatively low intensity of production.

The Phase D/E sample includes fourteen wasters and twenty-four pieces of kiln debris. In comparison, the Phase F sample contains more than four times as many wasters (61) and almost 50 percent more kiln debris (34). Thus, despite the overall decrease in production-related collections, proportionately more evidence for manufacture was recovered.

The number of collection units actually containing misfired sherds and kiln debris is also relevant. Phases D/E and F are comparable in both the number of squares containing wasters (11 vs. 9) and the percentage of squares containing wasters (4.11% vs. 4.41%). These data suggest that the number of waster-bearing squares does not change significantly through time.

Collection units containing kiln fragments reflect a different pattern. These data are especially informative since the presence and/or absence of kiln fragments is probably more meaningful than the overall amount of that debris. The Phase D/E sample contains fifteen squares with kiln debris, compared with twenty-nine squares in Phase F. The percentage difference is even more pronounced, with Phase F squares exhibiting almost three times the percentage of squares with kiln material (14.21%) as Phase D/E (5.61%). Unlike waster-containing survey units, collections with kiln debris increase toward the end of the Middle Classic.

These data suggest that pottery making is actually intensifying during this time period. Recall that low-intensity production at San Isidro is characterized by a waster dump to kiln ratio of 1:1. A comparable ratio is exhibited at Matacapan during Phase D/E, in which the percentage of waster squares to kiln debris squares is 1:1.3. In addition, surface materials in San Isidro houselots exhibit a pattern of high-density material immediately around the kiln with a low-density zone associated with the residence. The average distance from the kilns to the residence in San Isidro was 6.19 m. The average distance of the 21 high density loci to the nearest low-density area within the Phase D/E sample from Matacapan is 7 m.

During Phase F the ratio of waster squares to kiln squares in Matacapan increases to 1:3.2. If the greater frequency of kiln squares was a simple function of more individual producers, then the number of waster squares would also be expected to increase. The fact that more kilns are suggested while the number of waster squares remains relatively constant indicates that production is reorganizing into a more intensive system.

If this observation is valid, then waster squares should provide evidence of more intensive use. During Phase D/E the average waster square contained 1.27 firing errors. In the subsequent phase, this figure increases more than five times to an average of 6.77 wasters. This dramatic change supports the view that single waster dumps are being utilized more intensively during Phase F.

An emphasis on production organization indicates that ceramic production during the latter part of the Middle Classic may have been intensifying. The number of production loci appears to decrease, but at the same time comparatively more kilns are indicated and one waster dump is serving approximately three kilns. Ironically, if emphasis had been placed on the number of collection squares or even the number of waster-bearing squares, the conventional wisdom might have produced the exact opposite conclusion. By emphasizing the organizational structure of production, however, these data underscore important economic reorganization during the Middle Classic period.

Additional data from Matacapan also indicate that the late Middle Classic was a time of socioeconomic transition. For example, ceramic seriation data suggest that the intensive Comoapan production industry was predominately a Phase F phenomenon. It would seem from the data that an intensification of ceramic production was a consistent theme during this period.

Moreover, the end of the Middle Classic was also the time during which Teotihuacan influence at the site was minimal (Santley and Ortiz n.d.). In addition, evidence from spindle whorls suggests that cloth production, a comparatively high-status activity, was becoming more specialized at this time (Hall 1989). Finally, changes in female figurine presentation and elaboration also indicate that cloth production was intensifying toward the end of the Middle Classic (Kann 1989). From this perspective it is interesting to note the frequent association between ceramic intensification and male involvement in pottery manufacture (Kramer 1985:79–80; Rice 1987:188). If agricultural land was increasingly usurped for cotton production, then a reorganization of the domestic economy to nonsubsistence activities may have taken place (Kann, personal communication). It is possible, therefore, that by the end of the Middle Classic women were specializing in cloth manufacture, while ceramic production was falling under the purview of males.

Summary

In sum, an organizational approach to production activities provides two critical benefits. Like the more conventional scheme, it enables archaeologists to differentiate between modes and scales of pottery making. These differences are not simply a function of artifact frequencies or the number of "polishing stones" in one context versus the number of "polishing stones" in another. The archaeological record of most complex systems represents an accumulation of activity events. An emphasis simply on quantity could make it very difficult to differentiate between the same action repeated through time, or a palimpsest produced by several different activities working in concert. An emphasis on how those activities are organized, however, will provide the background for examining variability in the material patterns.

The second benefit of an organizational perspective is the potential to identify intra-modal change, even though our overall perception of the production mode may not vary appreciably. This capability is especially crucial for investigating tempos of change among different pottery production systems (e.g. Rice 1984a). The ethnographic record clearly demonstrates the wide variability in pottery manufacture and the ethnohistoric record provides some fascinating accounts of production dynamics through time (e.g. Adams 1979; Charlton 1968; Deetz 1965; Tschopik 1950). But at the same time, a static view of production organization may limit our chance to see archaeologically what we know occurs in more contemporary settings. The ability to monitor these differences archaeologically depends as much on perceiving variability within modes as between modes. A view of production that focuses on the organizational structure of activities is one means for identifying and investigating this important variability.

9

Conclusion

One of the more important advances stemming from the "essential polemics" (e.g. Dunnell 1986:25) of the last thirty years is the realization that archaeological materials are not self evident. Rather, it is the responsibility of the archaeologist to describe material patterns, identify meaningful variability, and interpret that variability. The current wealth of competing paradigms and programmatic statements is in one sense a tribute to archaeologists' increasing awareness of their role in generating inferences about the past (e.g. Watson 1986).

The theme of evaluating assumptions about the archaeological record has served as the centerpiece of the present work. If archaeologists wish to understand how ceramic production developed and integrated with prehispanic complex societies, research cannot simply focus on the archaeological record. Instead, studies dealing with contemporary production systems must be undertaken. Only in this way can both the behavior generating the pattern and the material consequences of that activity be controlled. It is the ability to document both cause and effect that enables archaeologists to establish the necessary relationships between pottery making and the material record.

For archaeologists interested in prehispanic ceramic production, the concept of actualistic research is nothing new. Anthropological accounts of contemporary potters have a long, established history (see Rice and Saffer 1982). The existing body of ethno-archaeological information on pottery making is similarly impressive and continues to grow (e.g. Arnold 1987; Deal 1983; Hagstrum 1989; Kramer 1985). Furthermore, ethnographic accounts of ceramic production have recently been synthesized and presented in a systems perspective (Arnold 1985). Information on the production and consumption of pottery is extensive and widely available to the archaeologist.

Despite this wealth of information, some theoretical limitations in addressing pottery manufacture persist (e.g. Rice 1984a; Stark 1985). These limitations are especially relevant to archaeologists studying prehistoric economic systems. While craft production is an acknowledged concomitant of socioeconomic complexity, increasing levels of specialization may be difficult to detect archaeologically. This difficulty, however, is not necessarily a function of the archaeological record, nor is it a consequence of inappropriate research questions. Rather, the problem stems from a lack of information that can be used to identify production organization in the material record:

> Understanding the prehistoric socioeconomic organization of production also demands attention to both scale and mode of production . . . In the absence of satisfactory concepts and "middle-range theory" spanning the gap between

> economic anthropology theory and the empirical realities of the archaeological
> data base, archaeologists have pursued production arrangements indirectly
> ... Until such [ethnoarchaeological] data are gathered, the finer points of
> full-time versus part-time specialization and degree of centralized control of
> production are likely to be unanswered, and the whole subject of scale and
> mode of pottery production will have to be treated in very general and
> simplistic terms.
>
> (Rice 1987:171)

This sobering characterization reaffirms the necessity of research into production organization. It also identifies middle-range research as a useful vehicle for pursuing that goal.

This suggestion, however, by no means implies a consensus on what constitutes middle-range theory and middle-range research (e.g. Schiffer 1988:462–464). For example, Raab and Goodyear (1984) comment that the concept of middle-range theory associated with sociology is very different from that promulgated by many archaeologists. Statements concerning the term's introduction aside (cf. Binford 1983b:18–19; Raab and Goodyear 1984:255), in the sociological literature middle-range theory provides a guide for evaluating more abstract, general theories through empirical testing (Raab and Goodyear 1984:257). As understood by the vast majority of archaeologists, however, middle-range theory focuses on the "invariant linkages between the archaeological record and the behavior that produced it" (Thomas 1986:245; also see Grayson 1986). The position adopted in this work is that actualistic research does not constitute an empirical "test" of general theory. Rather, middle-range studies provide a means for identifying causal relationships that can be used to evaluate our ideas about the past (e.g. Binford 1981:25).

Addressing ambiguity

The general lack of methods for linking ceramic production behavior to the archaeological record of production locations has provided the point of departure for the present study. Ambiguity in interpretation was cited as the justification for this research. Of course, ambiguous conclusions have been around much longer than middle-range research. Moreover, not all archaeologists agree that actualistic studies constitute an appropriate research program. It would be informative, therefore, to compare the approach of the current work with a study that also addresses ambiguity in assemblage data, but has questioned the value of actualistic research (Sullivan and Rozen 1985; Rozen and Sullivan 1989). The study used in this comparison is devoted to debitage analysis; one of the co-authors, however, has also discussed difficulties in interpreting pottery-making loci (Sullivan 1988). This comparison demonstrates the degree of potential interpretive divergence despite similar points of departure. This section also addresses the cited authors' criticisms of middle-range research.

A recent article on debitage analysis provides an excellent parallel to the research presented in this work. Sullivan and Rozen (1985) have voiced dissatisfaction with current procedures for studying chipped stone tools, identifying two central difficulties with debitage analysis. First, they note a lack of concordance between lithic reduction activities and attribute patterning within stone tool assemblages (Sullivan and Rozen 1985:756, 758). Second, they suggest that typologies currently used to analyze debitage are "linked a priori to specific conclusions about lithic technology" (Sullivan and Rozen 1985:758). Thus, the categories used to characterize reduction activities may predetermine some of the conclusions reached through lithic analysis (Sullivan and Rozen 1985:774).

These observations parallel many of the comments made in the present study. This work discussed ambiguity in terms of the items used to identify and interpret ceramic production. Difficulties with ceramic production typologies may obscure intra-mode variability and impede studies of inter-mode transition. Both studies, therefore, begin with similar characterizations of the archaeological methods applied to their respective areas of interest.

Beyond the recognition of these problems, however, the two studies take extremely different approaches to resolving their respective predicaments. In response to observed ambiguity, Sullivan and Rozen call for a new typological scheme, one that limits the amount of subjectivity in categorizing debitage: "We argue that the categories employed in debitage analysis should not be linked a priori to specific conclusions about lithic technology. Rather, debitage analyses should be conducted with interpretation-free categories to enhance objectivity and replicability" (1985:758). The authors seek to reduce ambiguity through an approach that "does not depend on making technological inferences at the artifact level" (Sullivan and Rozen 1985:755). Greater objectivity is thought to improve artifact descriptions and allows archaeologists to control and evaluate factors contributing to archaeological variability (Sullivan and Rozen 1985:759–760).

The present study, in contrast, emphasizes the need for improved understanding, rather than improved "objectivity," in addressing our ignorance of the past. The position taken throughout this work is that linkages between the present and past are established through actualistic research, focusing on behavioral characteristics that produce consistent patterning in the material record. A more "objective" typology of ceramic production would not significantly advance our knowledge of prehistoric pottery making. The fault does not simply lie with naive appeals for "objectivity" (e.g. Binford and Sabloff 1982; Ensor and Roemer 1989). The difficulty is also in determining a priori what "objective" measures are relevant to archaeological questions. Determining relevance cannot be established by simply describing material phenomena (see below). Middle-range research, on the other hand, can identify those properties of ceramic production systems that are relevant to evaluating statements about the archaeological record. Furthermore, middle-range research can establish the causal relationships between production activities and material patterns.

It is within the process of evaluating arguments about the past that a call for objectivity is appropriate. Objectivity can be expressed as the degree of independence between ideas and the methods used to evaluate those ideas (Binford 1982a:127–128). Ideas derived from archaeological data cannot be independently evaluated with the same archaeological data, no matter how "objective" the classificatory scheme (e.g.

Amick and Mauldin 1989:167). Objectivity is achieved by evaluating archaeological patterning with independently derived data, such as that generated through middle-range research.

In replying to comments regarding their article, Rozen and Sullivan (1989) exhibit considerable confusion over this point. For example, Amick and Mauldin (1989:167) observe that inference evaluation "necessarily involves utilizing existing knowledge to isolate and investigate ambiguity." This procedure, of course, is middle-range in scope. Rozen and Sullivan (1989:173) respond that Amick and Mauldin "are concerned only with the methodology by which meaning is assigned to the archaeological record, and not with the meaning itself." Where, then, does that "meaning itself" originate if not through research that controls for the activities producing material patterns? As discussed in Chapter 5, meaning is certainly not generated through new typologies or "improved" methods of description. Meaning is derived from an understanding of the situational factors that affect decision making and a knowledge of the causal relationships that transform decisions into archaeological patterns.

Sullivan and Rozen's misunderstanding of this point calls to mind the oft-cited distinction between precision and accuracy. Precision, of course, is determined by our methods for documenting degrees of variability. Precision is often associated with increasing the resolution of observations. Accuracy, in contrast, is a measure of error or inconsistency in observation with reference to a standard. As most archaeologists are aware, more precise tools for measuring do not by themselves insure the accuracy of observations made with those tools (e.g. Pinder et al. 1979:442; Plog 1985:243).

When evaluating archaeological inferences, accuracy requires a determination of the relevance of one's observations of contemporary phenomena to topics of archaeological concern. A more "objective" classification *may* provide greater precision in artifact analyses (i.e. description) and certainly a concern for analytical precision is commendable. Increased precision, however, will not substitute for evaluations of relevance. Simply because greater analytical resolution is possible does not eliminate the need to insure that attributes used in classification are appropriate to the ideas being evaluated.

For example, a classification of pottery production systems might utilize firing temperature (obtained through refiring experiments) as the classificatory criterion. This typology may even be considered "objective," since no "technological inferences" (Sullivan and Rozen 1985:755) are made and no assumptions regarding production scale or market orientation are necessary. Using this classification we may be able to precisely measure and categorize various archaeological ceramic assemblages. Unfortunately, we still have not justified why firing temperature is necessarily relevant to the archaeological consequences of ceramic production organization. Nor are such justifications validated through reference to *assumptions*. Establishing relevance would require actualistic investigations of the relationship between variability in firing temperature and differences in the organization of pottery making. It is quite conceivable that firing temperature would constitute an inappropriate criterion for investigating variability in production organization. And if this were true, considerable time and energy would have been wasted by categorizing pottery manufacture in terms of an irrelevant criterion. The assumption that temperature is relevant simply because it can be measured precisely and it is "objective" bespeaks a strict empiricist's approach to archaeological research. This perspective presumes the self-evidence of meaning as exhibited by the arrangement of the material record (e.g. Binford 1985; cf. Gould 1985:638).

A similar paradigm is reflected in Sullivan's (1988) critique of pottery-making evidence in the Southwestern U.S. – "Prehistoric Southwest Ceramic Manufacture: The Limitations of the Current Evidence." The article's title is a telling statement concerning the investigation of ceramic production *sensu* strict empiricism. Methods for evaluating the identification of production areas are not problematic; according to the title the *evidence* for ceramic production is limited. Sullivan responds to these perceived limitations in classically empirical fashion: "the artifacts and features typically used to identify pottery-making and pottery-firing areas may not have been encountered during excavation … it is essential to expand excavation strategies to include narrow-spaced trenching and extensive stripping of extramural areas, midden, and trash areas" (1988:32–33). In other words, archaeologists would learn more about ceramic production if they simply collected more archaeological data! The process by which meaning is given to those data is not considered, since their "meaning" is apparently taken for granted. From this perspective, meaning as represented by the artifacts is self-evident and, by extension, middle-range studies designed to evaluate this meaning are misdirected experiments concerned "only with the methods by which meaning is *assigned* to the archaeological record" (Rozen and Sullivan 1989:173; emphasis added).

The present work, like Sullivan's (1988) discussion, argues that problems exist with archaeological approaches to ceramic production. But unlike the strict empiricist's approach adopted by Sullivan (1988; Sullivan and Rozen 1985), the current study suggests that collecting more archaeological data will not generate improved linkages between the present and the past. The problem is not so much with our excavation techniques; rather the "limitations" are a function of our inferential techniques:

> The practical limitations on our knowledge of the past are not inherent in the nature of the archaeological record; the limitations lie in our methodological naivete, in our lack of principles determining the relevance of archaeological remains to propositions regarding processes and events of the past.
> (Binford 1968:23)

A better understanding of the archaeological "evidence" for ceramic production in the Southwest, or anywhere else for that matter, depends on our ability to accomplish two goals. First, studies of contemporary ceramic manufacture are necessary to establish the linkages between production organization and archaeological patterns. Second, the relevance of those observations to questions of archaeological concern must be established. The first goal is accomplished through a program of middle-range research. The success of the second goal depends on several variables, including the particular question being investigated, the archaeological visibility of behavior being addressed, and the uniformitarian properties of factors presented as relevant.

Addressing relevance

It follows from the first goal noted above that middle-range research should not be limited in scope; that is, variability is the stuff of middle-range studies. Actualistic studies should not be restricted to groups that supposedly supply a "direct historical" analogy to the past (e.g. Ascher 1961). I once mentioned to a colleague my desire to contrast the domestic pottery-making data discussed here with a larger-scale, more standardized example of production. Brick manufacture is also conducted in the Tuxtlas, and I felt (and continue to believe) that such an industry would supply an excellent organizational counterpoint to the part-time potters. My colleague's response, however, was on the order of "Why are you interested in brick making? The prehistoric potters in the Tuxtlas weren't making bricks, were they?" This statement implies that contemporary brick makers do not provide a relevant analog to ceramic producers in the past. Thus, some critics attempt to dismiss the value of actualistic research by noting a lack of correspondence between various properties of the contemporary example and assumed properties of the archaeological case under investigation. These dismissals take the form of arguments that question the relevance of relationships between observations and ideas about the past (e.g. Binford 1983b:157–167).

As noted in this volume's introduction, however, middle-range theory building is not devoted to establishing analogs or justifying relevance through empirical generalizations. Theory building attempts to understand the "whys" of relationships in addition to documenting the "whats." If theory is ever to account for undocumented patterning, it must necessarily be more than a compilation of ethnographic or historical facts applied in an analogical format. Thus, a middle-range research program need not suffer the criticism leveled at analogical arguments (e.g. Gould 1980:29; Wylie 1982:393). Moreover, the formulation of middle-range theory should profit from studies conducted in a variety of contexts and employing a wide range of data. Actualistic research provides "a practical way for archaeologists to establish the necessary operational linkages between behavioral and empirical worlds. It likewise highlights the often-overlooked point that mid-range theory building need not be restricted to ethnoarchaeology ... Mid-range theory is, after all, where you find it" (Thomas 1986:247).

The second goal noted above also focuses on relevance. How do we gain confidence in the attributes used to anchor statements about the past? Obviously, an emphasis on causal relationships that leave no material traces provides a poor referent. For example, a ceramic production theory that is ultimately founded on variability in oral, pre-firing ritual may have little archaeological utility. Determining the relevance of attributes, therefore, must be accomplished with reference to the material record: "As pointed out, we cannot use the record to evaluate our ideas of causal dynamics in any direct sense. We can, however, use the properties of the archaeological record to make *a judgment* whether a particular idea regarding dynamics may or may not apply to a given archaeological case (Binford 1983b:163, original emphasis).

The present work suggests that organizational properties of spatial usage provide a relevant context for evaluating ideas about pottery manufacture in the past. The material consequences of spatial usage include artifact distributions and facilities on archaeological sites. The organizational properties of the production system are reflected in the size, location, and composition of those material consequences. To what extent are these attributes relevant to a consideration of ceramic manufacture?

As indicated above, one test of relevance is archaeological visibility. Are the organizational properties of spatial usage reflected in the material record? Chapters 7 and 8 were devoted to this issue. The data in Chapter 7 are presented as an independent assessment of the postulated relationship between activity organization and spatial availability. The discussion in Chapter 6 constructed an argument that activity structure must be reorganized as pressures on available space increase. This relationship was evaluated using the occurrence of kiln firing and open firing, and a close association was indicated.

Although patterning in firing variability is consistent with expectations, additional analyses were undertaken. Spatial pressure within the houselot should also have implications for non-production activities. Specifically, greater competition for space should result in more intensive maintenance, as a function of the increased number of activities per unit area. Moreover, the occurrence of larger, specific dumping loci was also anticipated:

> Where there is much area in comparison to the activity intensity, activities and object placements should be relatively randomly located and free to change location or vary over time. In contrast, where area is very limited in comparison to activity intensity, activities should repeatedly take place in specific locations, and objects (including refuse dumps) should have specific locations where they are consistently found.
> (Hayden and Cannon 1983:156)

The data on refuse distributions recovered from the residential compounds endorse the relevance of organizational principles to the study of pottery manufacture. There is consistent patterning in the size of discrete dumps, the density of surface material within the houselot, and the frequency and weight of various material types distributed across the patio. These observations were not made on behavior; rather, they documented the material consequences of domestic activities. As such, they were archaeologically identifiable phenomena.

Despite these findings, the skeptic might suggest that the time frame of actualistic analysis compromises the relevance of these patterns. In other words, since "real" archaeological assemblages are built up over a number of years, results of a synchronic study of ceramic production are inappropriate for evaluating ideas about the past. In anticipation of these concerns, Chapter 8 compares ideas that account for the middle-range data to a "real" archaeological example. This comparison employs controlled surface collections and excavations to evaluate the relevance of spatial organizational concepts to a specific archaeological context. The discussion, however, is not presented as a "test" of ceramic production theory (e.g. Binford 1983b:164). It is an evaluation of the relevance of the archaeological data to the questions of spatial organization.

The archaeological patterning identified in Chapter 8 also suggests that an emphasis on spatial organization is appropriate. Organizational variability in the material record is represented in two ways. First, differences in the location and arrangement of production facilities at Matacapan indicate a range of ceramic production intensities. The occurrence of feature clusters in various proportions is consistent with implications of organizational variability. Second, the spatial distributions of material within one portion of the site display significant change through time. This area was previously characterized as conforming to a single production mode. Changes in the spatial distribution of material are consistent with expectations of increasing production intensification based on the organizational attributes of pottery making. Independent evidence also suggests a re-organization of the economy during this period. These data clearly argue for the relevance of organizational dynamics to the archaeological record of Matacapan.

A second consideration in establishing relevance is the security of the uniformitarian principles being advanced. Most archaeologists are fully aware that to justify an inference about the past requires an assumption of constancy along some dimension (cf. Gould and Watson 1982:362). Generating archaeological inferences is performed without a knowledge of past behavior. Since the past is unobservable, arguments that seek to justify those inferences must assume certain properties of the system under investigation. These properties are uniformitarian in that relationships between variables are considered to be uniform across space and through time.

These uniformitarian statements serve two purposes. First, they provide inferential security so that causal arguments derived from contemporary experience may be considered retroactive. Anthropologists, cognizant of cultural variability, are hesitant to place inordinate emphasis on culturally based uniformitarian assumptions. Consequently, such disciplines as biology, ethology, physics, and chemistry provide the basis for most statements regarding constancy. For example, many archaeological questions related to ceramic production are addressed with the aid of physico-chemical analyses (e.g. Bronitsky 1986; Olin and Franklin 1982; Pool 1990; Rice 1987). Arnold's (1985) systems approach to modeling ceramic production similarly emphasizes physico-chemical properties: "All of these feedback relationships eventually build upon the chemical and physical characteristics of clays. These characteristics provide the basis for understanding the relationship of ceramics to environment and culture apart from any ideological or social structural factors" (1985:237).

While I am less comfortable attributing "all" the relationships to the properties of the raw materials, I certainly endorse Arnold's (1985) determination to secure inferences with uniformitarian assumptions. With this thought in mind I presented the data in Chapters 2–4 from the perspective of ceramic ecology. These data demonstrate that the potter's natural and social environment are most definitely relevant to patterns of ceramic production and consumption. A ceramic ecological focus is one necessary component of archaeological investigations into pottery manufacture.

It should also be emphasized that uniformitarianism is *not* determinism. The assumption that certain relationships are constant cannot provide an explanation for cultural variability. Explanations are generated in the present from a body of theory regarding cause and effect. Uniformitarian assumptions are simply tools that allow us to apply causal relationships to the past. The production environment does not determine what specific decisions are made. Rather, archaeologists can use assumed properties of the potter's environment to moor inferences about the production system.

Uniformitarian assumptions also have a second function. These assumptions provide a standard against which variability can be assessed (Binford 1982a:131). It is readily apparent that unique conditions operating in the past cannot be directly understood in terms of the present. No amount of actualistic research will allow us to directly infer past events that resulted from conditions no longer in existence. This reality, however, does not mean archaeological interpretation is limited to the data of today. Rather, uniformitarian assumptions can be used as a yardstick to monitor divergence from expectations. But as Gould notes, to "use the principle of uniformitarianism effectively . . . we must not only ask the right questions but also ask them in the right order" (Gould and Watson 1982:366; also Gould 1985:640). Before research into unanticipated archaeological variability can commence, we must first establish the uniformitarian principles that will allow us to recognize unexpected variability when it is encountered.

To what degree can the principles of intra-site spatial organization provide us with uniformitarian assumptions? First, we should understand that uniformitarian properties constitute another form of inference. That is, when applied to the past they literally are assumptions. Thus, research into the potential uniformitarian characteristics of activity organization is also a continuous, contemporary pursuit. Most of such research has occurred within the realm of hunter/gatherer studies (e.g. Binford 1978, 1983a; O'Connell 1987; Yellen 1977). Actualistic investigations into the spatial characteristics of activities within sedentary systems are a more recent phenomenon (e.g. Deal 1985; Dodd 1987; Hayden and Cannon 1983; Kent 1984; Smyth 1989). Analyses at both scales, however, are producing sufficient data to suggest that properties of spatial organization can supply potential uniformitarian statements (e.g. Kent 1987a; Schiffer 1987).

For the present study, activity placement is the most relevant aspect of organization. Research conducted in a number of diverse contexts indicates that activities are differentially located as a function of variability along several dimensions. Tasks producing noxious by-products or large quantities of refuse, for example, are situated away from areas of domestic focus (e.g. Binford 1983a:187; Dodd 1987; Nicklin 1979). The number of individuals involved in an activity will also condition the performance locus (e.g. Binford 1978:350–351; Hayden and Cannon 1983:156; O'Connell 1987:103–104). Activity duration, and thus the potential for interruption, will affect the distribution of tasks across space (Anderson 1982:124–126). Finally, and as a corollary to activity duration, the number of activities occurring simultaneously conditions the spatial placement of tasks (Binford 1978:354).

These various conclusions demonstrate that activities are structured, both spatially and temporally, in accordance with specific guiding principles (e.g. Kent 1987c). In view of the continuing research efforts along these lines, the present work offers a small contribution. Chapter 6 explicates some of the principles that condition the organizational structure of pottery-making. The influential role of spatial availability in organization was discussed above. Two additional factors to consider are the facilities being employed and the degree to which an activity requires constant participation.

Production facilities both condition, and are conditioned by, activity organization. The use of kilns in the Tuxtlas is significantly associated with activity segregation and the repetitive use of a given location. Open firing, in contrast, is conducted throughout the residential compound in response to wind conditions, the number of items being fired, and the simultaneous occurrence of additional activities.

This distinction was presented in terms of a continuum of spatial utilization. *Spatially flexible activities*, as represented by open firing, are located as much in a responsive fashion as their placement is predetermined. Consequently, the material technology associated with these activities is easily transportable and the activities themselves tend to be relatively short-term. *Spatially restrictive activities*, in comparison, require longer periods of time, are not easily interrupted, and often make use of nonportable facilities. Among the Tuxtlas potters, kiln firing is an example of this latter type of spatial organization. The importance of permanent facilities in dictating the location of activities, even among domestic producers, should not be overlooked. Deal (1988) has observed that some Highland Maya potters may segregate production activities for similar reasons: "However, grinding calcite for temper and modeling of vessels were not always done at the same time or in the same location . . . Because of their weight, grinding metates were often used in their storage locations" (1988:121).

Viewing production activities in this way enables us to de-emphasize manufacturing tools *per se* when justifying ideas about the past (e.g. Stark 1985:172). Rather than simply citing the quantity and/or diversity of production evidence, we need to understand the organizational principles that result in those archaeological patterns. This requirement is especially important, given that assemblage diversity in archaeological collections appears to be as much a function of sample size as a reflection of behavioral variability (Jones et al. 1983; Thomas 1986:242).

A second point made in the discussion of activity scheduling was that certain activities require constant attention, while other tasks are conducted with little participant involvement. Activities thus reflect comparatively high degrees of participation or they are relatively low along the scale. Kiln firing requires low amounts of participant interaction and thus enables a potter to conduct other tasks while vessels are being fired. In contrast, vessel manufacture among the Tuxtlas potters is highly participatory and the potter is not able to conduct other tasks while vessels are being formed. Participation also has implications for the location of tasks. Domestic tasks within some Maya households of the Puuc region, Yucatan, Mexico, are also conditioned by the degrees of activity participation (Smyth 1989:118–121).

In combination, these findings serve notice that activity location is responsive to specific organizational properties of behavior. Moreover, the material correlates of these properties are identifiable and recoverable archaeologically. While further work along these lines is mandatory, an emphasis on the organizational structure of activities can produce justified uniformitarian assumptions.

Summary

This study has purposefully adopted a comparatively narrow research focus. It presents data on a small number of domestic potters producing for a relatively restricted market in one area of Mexico. The vessels made by these potters are neither diverse nor ornate, and ceramic production and consumption occur within a theater of traditional socioeconomic activities.

Although the focus has been narrow, the data have broader implications for the archaeological study of ceramic production. Using the Tuxtlas potters as a spring board, the present study argues that conventional methods for monitoring ceramic manufacture must be re-evaluated. Assumptions that different production modes or scales are necessarily linked to variability in production facilities must be reconsidered. The argument, however, is not reactionary; the baby should not be tossed out with the bath water. Certainly, differences in the diversity of production tools and the quantity of debris are associated with variability in pottery manufacture. But more frequently than not, these generalizations are applied uncritically. The citation of ethnographic anecdotes often serves as the justification for making statements about the past. And while the cited relationships may be valid, they do not move archaeology any closer toward explanation. In fact, they are just as likely to move us toward tautological reasoning.

A good example would be the application of models derived from contemporary Mexican potters producing for a tourist market to prehispanic political, social, and economic systems. As an analogical argument, we must accept that similar economic circumstances characterized the past. That is, we must also assume that the prehispanic potters were confronted with a comparatively rapid, large-scale demand for nontraditional pottery. If true, it is an extremely crucial piece of information for understanding prehispanic socioeconomic organization. But can we simply make that assumption? *Not if the character of prehispanic socioeconomic organization is also what we are attempting to understand.* "There is an important characteristic of all inferential arguments, simply that *we can never reason in a valid manner from premises to a conclusion that contradicts the premise with which we start*" (Binford 1981:29, original emphasis).

It is imperative, therefore, that archaeologists invest considerably more effort in substantiating their assumptions about the past. The approach adopted here focuses on the relationships between activity organization and the material correlates of domestic pottery-making. While many of the patterns are suggestive, they require evaluation within a range of production contexts. It is not the purpose of this work to accommodate the entirety of potential production variability. Rather, the present study demonstrates the utility of an organizational perspective and a middle-range approach for investigating ceramic production.

Middle-range research is designed to move arguments away from analogy and stipulate the causal connections between activities and material consequences. Archaeological inference ultimately rests on the ability to make accurate identifications of process in relation to the material record. We must be secure in our ability to differentiate between various ceramic production systems based on the distribution of material remains. This study suggests that an emphasis on spatial organization will contribute toward that goal. An understanding of spatial organization will not come from the archaeological record itself. There is a growing body of information, collected from a variety of contexts, establishing the relevance of activity analyses to archaeological questions. There is no reason to exclude ceramic production from the benefits of that research.

REFERENCES

Adams, W. Y. 1979. On the argument from ceramics to history: A challenge based on evidence from Medieval Nubia. *Current Anthropology* 20:727–734.

Amick, D. and R. Mauldin 1989. Comments on Sullivan and Rozen's "Debitage analysis and archaeological interpretation." *American Antiquity* 54:166–168.

Anderson, D. 1982. Space use and site structure. *Haliksa'i* 1:120–141.

Andrle, R. F. 1964. A Biogeographical Investigation of the Sierra de Tuxtla in Veracruz, Mexico. Unpublished Ph.D. dissertation, Department of Geography and Anthropology, Louisiana State University. University Microfilms, Ann Arbor.

Arnold, D. E. 1971. Ethnomineralogy of Ticul, Yucatan potters. *American Antiquity* 36:20–40.

    1975. Ceramic ecology of the Ayacucho Basin, Peru: Implications for prehistory. *Current Anthropology* 16:183–194.

    1985. *Ceramic Theory and Cultural Process.* Cambridge University Press, Cambridge.

Arnold, P. J., III 1986. Ceramic production and the archaeological record: Some questions and considerations. *Haliksa'i* 6:57–73.

    1987. The Household Potters of Los Tuxtlas: An Ethnoarchaeological Study of Ceramic Production and Site Structure. Unpublished Ph.D. dissertation, Department of Anthropology, University of New Mexico, Albuquerque.

    1988. Household ceramic assemblage attributes in the Sierra de los Tuxtlas, Veracruz, Mexico. *Journal of Anthropological Research* 44:357–383.

    1989. Prehispanic household ceramic production variability at Matacapan, Veracruz, Mexico. In *Households and Communities*, edited by S. MacEachern, D. Archer, and R. Gavin, pp. 388–397. Proceedings of the 21st Annual Chacmool Conference, Archaeological Association of the University of Calgary, Calgary.

Arrot, C. R. 1967. Ceramica actual de Guatemala: San Luis Jilotepeque. *Antropologia e Historia de Guatemala* 19(2):38–47.

Ascher, R. 1961. Analogy in archaeological interpretation. *Southwestern Journal of Anthropology* 17:317–325.

Baez-Jorge, F. 1973. *Los Zoque-Popolucas: Estructura Social.* Instituto Nacional Indegenista, Secretaria de Educacion Publica. Mexico, D. F.

Balfet, H. 1965. Ethnographic observations in North Africa and archaeological interpretation: The pottery of the Maghreb. In *Ceramics and Man*, edited by F. R. Matson, pp. 161–177. Aldine, Chicago.

    1984. Methods of formation and the shape of pottery. In *The Many Dimensions of Pottery*, edited by S. E. van der Leeuw and A. C. Pritchard, pp. 171–197. Universiteit van Amsterdam, Albert Egges van Giffen Instituut voor Prae- en Protohistorie, Amsterdam.

Bayard, D. 1969. Science, theory, and reality in the "New Archaeology." *American Antiquity* 34:376–384.

Becker M. J. 1973. Archaeological evidence for occupational specialization among the Classic Period Maya at Tikal, Guatemala. *American Antiquity* 38:372–376.

Benco, N. L. 1987. *The Early Medieval Pottery Industry at al-Basra, Morocco.* BAR International Series 341. BAR, Oxford.

Binford, L. R. 1968. Archaeological perspectives. In *New Perspectives in Archaeology*, edited by L. R. Binford and S. Binford, pp. 5–32. Aldine, Chicago.

1977. General introduction. In *For Theory Building in Archaeology*, edited by L. R. Binford, pp. 1–10. Academic Press, New York.

1978. Dimensional analysis of behavior and site structure: Learning from an Eskimo hunting stand. *American Antiquity* 44:4–20.

1981. *Bones: Ancient Men and Modern Myths*. Academic Press, New York.

1982a. Objectivity, explanation, and archaeology 1980. In *Theory and Explanation in Archaeology*, edited by C. Renfrew, M. J. Rowlands, and B. Segraves-Whallon, pp. 125–138. Academic Press, New York.

1982b. Meaning, inference, and the material record. In *Ranking, Resource, and Exchange*, edited by C. Renfrew and S. Shennan, pp. 160–163. Cambridge University Press, Cambridge.

1983a. *In Pursuit of the Past*. Thames and Hudson, London.

1983b. *Working at Archaeology*. Academic Press, New York.

1985. "Brand X" versus the recommended product. *American Antiquity* 50:580–590.

Binford, L. R. and J. A. Sabloff 1982. Paradigms, systematics, and archaeology. *Journal of Anthropological Research* 38:137–153.

Bishop, R. L. and R. L. Rands 1982. Maya fine paste ceramics: A compositional perspective. In *Analyses of Fine Paste Ceramics, Excavations at Siebal, Department of Peten Guatemala No. 2*, edited by J. A. Sabloff, pp. 283–314. Peabody Museum of Archaeology and Ethnology, Harvard University Press, Cambridge.

Blalock, H. M. 1972. *Social Statistics*. McGraw-Hill, New York.

Bordaz, J. 1964. Pre-Columbian Ceramic Kilns at Penitas, a Post-Classic Site in Coastal Nayarit, Mexico. Unpublished Ph.D. dissertation, Department of Anthropology, Columbia University. University Microfilms, Ann Arbor.

Borhegyi, S. F. de 1961. Miniature mushroom stones from Guatemala. *American Antiquity* 26:498–504.

Brew, J. O. 1946. *Archaeology of Alkali Ridge, Southeastern Utah*. Paper of the Peabody Museum, Vol. 22. Cambridge.

Bronitsky, G. 1986. The use of materials-science techniques in the study of pottery construction and use. In *Advances in Archaeological Method and Theory*, Vol. 9, edited by M. Schiffer, pp. 209–276. Academic Press, New York.

Brumfiel, E. M. and T. K. Earle 1987. Specialization, exchange, and complex societies: An introduction. In *Specialization, Exchange, and Complex Societies*, edited by E. M. Brumfiel and T. K. Earle, pp. 1–9. Cambridge University Press, Cambridge.

Charlton, T. 1968. Post-conquest Aztec ceramics: Implications for archaeological interpretation. *Florida Anthropologist* 21:96–101.

Chinas, B. 1973. *The Isthmus Zapotecs: Women's Role in Cultural Context*. Holt, Rinehart, and Winston, New York.

Clark, J. E. 1986. From mountains to molehills: A critical review of Teotihuacan's obsidian industry. In *Research in Economic Anthropology, Supplement 2, 1986 Economic Aspects of Prehispanic Highland Mexico*, edited by B. L. Isaac, pp. 23–74. JAI Press, Greenwich.

Colton, H. S. 1951. Hopi pottery-firing temperatures. *Plateau* 24:73–76.

Cook, S. 1984. *Peasant Capitalist Industry: Piecework and Enterprise in Southern Mexican Brickyards*. University Press of America, New York.

D'Altroy, N. T. and T. K. Earle 1985. Staple finance, wealth finance, and storage in the Inka political economy. *Current Anthropology* 26:187–206.

David, N. 1972. On the life span of pottery, type frequencies, and archaeological inference. *American Antiquity* 37:141–142.

David, N. and H. Hennig 1972. *The Ethnography of Pottery: A Fulani Case Seen in Archaeological Perspective*. Addison Wesley Modular Publications No. 21. Addison Wesley, Reading, Mass.

Deal, M. 1983. Pottery Ethnoarchaeology Among the Tzeltal Maya. Unpublished Ph.D. dissertation, Department of Anthropology, Simon Frazer University, Burnaby, British Columbia.

1985. Household pottery disposal in the Maya Highlands: An ethnoarchaeological interpretation. *Journal of Anthropological Archaeology* 4:243–291.

1988. An ethnoarchaeological approach to the identification of Maya domestic pottery production. In *Ceramic Ecology Revisited 1987: The Technology and Socioeconomics of Pottery*, edited by C. Kolb, pp. 111–142. BAR International Series 436(ii). BAR, Oxford.

Deal, M. and B. Hayden 1987. The persistence of pre-Columbian lithic technology. In *Lithic Studies Among the Contemporary Highland Maya*, edited by B. Hayden, pp. 235–331. University of Arizona Press, Tucson.

DeBoer, W. R. 1974. Ceramic longevity and archaeological interpretation: An example from the Upper Ucayali, Peru. *American Antiquity* 39:335–343.

1983. The archaeological record as preserved death assemblage. In *Archaeological Hammers and Theories*, edited by J. Moore and A. Keene, pp. 19–36. Academic Press, New York.

1985. Pots and pans do not speak nor do they lie: The case for occasional reductionism. In *Decoding Prehistoric Ceramics*, edited by B. A. Nelson, pp. 347–357. Southern Illinois University Press, Carbondale.

DeBoer, W. R. and D. W. Lathrap 1979. The making and breaking of Shipibo-Conibo ceramics. In *Ethnoarchaeology: Implications of Ethnography for Archaeology*, edited by C. Kramer, pp. 102–138. Columbia University Press, New York.

Deetz, J. 1965. *The Dynamics of Stylistic Change in Arikara Ceramics*. University of Illinois Press, Chicago.

Diaz, M. N. 1966. *Tonala: Conservatism, Responsibility, and Authority in a Mexican Town*. University of California Press, Berkeley.

Dodd, W. 1987. Factors conditioning the placement of fire-related facilities and refuse. Paper presented at the 52nd Annual Meeting of the Society for American Archaeology, Toronto.

Donnan, C. B. 1971. Ancient Peruvian potters' marks and their interpretation through ethnographic analogy. *American Antiquity* 36:460–466.

Dunnell, R. C. 1971. *Systematics in Prehistory*. Free Press, New York.

1986. Five decades of American archaeology. In *American Archaeology Past and Future*, edited by D. Meltzer, D. Fowler, and J. A. Sabloff, pp. 23–49. Smithsonian Institution Press, Washington, D. C.

Earle, T. K. 1987. Specialization and the production of wealth: Hawaii chiefdoms and the Inka empire. In *Specialization, Exchange, and Complex Societies*, edited by E. M. Brumfiel and T. K. Earle, pp. 64–75. Cambridge University Press, Cambridge.

Ensor, H. B. and E. R. Roemer, Jr. 1989. Comments on Sullivan and Rozen's "Debitage analysis and archaeological interpretations." *American Antiquity* 54:175–178.

Feinman, G. M. 1980. The Relationship Between Administrative Organization and Ceramic Production in the Valley of Oaxaca, Mexico. Unpublished Ph. D. dissertation, Department of Anthropology, City University of New York, University of Microfilms, Ann Arbor.

1985. Changes in the organization of ceramic production in pre-hispanic Mexico. In *Decoding Prehistoric Ceramics*, edited by B. A. Nelson, pp. 195–223. Southern Illinois University Press, Carbondale.

1986. The emergence of specialized ceramic production in Formative Oaxaca. In *Research in Economic Anthropology, Supplement 2, Economic Aspects of Prehispanic Highland Mexico*, edited by B. L. Isaac, pp. 347–373. JAI Press, Greenwich.

Feinman, G. M., R. Blanton, and S. Kowalewski 1984. Market system development in the prehispanic Valley of Oaxaca, Mexico. In *Trade and Exchange in Early Mesoamerica*, edited by K. G. Hirth, pp. 157–178. University of New Mexico Press, Albuquerque.

Feinman, G. M., S. Kowalewski, and R. Blanton 1984. Modelling ceramic production and organizational change in the pre-hispanic Valley of Oaxaca, Mexico. In *The Many*

Dimensions of Pottery, edited by S. E. van der Leeuw and A. C. Pritchard, pp. 267–333. Albert Egges van Giffen Instituut voor Prae- en Protohistorie, Universiteit van Amsterdam, Amsterdam.

Feinman, G. M., S. Upham, and K. Lightfoot 1981. The production step measure: An ordinal index of labor input in ceramic manufacture. *American Antiquity* 48:871–884.

Fontana, B., W. Robinson, C. Cormack, and E. Leavitt, Jr. 1962. *Papago Indian Pottery*. University of Washington Press, Seattle.

Foster, G. M. 1948. *Empire's Children: The People of Tzintzuntzan*. Institute of Social Anthropology Publication No. 6. Smithsonian Institution, Washington, D.C.

1955. Contemporary pottery techniques in southern and central Mexico. *Middle American Research Institute Publications* 22:1–48.

1960a. Archaeological implications of the modern pottery of Acatlan Pueblo, Mexico. *American Antiquity* 26:205–214.

1960b. Life-expectancy of utilitarian pottery in Tzintzuntzan, Michoacan, Mexico. *American Antiquity* 25:606–609.

1965. The sociology of pottery: Questions and answers arising from contemporary Mexican work. In *Ceramics and Man*, edited by F. Matson, pp. 43–61. Viking Fund for Publications in Anthropology No. 41. Wenner-Gren Foundation for Anthropological Research, New York.

1966. *A Primitive Mexican Economy*. Second printing. University of Washington Press, Seattle.

1967. *Tzintzuntzan: Mexican Peasants in a Changing World*. Little Brown, Boston.

Fournier, R. 1973. *Illustrated Dictionary of Practical Pottery*. Van Nostrand Reinhold, New York.

Fry, R. E. 1981. Pottery production-distribution systems in the southern Maya lowlands. In *Production and Distribution: A Ceramic Viewpoint*, edited by H. Howard and E. L. Morris, pp. 145–167. BAR International Series 120. BAR, Oxford.

Garcia, E. 1970. Los climas del estado de Veracruz. *Anales del Instituto de Biologia, Universidad Nacional de Mexico, Seria Botanica* 41(1):3–42.

Gero, J. 1983. Material Culture and the Reproduction of Social Complexity: A Lithic Example from the Peruvian Formative. Unpublished Ph.D. dissertation, Department of Anthropology, University of Massachusetts.

Gomez-Pompa, A. 1973. Ecology of the Vegetation of Veracruz. In *Vegetation and Vegetational History of Northern Latin America*, edited by A. Graham, pp. 73–148. Elsevier, Amsterdam.

Gould, R. A. 1980. *Living Archaeology*. Cambridge University Press, London.

1985. The empiricist strikes back: Reply to Binford. *American Antiquity* 50:638–644.

Gould, R. A. and P. J. Watson 1982. A dialogue on the meaning and use of analogy in ethnoarchaeological reasoning. *Journal of Anthropological Archaeology* 1:355–381.

Grayson, D. K. 1986. Eoliths, archaeological ambiguity, and the generation of "middle-range" research. In *American Archaeology Past and Future*, edited by D. Meltzer, D. Fowler, and J. A. Sabloff, pp. 77–133. Smithsonian Institution Press, Washington, D. C.

Grim, R. E. 1962. *Applied Clay Mineralogy*. McGraw-Hill, New York.

Guthe, C. E. 1925. *Pueblo Pottery Making: A Study at the Village of San Ildefonso*. Yale University Press, New Haven.

Hagstrum, M. 1985a. Village-level ceramic craft specialization in the Mantaro Valley, Peru: An ethnographic/archaeological account. Paper presented at the 50th Annual Meeting of the Society for American Archaeology, Denver.

1985b. Measuring prehistoric ceramic craft specialization: A test case in the American Southwest. *Journal of Field Archaeology* 12:65–75.

1987. Supply and demand of ceramic products: An ethnoarchaeological study of community specialization in the Central Andes, Peru. Paper presented at the 52nd Annual Meeting of the Society for American Archaeology, Toronto.

1989. Technological Continuity and Change: Ceramic Ethnoarchaeology in the Peruvian Andes. Unpublished Ph.D. dissertation, Department of Anthropology, University of California at Los Angeles, Los Angeles.

Hall, B. 1989. Spindle whorls and textile manufacture at Matacapan, Veracruz. Paper presented at the 88th Annual Meeting of the American Anthropological Association, Washington, D.C.

Hammond, G. and N. Hammond 1981. Child's play: A disturbance factor in archaeological distribution. *American Antiquity* 46:634–636.

Harris, M. 1968. *The Rise of Anthropological Theory*. Thomas Y. Crowell, New York.

Hayden, B. and A. Cannon 1983. Where the garbage goes: Refuse disposal in the Maya Highlands. *Journal of Anthropological Archaeology* 4:117–163.

1984. Interaction inferences in archaeology and learning frameworks of the Maya. *Journal of Anthropological Archaeology* 3:325–367.

Hempel, C. 1977. Formulation and the formalization of scientific theories. In *The Structure of Scientific Theories* (2nd edn.), edited by F. Suppe, pp. 244–256. University of Illinois Press, Urbana.

Hendry, J. C. 1957. Atzompa: A Pottery Producing Village of Southern Mexico. Unpublished Ph.D. dissertation, Department of Anthropology, Cornell University. University Microfilms, Ann Arbor.

Hill, R. M. II 1985. Potttery production and change: Models from ethnography and ethnohistory. Paper presented at the 50th Annual Meeting of the Society for American Archaeology, Denver.

Hodder, I. 1981. Comment on "Evolution of specialized pottery production: A trial model." *Current Anthropology* 22:231–232.

1982. *Symbols in Action*. Cambridge University Press, Cambridge.

1987. The meaning of discard: Ash and domestic space in Baringo. In *Method and Theory for Activity Area Research*, edited by S. Kent, pp. 424–448. Columbia University Press, New York.

Holmes, C. G. 1952. *Sayula*. Temas de Mexico, Seria Geografia. Sociedad Mexicana de Geografia y Estadistica, Mexico, D.F.

Irwin, G. J. 1977. The Emergence of Mailu as a Central Place in the Prehistory of Coastal Papua. Unpublished Ph.D. thesis, Department of Prehistory, Australian National University, Canberra.

Isaac, B. L. 1986. Introduction. In *Research in Economic Anthropology, Supplement 2, 1986, Economic Aspects of Prehispanic Highland Mexico*, edited by B. L. Isaac, pp. 1–19. JAI Press, Greenwich.

Jones, G. T., D. K. Grayson, and C. Beck 1983. Artifact class richness and sample size in archaeological surface assemblages. In *Lulu Linear Punctated: Essays in Honor of George Irving Quimby*, edited by R. C. Dunnell and D. K. Grayson, pp. 55–73. Anthropological Papers of the Museum of Anthropology No. 72. University of Michigan, Ann Arbor.

Kann, V. 1989. The production of social imagery: Matacapan social roles as defined through representational practice. Paper presented at the 88th Annual Meeting of the American Anthropological Association, Washington, D.C.

Kaplan, A. 1964. *The Conduct of Inquiry*. Chandler, Scranton.

Kent. S. 1984. *Analyzing Activity Areas: An Ethnoarchaeological Study of the Use of Space*. University of New Mexico Press, Albuquerque.

1987a. *Method and Theory for Activity Area Research* (editor). Columbia University Press, New York.

1987b. Understanding the use of space: An ethnoarchaeological approach. In *Method and Theory for Activity Area Research*, edited by S. Kent, pp. 1–60. Columbia University Press, New York.

1987c. Parts as wholes – A critique of theory in archaeology. In *Method and Theory for Activity Area Research*, edited by S. Kent, pp. 513–546. Columbia University Press, New York.

Kerley, J. 1989. The lithic assemblage variability at Matacapan. Paper presented at the 88th Annual Meeting of the American Anthropological Association, Washington, D. C.

Killion, T. W. 1987. Agriculture and Residential Site Structure Among Campesinos in Southern Veracruz, Mexico: Building a Foundation for Archaeological Inference. Unpublished Ph.D. dissertation, Department of Anthropology, The University of New Mexico, Albuquerque.

Kneebone, R. R. and C. A. Pool 1985. Archaeological investigations of intensive ceramic production: A recent discovery at Comoapan, Veracruz, Mexico. Paper presented at the 50th Annual Meeting of the Society for American Archaeology, Denver, Colorado.

Kohler, U. 1976. Mushrooms, drugs, and potters: A new approach to the function of precolumbian Mesoamerican mushroom stones. *American Antiquity* 41:145–153.

Kolb, C. 1976. The methodology of Latin American ceramic ecology. *El Dorado: Bulletin of South American Archaeology* 1:44–82.

1981. Comment on "Evolution of specialized pottery production: A trial model." *Current Anthropology* 22:232–233.

1989. Ceramic ecology in retrospect: A critical review of methodology and results. In *Ceramic Ecology, 1988: Current Research on Ceramic Materials*, edited by C. Kolb, pp. 261–375. BAR International Series 513. BAR, Oxford.

Kramer, C. 1979. *Ethnoarchaeology: Implications of Ethnography for Archaeology*. Columbia University Press, New York.

1985. Ceramic ethnoarchaeology. *Annual Review of Anthropology* 14:77–102.

Krause, R. A. 1985. *The Clay Sleeps: An Ethnoarchaeological Study of Three African Potters*. University of Alabama Press, Alabama.

Krotser, P. H. 1974. Country potters of Veracruz, Mexico: Technological survivals and culture change. In *Ethnoarchaeology*, edited by C. B. Donnan and C. W. Clewlow, Jr., pp. 131–146. UCLA Institute of Archaeology Monograph 4. Los Angeles.

1980. Potters in the land of the Olmec. In *In the Land of the Olmec*, Vol. 2, *The People of the River*, edited by M. D. Coe and R. A. Diehl, pp. 125–138. University of Texas Press, Austin.

Krotser, P. H. and E. Rattray 1980. Manufactura y distribucion de tres grupos ceramics de Teotihuacan. *Anales de Antropologia* Tomo I Volumen VXII:91–104.

Lackey, L. M. 1982. *The Pottery of Acatlan: A Changing Mexican Tradition*. University of Oklahoma Press, Norman.

Lauer, P. 1974. *Pottery Traditions in the D'Entrecasteaux Islands of Papua*. Occasional Papers in Anthropology 3. Anthropology Museum, University of Queensland, St. Lucia, Queensland, Australia.

Leuzinger, E. 1960. *Africa: The Art of the Negro People*. Translated by A. E. Keep. McGraw Hill, New York.

Longacre, W. 1981. Kalinga pottery: An ethnoarchaeological study. In *Patterns of the Past: Studies in Honour of David Clarke*, edited by I. Hodder, G. Isaac, and N. Hammond, pp. 49–66. Cambridge University Press, Cambridge.

1985. Pottery use-life among the Kalinga, Northern Luzon, the Philippines. In *Decoding Prehistoric Ceramics*, edited by B. A. Nelson, pp. 334–346. Southern Illinois University Press, Carbondale.

Matson, F. R. 1965. Ceramic ecology: An approach to the study of the early cultures of the Near East. In *Ceramics and Man*, edited by F. R. Matson, pp. 202–217. Viking Fund Publications in Anthropology No. 41. Aldine, Chicago.

McKellar, J. A. 1983. Correlates and the explanation of distribution. *Atlatl*, Occasional Papers 4, Anthropology Club. University of Arizona, Tucson.

Medel y Alvarado, L. 1963. *Historia de San Andres Tuxtla, 1532–1950*. Coleccion Suma Veracruzana, Seria Historigrafia. Editorial Citlaltepetl, Mexico D.F.

Mills, B. J. 1989. Integrating functional analyses of vessels and sherds through models of ceramic assemblage formation. *World Archaeology* 21:133–147.

Muller, J. 1984. Mississippian specialization and salt. *American Antiquity* 49:489–507.

Myers, J. E. 1984. The Political Economy of Ceramic Production: A Study of the Islamic Commonware Pottery of Medieval Osar Es-Seghir. Unpublished Ph.D. dissertation, Department of Anthropology, State University of New York at Binghamton. Binghamton, New York.

Nagel, E. 1961. *The Structure of Science.* Harcourt, Brace, and World, New York.

Nelson, B. A. 1981. Ethnoarchaeology and paleodemography: A test of Turner and Lofgren's hypothesis. *Journal of Anthropological Research* 37:107–129.

1985. Ceramic frequencies and use lives: A Highland Mayan case in cross-cultural perspective. Paper presented at School of American Research, Santa Fe, New Mexico.

Nicklin, K. 1971. Stability and innovation in pottery manufacture. *World Archaeology* 3:13–48.

1979. The location of pottery manufacture. *Man* 14:436–458.

O'Connell, J. F. 1987. Alyawara site structure and its archaeological implications. *American Antiquity* 52:74–108.

Olin, J. S. and A. D. Franklin (eds.) 1982. *Archaeological Ceramics.* Smithsonian Institution, Washington, D.C.

Papousek, D. A. 1974. Manufactura de alfarería en Temascalcingo, Mexico, 1967. *America Indigena* 34(4):1009–1046.

1981. *The Peasant-Potters of Los Pueblos.* Van Gorcum, Assen, The Netherlands.

Pastron, A. G. 1974. Preliminary ethnoarchaeological investigations among the Tarahumara. In *Ethnoarchaeology,* edited by C. B. Donnan and C. W. Clewlow, Jr., pp. 93–114. Archaeology Survey, Institute of Archaeology Monograph 4. University of California, Los Angeles.

Peacock, D. P. S. 1981. Archaeology, ethnology, and ceramic production. In *Production and Distribution: A Ceramic Viewpoint,* edited by H. Howard and E. L. Morris, pp. 187–194. BAR International Series 120. BAR, Oxford.

1982. *Pottery in the Roman World.* Longman, London.

Pinder, D., I. Shimada, and D. Gregory 1979. The nearest-neighbor statistic: Archaeological application and new developments. *American Antiquity* 44:430–445.

Plog, S. 1985. Estimating vessel orifice diameters: Measurement methods and measurement error. In *Decoding Prehistoric Ceramics,* edited by B. A. Nelson, pp. 347–357. Southern Illinois University Press, Carbondale.

Pool, C. A. 1990. Ceramic Production, Resource Procurement, and Exchange at Matacapan, Veracruz, Mexico. Unpublished Ph.D. dissertation, Department of Anthropology, Tulane University, New Orleans.

Raab, L. M. and A. Goodyear 1984. Middle-range theory in archaeology: A critical review of origins and applications. *American Antiquity* 49:255–268.

Rathje, W. 1975. The last tango in Mayapan: A tentative trajectory of production-distribution systems. In *Ancient Civilization and Trade,* edited by J. A. Sabloff and C. C. Lamberg-Karlovsky, pp. 409–448. University of New Mexico Press, Albuquerque.

Redman, C. L. and J. E. Myers 1981. Interpretation, classification, and ceramic production: A medieval North African case study. In *Production and Distribution: A Ceramic Viewpoint,* edited by H. Howard and E. L. Morris, pp. 285–307. BAR International Series 120. BAR, Oxford.

Redmond, E. M. 1979. A Terminal Formative ceramic workshop in the Tehuacan Valley. In *Prehistoric Social, Political, and Economic Development in the Area of the Tehuacan Valley: Some Results of the Palo Blanco Project,* edited by R. Drennan, pp. 111–125. Museum of Anthropology, University of Michigan, Ann Arbor.

Reina, R. E. 1963. The potter and the farmer: The fate of two innovators in a Maya village. *Expedition* 5(4):18–30.

1966. *The Law of the Saints: A Polomam Pueblo and Its Community Culture.* Bobbs-Merrill, Indianapolis.

Reina, R. E. and R. M. Hill II 1978. *The Traditional Pottery of Guatemala*. University of Texas Press, Austin.

Rice, P. M. 1976. Ceramic Continuity and Change in the Valley of Guatemala: A Study of Whiteware Pottery Production. Unpublished Ph.D. dissertation, Department of Anthropology, The Pennsylvania State University. University Microfilms, Ann Arbor.

  1981. Evolution of specialized pottery production: A trial model. *Current Anthropology* 22:219–240.

  1984a. Change and conservatism in pottery-producing systems. In *The Many Dimensions of Pottery*, edited by S. E. van der Leeuw and A. C. Pritchard, pp. 233–288. Albert Egges van Giffen Instituut voor Prae- en Protohistorie, Universiteit van Amsterdam, Amsterdam.

  1984b. The archaeological study of specialized pottery production: Some aspects of method and theory. In *Pots and Potters: Current Approaches in Ceramic Archaeology*, edited by P. Rice, pp. 45–54. Institute of Archaeology Monograph XXIV. University of California, Los Angeles.

  1985. Maya pottery techniques and technology. In *Ancient Technology to Modern Science, Ceramic and Civilization Vol. 1*, edited by W. Kingery, pp. 113–132. American Ceramic Society, Columbus.

  1987. *Pottery Analysis: A Sourcebook*. University of Chicago Press, Chicago.

Rice, P. M. and M. E. Saffer 1982. *Ceramic Notes, No. 1: Annotated Bibliography of Ceramic Studies, Part I: Analysis. Technical and Ethnographic Approaches to Pottery Production and Use*. Occasional Papers of the Ceramic Technology Lab. Florida State Museum, Gainesville.

Riley, J. A. 1984. Pottery analysis and the reconstruction of ancient exchange systems. In *The Many Dimensions of Pottery*, edited by S. E. van der Leeuw and A. C. Pritchard, pp. 55–73. Universiteit van Amsterdam, Albert Egges van Griffen Instituut voor Prae- en Protohistorie, Amsterdam.

Rios Macbeth, F. 1952. Estudio geological de la region de Los Tuxtlas. *Boletin de la Asociacion Mexicana de Geologos Petroleros* 4:325–376.

Rouse, I. 1960. The classification of artifacts in archaeology. *American Antiquity* 25:313–323.

Rozen, K. C. and A. P. Sullivan III 1989. Measurements, method, and meaning: Problems with Amick and Mauldin's middle-range approach. *American Antiquity* 54:169–174.

Rye, O. S. 1976. Keeping your temper under control: Materials and the manufacture of Papuan potter. *Archaeology and Physical Anthropology in Oceania* 11:106–137.

  1981. *Pottery Technology: Principles and Reconstruction*. Taraxacum Manuals on Archaeology No. 4. Washington, D.C.

Rye, O. S. and C. Evans 1976. *Traditional Pottery Techniques of Pakistan: Field and Laboratory Studies*. Smithsonian Contributions to Anthropology No. 21. Smithsonian Institution, Washington, D.C.

Sahlins, M. D. 1958. *Social Stratification in Polynesia*. University of Washington Press, Seattle.

Salmon, M. H. 1982. *Philosophy and Archaeology*. Academic Press, New York.

Sanders, W. T., J. Parsons, and R. S. Santley 1979. *The Basin of Mexico: Ecological Processes in the Evolution of a Civilization*. Academic Press, New York.

Sanders, W. T. and R. S. Santley 1983. A tale of three cities: Energetics and urbanization in prehispanic Central Mexico. In *Prehistoric Settlement Patterns*, edited by E. Vogt and R. Leventhal, pp. 243–291. University of New Mexico Press, Albuquerque.

Santley, R. S. and P. J. Arnold III 1986. Variability in specialized ceramic production at Matacapan, Veracruz, Mexico. In *The Social and Economic Contexts of Technological Change*, compiled by S. E. van der Leeuw and R. Torrence. Allen and Unwin, London.

Santley, R. S., P. J. Arnold III, and C. A. Pool 1989. The ceramic production system at Matacapan, Veracruz, Mexico. *Journal of Field Archaeology* 16:107–132.

Santley, R. S., J. M. Kerley, and R. R. Kneebone 1986. Obsidian working, long-distance exchange, and the politico-economic organization of early states in Central Mexico. In

Research in Economic Anthropology Supplement 2, 1986, Economic Aspects of Prehispanic Highland Mexico, edited by B. L. Isaac, pp. 101–132. JAI Press, Greenwich.

Santley, R. S. and P. Ortiz C. n.d. *La Ceramica de Matacapan.* Colleccion Cientifica, Instituto Nacional de Antropologia e Historia, Mexico City.

Santley, R. S., P. Ortiz C., P. J. Arnold III, R. R. Kneebone, M. Smyth, and J. M. Kerley 1985. Reporte final de campo Proyecto Matacapan: Temporada 1983. *Cuadernos del Museo* 4:3-97. Universidad Veracruzana, Xalapa, Mexico.

Santley, R. S., P. Ortiz C., T. W. Killion, P. J. Arnold III, and J. M. Kerley 1984. *Final Field Report of the Matacapan Archaeological Project: The 1982 Season.* Research Paper Series No. 15. Latin American Institute, University of New Mexico, Albuquerque.

Saraswati, B. and N. K. Behura 1966. *Pottery Techniques of Peasant India.* Anthropological Survey of India, Memoir No. 13.

Schiffer, M. B. 1976. *Behavioral Archaeology.* Academic Press, New York.

1987. *Formation Processes of the Archaeological Record.* University of New Mexico Press, Albuquerque.

1988. The structure of archaeological theory. *American Antiquity* 53:461–485.

Shepard, A. O. 1956. *Ceramics for the Archaeologist.* Carnegie Institution of Washington Publication 609. Washington, D.C.

Sierra M., R. 1969. La variabilidad de la lluvia al sur del paralelo 20° norte en el estado de Veracruz. *Boletin del Instituto Geografia* II:27-58. Universidad Nacional Autonoma de Mexico, Mexico.

1971. La variabilidad de la lluvia y su relacion con la productividad agricola en el estado de Veracruz. *Boletin del Instituto Geografia* IV:49–77. Universidad Nacional Autonoma de Mexico, Mexico.

Simmons, M. P. and B. Brem 1979. The analysis and distribution of volcanic ash tempered pottery in the Lowland Maya. *American Antiquity* 44:79–91.

Sinopoli, C. 1988. The organization of craft production at Vijayanagara, South India. *American Anthropologist* 90:580-597.

Skibo, J., M. B. Schiffer, and K. Reid 1989. Organic-tempered pottery: An experimental study. *American Antiquity* 54:122–146.

Smith, R. E. 1971. *The Pottery of Mayapan: Including Studies of Ceramic Material from Uxmal, Kabah, and Chichen Itza.* Papers of the Peabody Museum Vol. 66. Harvard University, Cambridge.

Smyth, M. P. 1989. Domestic storage behavior in Mesoamerica: An ethnoarchaeological approach. In *Archaeological Method and Theory, Vol. 1*, edited by M. B. Schiffer, pp. 89–138. University of Arizona Press, Tucson.

Spence, M. W. 1981. Obsidian production and the state in Teotihuacan. *American Antiquity* 46:769–788.

1986. Locational analysis of craft specialization areas in Teotihuacan. In *Research in Economic Anthropology, Supplement 2, 1986, Economic Aspects of Prehispanic Highland Mexico*, edited by B. L. Isaac, pp. 75–100. JAI Press, Greenwich.

SPP 1981. Carta de Precipitacion: Total Annual, Villahermosa, 1:1,000,000. SPP Programacion y Presupuestos, Coordinacion General de los Servicios Nacionales de Estadistica, Geografia e Informatica. Mexico, D.F.

1982. Carta Topografica de San Andres Tuxtla, Veracruz, E157A73. SPP Programacion y Presupuestos, Coordinacion General de los Servicios Nacionales de Estadistica, Geografia e Informatica. Mexico, D.F.

Stanislawski, M. B. 1978. If pots were mortal. In *Explorations in Ethnoarchaeology*, edited by R. A. Gould, pp. 201–228. University of New Mexico Press, Albuquerque.

Stark, B. L. 1984. An ethnoarchaeological study of a Mexican pottery industry. *Journal of New World Archaeology* 6(2):4-14.

1985. Archaeological identification of pottery-production locations: Ethnoarchaeological and archaeological data in Mesoamerica. In *Decoding Prehistoric Ceramics*, edited by B. A. Nelson, pp. 158–194. Southern Illinois University Press, Carbondale.

Steponaitis, V. P. 1984. Technological studies of prehistoric pottery from Alabama: Physical properties and vessel function. In *The Many Dimensions of Pottery*, edited by S. E. van der Leeuw and A. C. Pritchard, pp. 79–122. Universiteit van Amsterdam, Albert Egges van Giffen Instituut voor Prae- en Protohistorie, Amsterdam.

Stone, D. and C. Turnbull 1941. A Sula-Ulua pottery kiln. *American Antiquity* 7:39–47.

Sullivan, A. P. III 1988. Prehistoric southwestern ceramic manufacture: The limitations of the current evidence. *American Antiquity* 53:23–35.

Sullivan, A. P. III and K. C. Rozen 1985. Debitage analysis and archaeological interpretation. *American Antiquity* 50:755–779.

Tamayo, J. L. 1949. *Geografia general de Mexico, Tomo I, Geografia Fisica*. Talleres Graficos de la Nacion, Mexico.

Thomas, D. H. 1986. Contemporary hunter-gatherer archaeology in America. In *American Archaeology Past and Future*, edited by D. Meltzer, D. Fowler, and J. A. Sabloff, pp. 237–276. Smithsonian Institution Press, Washington, D. C.

Thompson, R. H. 1958. *Modern Yucatecan Maya Pottery Making*. Memoirs of the Society for American Archaeology No. 15. Washington, D.C.

Tschopik, H. Jr. 1950. An Andean ceramic tradition in historical perspective. *American Antiquity* 15:196–218.

Valenzuela, J. 1945. Las exploraciones efectuadas en Los Tuxtlas, Veracruz. *Anales del Museo Nacional de Arquelogia, Historia y Etnologia* 3:83–107.

van der Leeuw, S. E. 1976. *Studies in the Technology of Ancient Pottery*. Organization for the Advancement of Pure Research, Amsterdam.

1977. Towards a study of the economics of pottery making. In *Ex Horreo*, edited by B. L. van Beek, R. W. Brandt, and W. Groenman-Van Woaterange, pp. 68–76. Albert Egges van Giffen Instituut voor Prae- en Proto-Historie. Universiteit van Amsterdam, Amsterdam.

1984. Dust to dust: A transformational view of the ceramic cycle. In *The Many Dimensions of Pottery: Ceramics in Archaeology and Anthropology*, edited by S. E. van der Leeuw and A. C. Pritchard, pp. 707–773. Albert Egges van Giffen Instituut voor Prae- en Protohistorie, Universiteit van Amsterdam, Amsterdam.

van de Velde, P. and H. R. van de Velde 1939. The black pottery of Coyotepec, Oaxaca, Mexico. *Southwest Museum Papers* 13:7–43.

Vogt, E. Z. 1970. *The Zinacantecos of Mexico*. Holt, Rinehart, and Winston, New York.

Voyatzoglou, M. 1974. The jar makers of Thrapsano in Crete. *Expedition* 16:18–24.

Watson, P. J. 1986. Archaeological interpretations, 1985. In *American Archaeology Past and Future*, edited by D. Meltzer, D. Fowler, J. A. Sabloff, pp. 439–457. Smithsonian Institution Press, Washington, D.C.

Weatherill, R. 1971. *The Pottery Trade of North Staffordshire 1660–1760*. Manchester.

West, R. C. 1964. Surface configuration and associated geology of Middle America. In *Handbook of Middle American Indians Vol. 1, Natural Environment and Early Cultures*, edited by R. C. West, pp. 33–83. University of Texas Press, Austin.

Wilk, R. R. and R. McC. Netting 1984. Households: Changing form and function. In *Households: Comparative and Historical Studies of the Domestic Group*, edited by R. McC. Netting, R. R. Wilk, and E. J. Arnould, pp. 1–28. University of California Press, Berkeley.

Wilk, R. R. and W. L. Rathje 1982. Archaeology of the household: Building a prehistory of domestic life. *American Behavioral Scientist* 25:611–624.

Willey, G. R. 1961. Volume in pottery and the selection of samples. *American Antiquity* 27:230–231.

Winter, M. and W. O. Payne 1976. Hornos para ceramica hallados en Monte Alban. *Instituto Nacional de Antropologia e Historia* Boletin 16 (epoca II):37–40.

Wright, H. 1986. The evolution of civilizations. In *American Archaeology Past and Present*, edited by D. Meltzer, D. Fowler, and J. A. Sabloff, pp. 323–365. Smithsonian Institution Press, Washington, D.C.

Wright, H. and G. Johnson 1975. Population, exchange and early state formation in southwestern Iran. *American Anthropologist* 77:267–289.

Wylie, A. 1982. An analogy by any other name is just as analogical. *Journal of Anthropological Archaeology* 1:382–401.

Yellen, J. E. 1977. *Archaeological Approaches to the Present*. Academic Press, New York.

INDEX